P9-ELW-903

Great American Music: Broadway Musicals
Part II

Professor Bill Messenger

THE TEACHING COMPANY ®

PUBLISHED BY:

THE TEACHING COMPANY
4840 Westfields Boulevard, Suite 500
Chantilly, Virginia 20151-2299
1-800-TEACH-12
Fax—703-378-3819
www.teach12.com

Copyright © The Teaching Company, 2006

Printed in the United States of America

This book is in copyright. All rights reserved.

Without limiting the rights under copyright reserved above,
no part of this publication may be reproduced, stored in
or introduced into a retrieval system, or transmitted,
in any form, or by any means
(electronic, mechanical, photocopying, recording, or otherwise),
without the prior written permission of
The Teaching Company.

ISBN 1-59803-203-8

Bill Messenger

American Music Lecturer, The Peabody Institute
of the Johns Hopkins University

Bill Messenger studied musical composition, on scholarship, at The Peabody Institute of the Johns Hopkins University in Baltimore, Maryland, under Louis Cheslock. He attended a master class in 1963 with Nadia Boulanger, the teacher of Roy Harris, Virgil Thomson, and Aaron Copland. Mr. Messenger has two master's degrees, both from the Johns Hopkins University in Baltimore. He has done additional graduate work in musicology at the University of Maryland.

Mr. Messenger has taught composition, music history, and music theory at Goucher College in Baltimore and at a number of community colleges. He regularly lectures on American music at The Peabody Institute of the Johns Hopkins University. Mr. Messenger's latest book, *The Melody Lingers On*, has elicited the following from reviewer and college dean Linda Nielson: "This book should be a mandatory part of the library of every senior citizen."

Mr. Messenger's musical career includes studio work on many early rock 'n' roll recordings. He has accompanied many nationally known performers during his years in the music business, including Cass Elliot before her tenure with the Mamas and the Papas. In 1983, he was voted Baltimore's best piano player by *Baltimore* magazine. For the Peabody Elderhostel, he currently teaches a total of 11 different courses on various aspects of American musical theater.

Table of Contents
Great American Music: Broadway Musicals
Part II

©2006 The Teaching Company.

Great American Music: Broadway Musicals

Scope:

This course covers the 200-year evolution of American musical theater, including the minstrel era, the vaudeville era, the age of ragtime, the revue, and the book musical. Because recorded examples of music from recent Broadway musicals are readily available in retail stores, these are used less frequently here than the older, rarer recordings, without which most listeners would have little knowledge of the sound of early musicals. The shows chosen to be discussed in this course are each important links in musical theater's evolution.

"Give My Regards to Broadway," the theme song that opens each of the 16 lectures in this course, was written by George M. Cohan, the most popular star on Broadway during the 20th century's first decade and the grandfather of the integrated book musical. Every creator of Broadway musicals, from Kern and Hammerstein to Kander and Ebb and beyond, owes a debt to Cohan's innovations in musical theater.

The minstrel show represents America's first original form of musical theater. After the Civil War, it became an important source of employment for newly freed black performers.

In the songs of the minstrel and vaudeville eras, the form that dominates is the verse/chorus song. Such songs contained one chorus and several verses, usually constructed to tell a story. This was a sophisticated outgrowth of the folk ballad (including such songs as "On Top of Old Smokey" and "My Darling Clementine"), which constructed stories by accumulating verses. Understanding the way these songs are constructed musically (out of contrasting musical phrases) will aid the listener in understanding the processes involved in creating a musical.

Ragtime is, essentially, the use of marked and frequent melodic syncopation against an unsyncopated accompaniment. During the period from 1890 to 1910, it dominated American popular music. Even today, the rhythms of ragtime lie under the surface of much modern theater song.

Vaudeville appealed to men, women, and children and contained none of the offensive elements of the minstrel show. Consequently, by the early 20th century, it had largely replaced the minstrel show as

America's primary source of musical stage entertainment. The great vaudeville chains that circled the continent became a training ground for thousands of young performers who later appeared in movies, on radio, and on television.

For more than a century, the music publishing industry and the Broadway stage worked together to create America's hit songs. With the advent of talking-singing films, that relationship slowly began to deteriorate. Tin Pan Alley focused on selling sheet music; today, sheet music accounts for only a tiny fraction of song sales compared to recordings and music videos.

Musical theater as we now know it began in 1866 with a crude but popular show called *The Black Crook*. By the dawn of the 20th century, George M. Cohan was creating shows in which the songs had a dramatic purpose and the stories engaged the audience. Though most of Cohan's characters (such as little Johnny Jones) are drawn from his own personality, they are consistently lively and believable.

By 1909, Flo Ziegfeld and his extravaganzas were on Broadway to stay. Beautifully gowned girls and fabulous special effects (including an airplane that flew over the heads of the audience) made the Ziegfeld Follies the most popular item on Broadway.

Meanwhile, Jerome Kern (a decade before *Show Boat*) was creating intimate shows at the tiny 299-seat Princess Theatre that focused more on low-key plots, believable characters, and well-crafted songs.

Despite *Show Boat*'s great innovations as a musical in which story, song, and dance were integrated, the revue dominated the 1920s and 1930s. Revues showcased a variety of songs and sketches, often unrelated but sometimes unified by a broad theme, such as *Paris Nights* or *New Faces on Broadway*.

A year before World War I, America seemed to be getting ready for the jazz age. The new music appeared on recordings and began to emerge on Broadway. Between 1916 and 1920, Cole Porter and George Gershwin were writing their first Broadway songs. The George White Scandals (Ziegfeld's greatest competition) helped develop the talents of composer George Gershwin. Both American clothing styles and American music were becoming streamlined.

If any one person can be said to be the musical soul of the 1920s, it is George Gershwin. Using jazz ideas in both his concert and his

©2006 The Teaching Company.

theater works, he helped make the formerly despised idiom acceptable to America's intellectual elite.

With the exception of Gershwin's *Porgy and Bess*, what seems to be permanent about the Depression era is not the shows but the songs— the great standards of Rodgers and Hart, Jerome Kern, and Cole Porter. The collaboration of Rodgers and Hammerstein, however, created a large body of classic musicals, beginning in 1943 with *Oklahoma!*.

While this team dominated the 1940s, new greats shared the scene during the 1950s, including Leonard Bernstein, Frank Loesser, and Lerner and Loewe. The huge number of classic musicals produced during the 1950s included *The King and I*, *The Music Man*, *West Side Story*, *Guys and Dolls*, *The Sound of Music*, and *My Fair Lady*. As a result, the decade is often referred to as the "golden age of Broadway."

The 15 years from 1960–1975 represent an incredible variety of different kinds of classic Broadway shows. From 1960, *Bye Bye Birdie* is a hilarious, fast-paced satire of rock 'n' roll. That same year saw the beginning of the 40-year run of *The Fantasticks* at Greenwich Village's Sullivan Street Playhouse. Each new blockbuster seemed determined to surpass the attendance record of its predecessor. Starting in 1964, *Hello, Dolly!* ran for 2,844 performances. *Fiddler on the Roof*, mounted a few months later, ran for 3,242 performances. And 1975's *A Chorus Line* beat them all with a run of 6,137 performances.

The dark themes introduced by *West Side Story* in the 1950s and *Cabaret* in the 1960s dominated the remainder of the century, with such shows as Sondheim's *Sweeney Todd*, Schönberg's *Les Misérables*, Webber's *The Phantom of the Opera*, and Kander and Ebb's *Chicago* and *Kiss of the Spider Woman*. But by the late 1980s, Broadway lightened up and offered something for everyone— remakes of *Oklahoma!* and *Anything Goes*, along with all-dance shows, such as Jerome Robbins's *Broadway* and *Fosse*. As the century turned, *Hairspray* and *The Producers* brought back the old-fashioned fun that had dominated the street in its golden age.

Lecture Nine
Superstars on the Horizon

Scope:

The period from 1909–1915 was a particularly active time in musical theater, but it was not dominated by a single figure, as the period of 1900–1908 had been dominated by George M. Cohan or as the 1940s would be dominated by Rodgers and Hammerstein. These early years were the incubation period for songwriters who, in the following decade or two, were to become giants of the musical theater. Young Jerome Kern was writing interpolations for British and American musicals. Still in the process of acquiring his style, Kern wrote only one song during this period that shows the promise of things to come: "They Didn't Believe Me." Young Irving Berlin was also writing his first hit songs, among them "Alexander's Ragtime Band." But the profoundly tender waltzes, such as "All Alone by the Telephone" and "What'll I Do?" were still a decade away. In this lecture, we'll look at a few examples of the remarkable number of shows from this period, and we'll examine the careers of some of its well-known performers and songwriters, including Al Jolson and Cole Porter, along with Kern.

Outline

I. We begin with Chris Smith's "Ballin' the Jack" from the 1914 Broadway musical *The Girl from Utah*, the same show that introduced Jerome Kern's "They Didn't Believe Me." This was one of the more successful musicals of the period we'll be discussing in this lecture.

II. In 1909, Nora Bayes returned to the Ziegfeld Follies, singing her trademark, "Shine on Harvest Moon." Eve Tanguay also sang the song that had made her famous—"I Don't Care."

   A. In the second act of the 1909 Follies, with Lillian Lorraine at the controls, a life-sized airplane actually flew off the stage and over the heads of the audience.

   B. The show's most memorable production number involved the suggestion that each state should present a battleship to the nation's fleet. In this number, each chorus girl was dressed to represent a state, with a huge hat on her head designed to look like a different battleship.

III. During this period, there were more than twice as many theaters in New York City than there are today. And because shows had far shorter runs than they do today, a period such as 1909–1915 covered a large number of musicals. In this lecture, we'll select a few examples to represent the period.

    A. On July 18, 1910, *Up and Down Broadway*, one of the biggest hits of the season, premiered at the Casino Theatre.

        1. The plot revolved around the Greek gods arriving in New York City and vowing to reform theatrical taste. The gods' janitor, Momus, tags along for laughs. In the end, the gods conclude that Broadway knows more about good entertainment than they do.

        2. Eddie Foy, as Momus, led a cast that included Irving Berlin singing his song "Sweet Italian Love." Most of the score, however, was written by Jean Schwartz. One of Schwartz's songs, sung by a police officer in a Chinese neighborhood, became one of the top 10 songs of 1910. We hear "Chinatown, My Chinatown."

    B. One of the most popular shows of 1910, starring Nora Bayes, was *The Jolly Bachelors*. Much of the score was written by Bayes with her husband, Jack Norworth.

        1. Bayes played Miss Vandergould, a fabulously wealthy heiress who takes a job as a cashier in a drugstore. There, she hopes to find romance among the less effete men of the middle class. When she mistakenly gives a customer the wrong medicine, she and her beau scour the city to retrieve it.

        2. Their search takes them to a college campus, where Norworth leads a chorus of students in a medley of college songs. The production included a life-sized ocean liner and an airship sailing through the clouds. The popularity of this show obviously came less from the story than from the spectacular props and scenery.

        3. The score of *The Jolly Bachelors* included one song, by C. W. Murphy and Will Letters, that became Bayes's third biggest hit recording. We listen to it now: "Has Anybody Here Seen Kelly?"

C. Joe Howard, in the 1909 show *The Prince of Tonight*, introduced another immensely popular song. The show's program gave Howard credit for writing "I Wonder Who's Kissing Her Now," but the song was actually written by Howard's shy piano accompanist, Harold Orlob. Orlob didn't receive credit for the song until almost the end of his life. We listen to it now.

D. Before 1910, African-American comedian, songwriter, and singer Bert Williams had resisted Flo Ziegfeld's entreaties to join the Follies. However, when Williams's partner became ill, he no longer felt restrained from appearing as a solo act. He joined the Follies in 1910, along with the legendary Fannie Brice.

IV. The year 1911 saw Al Jolson starring in musical theater on Broadway for the first time. The show, which appeared at the Winter Garden, was called *La Belle Paree* (Schubert's answer to Ziegfeld's French Follies).

A. The Winter Garden, a spacious house with 1,600 seats, had been built by the Schuberts. With a disproportionately large number of its 1,600 seats on the orchestra level, the house was assured a handsome gross when it was filled to capacity, which it always was when Jolson played there. Jolson did so well for the Schuberts that they continued to produce his shows for the next 15 years.

B. The year after *La Belle Paree*, the Winter Garden produced *Hollywood Express*, in which Jolson introduced one of the most popular standards of the 20th century, "You Made Me Love You."

C. Jolson (1886–1950) was born in the Russian *shtetl* of Srednike, but he moved with his family to America at the age of 8. America's most popular star during the earlier part of his career, Jolson almost single-handedly held back the evolution of American musical theater.

1. A Cohan show, although it was centered around the star, was still a show—with a plot, characters, and songs that had some relationship to the plot. But a Jolson show was just that—a Jolson show. His audiences loved his take-charge stage persona, but his co-workers were not so enamored of his methods.

2. George Burns, a contemporary and a friend of Jolson's, talked about Jolson in his book, *All My Best Friends*. According to Burns, Jolson would sometimes stop the show, walk to the footlights, tell the audience the ending of the show, then ask, "Now, you wanna see that or you wanna hear Jolson sing?"

D. Why were people so taken with Jolson's singing? Primarily because they'd never heard anything like it before.

1. Jolson, along with Crosby and Sinatra, is one of the three great innovators of popular singing in the first half of the 20th century. Singers before Jolson sang the song the way it was written and enunciated with the clarity of robots.

2. Jolson brought to singing spontaneity and an approach closer to jazz. He would change the melodies, repeat phrases or words for emphasis or to create excitement, and insert slang words when he thought they'd pack more power.

3. Though it may be hard to believe today, Jolson was, in the teens, what Elvis was to the 1950s. His unique style made early-20th-century musical theater more intimate, personal, and intense.

E. Jolson wrote an autobiographical article in April 1919 for the *American Magazine* (provided by the International Al Jolson Society), painting a picture of the uniqueness of the theater of his day.

1. The performers, not only in vaudeville but also in musical theater, were improvisational, injecting personal references into the scripts, which made the audiences come back again and again because they knew the show was never going to be precisely the same twice.

2. Further, though the plot of the show may have remained unchanged, many of the lines, unrelated to the plot, were simply there to give the actors something funny to say. In other words, what there was of a plot was continually interrupted with jokes.

V. The 1912 season opened with an Eddie Foy romp called *Over the River* at the Globe Theatre.

A. The show was based on a straight play of 1897 called *The Man from Mexico*. The plot concerned the problems of a man who must serve time in jail. Too ashamed to confess the truth to his wife, he pretends he is going on a trip to Mexico. After he has vanished, his wife's travels, by highly unlikely coincidence, lead her to his jail cell.

B. Most of the songs in *Over the River* were composed by Jean Schwartz, who later wrote the Jolson hit "Rock-a-Bye Your Baby with a Dixie Melody." The show featured all the latest dance crazes and may have inspired Irving Berlin's show of 1914, another dance-focused musical, *Watch Your Step*, starring Vernon and Irene Castle.

C. To perform dances the Castles had first introduced, including the tango, the producers of *Over the River* hired the Marvelous Millers. There was some ragtime dancing, including the turkey trot and the grizzly bear, and composer Jean Schwartz took to the piano to accompany Lillian Lorraine and the chorus in his "Chopsticks Rag."

VI. To compete with the Follies, the Schuberts produced *The Passing Show of 1912*.

A. They hired a line of beautiful girls, putting them in attractive, sometimes provocative, costumes. They created an ocean liner set, a harem scene, and an elaborate ragtime wedding scene. The comedy in *The Passing Show of 1912* came from burlesquing other shows that were on Broadway that year.

B. During this same period, Victor Herbert (1859–1924) was very active, composing both *Naughty Marietta* and *Sweethearts* (1913).

    1. Though we don't focus on operettas, we should at least hear from Herbert, whose *Babes in Toyland* has been revived every Christmas season for the past 100 years.

    2. We listen to a little bit of a pre-1920s instrumental by Herbert that was later made into a popular song and one of the Glenn Miller Band's biggest hits, "Indian Summer." Our recording features Ed Goldstein and company re-creating the piece.

C. In December 1914, The New Amsterdam Theatre premiered Irving Berlin's first Broadway musical, *Watch Your Step*, starring Vernon and Irene Castle. From *Watch Your Step*, we

©2006 The Teaching Company.

hear "When I Discovered You," which may have inspired a later George Gershwin song.

1. *Watch Your Step* was destined to be Vernon and Irene Castle's first and final Broadway musical. When World War I began in Europe, Vernon joined the RAF and was later killed when his plane crashed. Irene went on to a successful career in silent films.

2. Interestingly, the plot of *Watch Your Step* mysteriously vanished during the second act.

   a. Classic Broadway shows have both plots and subplots; this allows for several kinds of conflict and doesn't restrict the important musical numbers to the leads. In the end, the subplot, skillfully employed, makes for a far more interesting musical.

   b. In 1914, however, and all the years before the integrated musical, there was often no subplot, and variety was created by somewhat clumsy means. *Watch Your Step* is a good example.

   c. The plot had to do with a will leaving $2 million to anyone who had never been in love, but by the second act, the story was forgotten and the evening was turned into a facsimile of a 5th Avenue nightclub floor show.

VII. The next year, 1915, was the year a young man, destined to become one of America's greatest songwriters, mounted his first Broadway show. The young man was a recent graduate of Yale named Cole Porter (1891–1964), and the show was called *See America First*.

A. Intended to be a spoof on the flag-waving musicals of Cohan, the show's story concerns an American senator who leaves the effete East so that his daughter can find a red-blooded he-man in the Wild West.

B. By a coincidence, she meets a British duke thinly disguised as a cowboy. Once she discovers the subterfuge, she wants nothing more to do with the duke. But at the final curtain, after the cowboy-duke saves the whole cast from murderous bandits, the lovers reunite and win her parents' approval. "I've a Shooting Box in Scotland" was the only song singled out by critics as anything better than atrocious.

C. Interestingly, fishing among the Yale archives turned up a song written in 1912 for one of Porter's college shows. Porter's "Longing for Dear Old Broadway," obviously influenced by Cohan, even begins with the same rhythm as "Give My Regards to Broadway." We hear this song, orchestrated by Jari Villanueva and sung by Bob Robinson.

VIII. Jerome Kern would do his second Princess Theatre show in 1915, by far his best work to date, and though the show contained no lasting standards, Kern's music and Guy Bolton's lyrics were a step closer to the ideal integrated score Kern would later create for 1927's *Show Boat*.

A. The plot of this show, *Very Good Eddie*, revolved around everyday people and was nearly believable. In the musical, the Hudson River Day Lines' *Catskill* stops for 15 minutes at Poughkeepsie. Dick Rivers (played by Oscar Shaw) comes aboard. Much of the action takes place among the ship's passengers, including a pair of newlyweds.

B. The characters in *Very Good Eddie* were not cartoon clowns or cardboard heroes. Its situations were relatively plausible. Its songs, while not able to stand up without the supporting situations, were nonetheless serviceable and promised better things to come.

C. The Princess shows were a wonderful way for Kern to hone his skills. The budget for a show at the tiny 299-seat theater was under $8,000. The weekly costs were less than the weekly salary of one star at the larger theaters.

D. The limitations of the theater were a challenge to Kern. His solutions resulted in intimate productions.

    1. The Princess Theatre stage wasn't large enough for a conventional chorus, so ensemble quartets and sextets were used.

    2. The orchestra itself was unlike anything previously heard in a show that filled a theater to capacity. Frank Sadler, who wrote Kern's orchestrations, arranged the music so that it needed no more than 11 musicians.

    3. Instead of making the show seem like a cheapskate production, these factors created a degree of intimacy, subtlety, and sophistication that was quite new to

Broadway. At the show's end, people felt as if they had been privileged to attend an exclusive, private soiree.

IX. During the period 1909 to 1915, something new was on the artistic horizon.

   A. Harriet Monroe founded *Poetry Magazine* in 1912, making household names of such poets as Robert Frost and T. S. Eliot. In 1914, Edgar Lee Masters published *Spoon River Anthology*, the first collection of poems to become a bestseller. The visual arts were undergoing an explosion of modernism as well.

   B. Ragtime was still in vogue and so were the blues, first made popular in 1914 with the publication of Handy's "St. Louis Blues." The old order on Broadway with its musical roots in Europe was giving way to the newer sounds indigenous to America. The excitement of blue notes and syncopated rhythms was—at that point—the sound of modernism.

   C. The years 1909–1915 were a time of trial and error and a period of gestation for musical talents that were to triumph in the following decades.

Suggested Reading:

Gerald Bordman, *American Musical Theatre: A Chronicle*.

Stanley Green, *The World of Musical Comedy*.

Questions to Consider:

1. Discuss Jolson's view that the musical theater of this period was both more intimate and more improvisational. Do you see the loss of these qualities in musical theater as positive or negative?

2. What limitations and advantages does a small theater present for composers and producers?

Lecture Nine—Transcript
Superstars on the Horizon

(Plays piano—"Ballin the Jack.") That was Chris Smith's "Ballin the Jack" from the 1914 Broadway musical *The Girl from Utah*, the same show that introduced Jerome Kern's "They Didn't Believe Me." This was one of the more successful musicals of the period we'll be discussing in this lecture.

The period from 1909–1915 was a particularly active time in musical theater, but it was not dominated by a single figure, as the period from 1900 to 1908 had been dominated by George M. Cohan, or as the 1940s were to be dominated by Rodgers and Hammerstein.

These early years were the incubation period for songwriters who, in the following decade or two, were to become giants of the musical theater. Young Jerome Kern was writing interpolations for British and American musicals. Still in the process of acquiring his style, Kern wrote only one song during this period that shows the promise of things to come. He writes this song as an interpolation into the same show that premiered "Ballin the Jack," *The Girl from Utah*. Kern's song, which we'll hear in a later lesson, and which we mentioned at the start of this lesson, was called "They Didn't Believe Me."

And young Irving Berlin was writing his first hit songs, among them "Alexander's Ragtime Band." But the profoundly tender waltzes like "All Alone by the Telephone," "What'll I Do?" and "Always" were still a decade away.

In 1909, Nora Bayes returned to the Ziegfeld Follies, singing her trademark, a huge hit that she and her husband had written for her to sing on the stage, "Shine on Harvest Moon." Eve Tanguay, the "I Don't Care" girl, sang the song that had made her famous, "I Don't Care." In the second act of the Follies, with Lillian Lorraine at the controls, a life-sized airplane actually flew off the stage and over the heads of the audience. I doubt that any theater would try anything that dangerous today and that was a quite a challenge, obviously, for Ziegfeld's stage crew.

The show's most memorable production number involved the suggestion that each state should present a battleship to the nation's fleet. Now, all battleships, at that time, were named for states— remember the *S.S. Missouri*. In this production number, each chorus

©2006 The Teaching Company.

girl was dressed to represent a state, with a huge hat on each head designed to look like a different battleship.

One Philadelphia newspaper was so thrilled by the spectacle that it seriously suggested that the nation accept Ziegfeld's scheme as a quick and easy way to enlarge the nation's fleet.

During this period, there were more than twice as many theaters in New York City as there are today. And, because shows had far shorter runs than they do today, a period of time as short as from 1909 to 1915 covered a vast quantity of musicals, many of them successful. Now, trying to talk about all these musicals would be impossible in this space of time. What we're going to do in this lesson is select a few examples to represent the period.

On July 18, 1910, *Up and Down Broadway*—one of the biggest hits of the season—premiered at the Casino Theatre. The thin plot revolved around Apollo and the other Greek gods arriving in New York City and vowing to reform theatrical taste. Their janitor, Momus, tags along for laughs. In the end, the gods conclude that Broadway knows more about good entertainment than they do.

Eddie Foy—remember Bob Hope as Eddie Foy in the film *The Seven Little Foys*—Eddie Foy, as Momus, led a cast that included Irving Berlin singing his new song, "Sweet Italian Love." Most of the score, however, was written by Jean Schwartz. One of his songs—sung by a police officer in a Chinese neighborhood—became one of the top ten songs of 1910. Here it is; the song was called "Chinatown" and it usually began with consecutive fourths *(plays piano)* or consecutive fifths, which was a hallmark of much Chinese music—at least, Anglo music trying to be Chinese music. *(Plays piano—"Chinatown, My Chinatown.")* That was "Chinatown," one of the big, big hits of 1910.

One of the most popular shows of 1910—starring Nora Bayes—was called *The Jolly Bachelors*. Much of the score was written by Nora Bayes with her husband, Jack Norworth. By the way, Nora Bayes and Jack Norworth billed themselves as "the happiest married couple in show business." Their billing changed shortly after their divorce. Nora Bayes played Miss Vandergould, a fabulously wealthy heiress who takes a job as a cashier in a drugstore. There, she hopes to find romance among the less effete men of the middle class. When she mistakenly gives a customer the wrong medicine, she and her beau scour the city to retrieve it before someone ends up hurting themselves.

Their search takes them to a college campus where Jack Norworth, coincidentally, happens to be leading a chorus of students in a long medley of college songs. The production included a life-sized ocean liner and an airship sailing through the clouds. The popularity of this show obviously came less from the story than it did from the spectacular props and scenery and from the considerable force of Ms. Bayes's personality.

The score of *The Jolly Bachelors* included one song, this one by C. W. Murphy and Will Letters, that became Nora Bayes's third biggest hit recording. Her biggest hit, yet to be recorded, was 1917's "Over There." Her second biggest hit was, of course, "Shine on Harvest Moon." The big hit of 1910's *The Jolly Bachelors* was "Has Anybody Here Seen Kelly?" Now the narrator of the song is Kelly's girlfriend who lost him in the St. Patrick's Day crowd. When she shouts, "Has anybody here seen Kelly?" you can guess what happens. Here's the song. *(Plays recording—"Has Anybody Here Seen Kelly?")* "Has Anybody Here Seen Kelly?" It's interesting that she threw in the line about Levi because Nora Bayes was born Dora Goldberg. The emphasis on race in these early songs is interesting; there's a sort of good-natured kidding here that people seemed to tolerate and even laugh at, even though it may be kidding on, you know on, them.

Now, let me tell you about a show that Joe Howard did in the 1909; it was called *The Prince of Tonight* and it introduced another immensely popular song, one that continued to be popular in 1910, 1911, and 1912—and through the teens actually. The show's program gave Howard credit for writing the song and the song was "I Wonder Who's Kissing Her Now."

But, Howard did not write the song. He did introduce it in 1909 in his otherwise forgettable musical, *The Prince of Tonight*. But, no one forgot the song, which had actually been written by Joe's shy piano accompanist, Harold Orlob. Now, Orlob wanted credit for the song, but strong-willed Howard convinced the shy young man that because he'd written it while working for Howard, the song belonged to Howard. Now Orlob knew this wasn't so, but he didn't dare challenge Howard. Besides, he needed the work.

 ©2006 The Teaching Company.

Forty years later, Twentieth Century Fox was making a film bio of Joe Howard's life called *I Wonder Who's Kissing Her Now*, starring Mark Stevens as Joe Howard. Now by this time, both Howard and Orlob were old men. Orlob was ill and knew he didn't have long to live.

Orlob hired a lawyer to get his name on the song. The lawyer went to elderly Joe Howard and Howard refused, knowing that it would look as if his fame was based on a lie, which it was. The lawyer then went to Fox and they offered Orlob $10,000 hush money, a tidy sum in 1947. Orlob refused the money. "All I want," he said, "is credit for what I did."

So, when the film came out, the opening credits read "I Wonder Who's Kissing Her Now," music by Joe Howard and Harold Orlob. Orlob attended the film's premiere, saw his name in the credits, and was prepared to die a happy man. This is the song *(plays piano—"I Wonder Who's Kissing Her Now")*.

Before 1910, black comedian-songwriter-singer Bert Williams had resisted Flo Ziegfeld's entreaties to join The Follies. Williams would not join Ziegfeld unless Ziegfeld also hired his partner William Walker, but Ziegfeld was not interested in Walker. In 1909, Walker became ill, dying in 1911. With Walker unavailable, Williams no longer felt restrained from appearing as a solo act. He joined The Follies in 1910, along with the legendary Fanny Brice—the model for Barbra Streisand's character in the 1960s Broadway show *Funny Girl*.

The year 1911 saw Al Jolson starring in musical theater on Broadway for the first time. The show, which appeared at the Winter Garden—one of a handful of theaters, by the way, of that period that still stands—the show was called *La Belle Paree*. This was Schubert's answer to Ziegfeld's French Follies. The Winter Garden, a spacious house with 1,600 seats, had been built by the Schuberts on Broadway between 50th and 51st Streets. With a disproportionately large number of its 1,600 seats on orchestra level, the house was assured a handsome gross when it was filled to capacity, which it always was when Jolson played there. Jolson did so well for the Schuberts that they continued to produce his shows for the next 15 years.

The year after *La Belle Paree*, they began preparing a show for him called *Honeymoon Express* and, in that show, he introduced one of the most popular standards of the 20th century. Now according to Jolson, when he was about to sing this song, he was in great pain because he was suffering from a very painful, ingrown toenail, and so, right before the chorus, he decided to relieve the pain on that toe by getting down on one knee. That was the first time, apparently, that Jolson ever did that and he made it a permanent pose in his performances. Here's the song he introduced in *Honeymoon Express.* I'll tell you what it's called after you hear it. *(Plays piano—"You Made Me Love You.")* Of course, that was "You Made Me Love You," a song later recorded by Judy Garland, by Harry James, and dozens and dozens of other performers.

Now a little bit about Jolson, the man who introduced that song, "You Made Me Love You." He was born in the Russian *shtetl* of Srednike. He moved with his family to America at the age of seven; that was in 1893. America's most popular star during the earlier part of his career, Jolson almost single-handedly held back the evolution of American musical theater.

Now, a Cohan show, while it was centered around Cohan, was still a show, with a plot, with characters, and with songs that had something to do with the plot. But, a Jolson show was just that—a Jolson show. His audiences loved his completely take-charge stage persona, but his coworkers, who often didn't get to go on to perform, were not so enamored with Jolson and the way he did things.

George Burns, a contemporary and a friend of Jolson's, talked about Jolson in his book, *All My Best Friends*. I'm summarizing what Burns says. He says, sometimes when Jolie was starring in a Broadway show at the Winter Garden, he'd actually stop the show, walk to the footlights, and tell the audience, "You know how dis ends. The horse, he wins the race, and the boy gets de girl. Now, you wanna see that or you wanna hear Jolson sing?" And, for the rest of the show, Jolson would sing whatever he felt like singing. George Burns said, "Nobody ever dominated a theater like Jolson. And, nobody was ever as quick to admit it either. Maybe the only thing as big as Jolson's talent was his ego."

Now one example of that is the time he was on the stage with Enrico Caruso and it turned out Caruso had to go first, and this was a war relief benefit. Jolson had to come second, so how did he introduce himself? Well, as Caruso was taking his bows, young Jolson ran out on the stage and said, "Folks, you ain't heard nothin' yet!" If you

©2006 The Teaching Company.

look up the word chutzpah, you'll see a picture of Jolson in the dictionary; if you don't, you should.

Now, why were the audiences so taken with this guy before World War I and shortly afterwards? What was there about his singing that was special and different? Well, they'd never heard anything like it before. Jolson, along with Crosby and Sinatra, is one of the three great innovators of popular singing in the first half of the 20th century. Singers before Jolson sang the song the way it was written and they enunciated it with clarity, with an almost robot-like clarity. Jolson brought singing spontaneity and an approach closer to jazz. He would change the melodies, he would repeat phrases, or he'd take words and say them over and over again to create excitement. And, he pronounced his words clearly, but never stiltedly. He also knew— as modern rock artists know—that slang packs more power than the proper word at times. So, a word like "have not" isn't going to sound half as good as "ain't."

Though it may be hard to believe, Jolson was, in the teens, what Elvis was to the 1950s. His unique style is a key to qualities in early 20th-century musical theater that I've long been aware of, but until now, I haven't been able to describe in words. The early Jolson-era musical theater was more intimate, more personal, more, you could say, in your face. George M. Cohan, for example, coming out would wave to his friends and even say "hello" to people in the audience. Jolson's performances are an even better example.

Now thank goodness that Jolson wrote an autobiographical article in April 1919 for the *American Magazine*; he paints a picture of the uniqueness of the theater of his day with more vivid examples than anything I've ever seen described elsewhere. I want to thank the International Al Jolson Society for making this Jolson article available to me. I'll read a few excerpts:

> I used the runway to get confidential with the audience by running up and down it, stopping for a chat with the people, and by kidding the audience ... People who usually sit back and look at the show with one eye and at the audience with the other, lean forward and they begin to chuckle. A man smiles up at me and I smile back at him. Someone will make a funny remark and, hearing it, I'll repeat it to the audience and comment on it. Sometimes men hand me cigars and, to be agreeable, I take them.

Without using the word improvisational, the performers—not only in vaudeville, but also in musical theater—particularly Jolson, but not only Jolson, were improvisational, injecting personal references into the scripts, which made the audiences come back again and again because they knew the show was never going to be precisely the same any two times. Jolson goes on to write in that article:

> This desire for intimacy with the audience has become so well known to managers that almost every show has an intimate personal touch to it. Raymond Hitchcock (the producer/director) introduced his show, *Hitchy-Koo*, by rising out of his orchestra seat and saying "Well, I guess we're all here now, so let's begin the show." Everyone laughed and craned his head to see what was going on. He then turned around and explained the plot to the audience, making comments on various people as they came down to the seats. If a man came down to the first two or three rows, for which he had paid a spectacular $5 a seat, Hitch would suddenly break off and say "My, but he must be a rich man!" The house roared and the man felt flattered.

Another part of the improvisatory feeling of the show grew out of the fact that, though the plot of the show may have remained unchanged, many of the lines, unrelated to the plot, were simply there to give the actors something funny to say. In other words, what there was of a plot was continually interrupted by jokes. For the most part, that did not disturb the audiences; they loved it. Jolson said he changed jokes regularly to encourage his audiences to attend multiple performances.

The 1912 season opened with an Eddie Foy romp called *Over the River* at the Globe Theatre. It was based on a straight play of 1897 called *The Man from Mexico*. The plot concerned the problems of a man who must serve time in jail. Now too ashamed to confess the truth to his wife, he pretends he is going on a trip to Mexico. After he has vanished, his wife's travels, by highly unlikely coincidence, lead her to his jail cell.

Most of the songs in *Over the River* were composed by Jean Schwartz who later wrote the Jolson hit "Rock-A-Bye Your Baby with a Dixie Melody." The show featured all the latest dance crazes and may have inspired Irving Berlin's show of 1914, another dance-focused musical called *Watch Your Step*, starring Vernon and Irene

Castle—the most popular dance team in America and, arguably, the world.

Actually, the producers of *Over the River* had wanted Vernon and Irene Castle for their show, but those two were already negotiating with Berlin who was then the hottest young talent on Tin Pan Alley. His presence on Broadway would bring far more prestige to a production than Jean Schwartz could muster. So, the Castles chose the Berlin show.

To perform the dances that the Castles had first introduced—including the tango—the producers of *Over the River* hired the Marvelous Millers—now long forgotten—but at the time, the Millers were perhaps the Castles' closest competition. Of the Millers in *Over the Top* one critic said, "They whirl and whirl and whirl." There was some ragtime dancing, including the Turkey Trot and the Grizzly Bear, and composer Jean Schwartz took to the piano to accompany Lillian Lorraine and the chorus in his "Chopsticks Rag." Both the critics and the public liked this show.

Now to compete with The Follies, the Schuberts produced *The Passing Show of 1912*. They hired a line of beautiful girls, putting them in attractive—sometimes, provocative—costumes, as Ziegfeld had done in the Follies. They created an ocean liner set, a harem scene filled with bathing girls, and an elaborate ragtime wedding scene.

The comedy in *The Passing Show of 1912* came from burlesquing other shows that were on Broadway that same year. Among the stars of the show was long-limbed, high-kicking Charlotte Greenwood who would, 40 years later, play Auntie Eller in the film version of Rodgers and Hammerstein's *Oklahoma!*.

During this same period, Victor Herbert was very active, composing both *Naughty Marietta* and *Sweethearts* in 1913. Though we don't focus on operettas because they're a European form, we should at least hear from Victor Herbert whose *Babes in Toyland* has been revived every Christmas season for the past 100 years. Here's a little bit of a pre-1920s instrumental by Victor Herbert that was more than two decades later made into a very popular song and one of the Glenn Miller Band's biggest hits, "Indian Summer." Here's Ed Goldstein and company recreating the piece. *(Plays recording—"Indian Summer.")*

In December 1914, The New Amsterdam Theatre premiered Irving Berlin's first Broadway musical, *Watch Your Step*. It starred Vernon and Irene Castle, the most popular dance team in America. Already a sensation, this show made the Castles the toast of the world, and soon women began bobbing their hair like Irene Castle and wearing Irene Castle hats and Irene Castle makeup. Men smoked Vernon Castle cigars and danced in Vernon Castle shoes. Masters of self-promotion, the Castles, in their time, used merchandising in the way that Disney would 40 years later.

Here's a song from *Watch Your Step* that may have inspired a later George Gershwin song. In 1937, George and Ira Gershwin wrote a film for Fred Astaire and Ginger Rogers called *Shall We Dance?* One of the songs in that film was called, "They All Laughed." Some of the lyrics went, "They all laughed at Christopher Columbus when he said the world was round / They all laughed when Edison recorded sound." Well those same lines, slightly varied, exist in this much earlier Berlin song. Also, that song by the Gershwins and this song by Berlin is a list song. The similarities are so great that I strongly suspect Ira was thinking of this song when he wrote "They All Laughed." This is the Irving Berlin song from *Watch Your Step* and it's called, "When I Discovered You." *(Plays piano—"When I Discovered You.")*

Watch Your Step was destined to be Vernon and Irene Castle's first and final Broadway musical. When World War I began in Europe, Vernon joined the R.A.F. and was later killed when his plane crashed. Irene went on to a successful career in silent films. By the way, the plot of *Watch Your Step* mysteriously vanished during the second act.

Just a few words about plots, in general, 1914 style, so we can compare these to the later plot-centered shows of the '40s, '50s, and onward. Classic Broadway shows have both plots and subplots; that allows for several different kinds of conflict and doesn't restrict the important musical numbers to the leads in the show.

In the end, the subplot, skillfully employed, makes for a far more interesting musical. An example or two from more recent musicals: in *My Fair Lady*, Eliza's linguistic dilemma is balanced by her father's decision to marry the woman he's living with, as well as by his decision to become a lecturer at Higgins's prodding. In *The King and I*, the conflict between Anna and the King is balanced by the

©2006 The Teaching Company.

romance of the two young lovers. In *Showboat*, the subplot, Julie's being wronged because she is married to a white man, becomes as important as the vicissitudes of Magnolia and Ravenel, the two young lovers.

But, in 1914 and in all the years before the integrated musical, there was often no subplot and variety was often created by somewhat clumsy means. *Watch Your Step* is a perfect example. The plot had to do with a will leaving $2 million dollars to anyone who had never been in love, but by the second act, the story was just plain forgotten and the evening was turned into a facsimile of a Fifth Avenue nightclub floor show. One variety act after another appeared until the show's finale, and lots of wonderful dancing from Vernon and Irene Castle, which had zero to do with the long deserted plot. And yet, the show was unquestionably a success.

The next year, 1915, was the year a young man, destined to become one of America's greatest songwriters, mounted his first Broadway show. The young man was a recent graduate of Yale named Cole Porter. The show was called *See America First*. It was intended to be a spoof on the flag-waving musicals of George M. Cohan. Its convoluted story concerns an American senator who leaves the effete East so that his daughter can find a red-blooded he-man in the Wild West. By a coincidence, she meets a British duke disguised as a cowboy. Once she discovers the subterfuge, she wants nothing more to do with the duke. But, at the final curtain, after the cowboy-duke saves the whole cast from murderous bandits, the lovers reunite and win her parents' approval. "I've a Shooting Box in Scotland" was the only song the critics singled out as better than atrocious in this show. The Shooting Box song shows that there was a genius here, waiting for its day. Part of the words are:

> I've a shanty in the Rockies
>
> I've a castle on the Rhine
>
> If you care for hotter places,
>
> I've an African Oasis.

Nice rhymes. By the way, *See America First* was apparently the Broadway debut of the actor who would, during the 1950s, star in the *Mr. Belvedere* film series, Clifton Webb. Webb's one comment about *See America First* was, "I played a cowboy and an autumn flower. Others had roles not so believable."

The New York Tribune wasn't so kind. They called it "the newest and worst musical in town;" but still, the failure of his first Broadway musical didn't deter Cole Porter, thank goodness.

Now what's interesting is that there's nothing in this show that could hold up today, but fishing around in the Yale archives turned up one pretty good song written in 1912 for one of Porter's college shows. Porter's "Longing for Dear Old Broadway," obviously influenced by Cohan—it even begins with the same rhythm as "Give My Regards to Broadway."

Jari Villanueva, our brilliant arranger, saw the germ of Porter's later songs in this work and he orchestrated it with the kind of Latin background you'd expect to hear in later Porter songs like "Night and Day" and "I've Got You under My Skin." Bob Robinson does the vocal. Here it is—1912 Cole Porter at Yale, "Longing for Dear Old Broadway." *(Plays recording—"Longing for Dear Old Broadway.")* Very, very early Cole Porter.

Jerome Kern would do his second Princess Theatre show in 1915, by far his best work to date, and though the show contained no lasting standards, Kern's music and Guy Bolton's lyrics were a step closer to that ideal integrated score Kern was later to create for 1927's *Showboat.* The plot of his 1915 Princess Theatre show, *Very Good Eddie*, revolved around everyday people, for a change, and was nearly believable.

In the musical, the Hudson River Day Lines Catskill stops for 15 minutes at Poughkeepsie. Dick Rivers, played by Oscar Shaw, comes aboard. Much of the action takes place on the ship among its various passengers who include a pair of newlyweds. Various intrigues occur.

Now the strength here was that the people in *Very Good Eddie* were not cartoon clowns or cardboard heroes. Its situations were relatively plausible. Its songs, while not able to stand up without the supporting situations, were nonetheless serviceable and promised better things to come.

The Princess shows were a wonderful way for Kern to hone his skills. The entire budget for a show at the tiny 299-seat theater was

©2006 The Teaching Company.

under $8,000. The weekly costs were less than the weekly salary of one star at the larger theaters. The limitations of the theater—the small stage and the small budget—were a challenge to Kern. His solutions resulted in intimate productions. I'm reminded of the Fantasticks at the tiny Sullivan Street Playhouse in Greenwich Village. Both shows had to employ subtlety because grand effects would have thrown the entire budget out of control.

The Princess Theatre stage wasn't large enough for a conventional chorus, so there were ensemble quartets and sextets, and the orchestra itself was unlike anything previously heard in a show that filled a theater to capacity every evening. Frank Sadler, who wrote Kern's orchestrations, arranged the music so that it needed no more than 11 musicians. Now somehow, instead of making the show seem like a cheapskate production, all these factors created a degree of added intimacy, subtlety, and sophistication that was quite new to Broadway. At the show's end, people felt as if they had been privileged to attend an exclusive, private soiree.

The period between 1909 to 1915 saw not only the early flowering of Cole Porter, Irving Berlin, and Jerome Kern; it also saw the remaining two of the big five of the 20th century, George Gershwin and Richard Rodgers, learning by listening to the works of these slightly older role models. George Gershwin is said to have been inspired to write a higher kind of popular song when he heard Jerome Kern's "They Didn't Believe Me."

During this early period, something new was on the artistic horizon. Harriet Monroe founded *Poetry Magazine* in 1912, making household names of poets like Robert Frost, and Edward Arlington Robinson, and T S Eliot. In 1914, Edgar Lee Masters published *Spoon River Anthology*, the first collection of poems to become a bestseller. The visual arts were undergoing an explosion of Modernism. Think of Duchamp, Modigliani, and Picasso. Ragtime was still in vogue and so were the blues, first made popular in 1914 with the publication of Handy's *St. Louis Blues*. The old order of Broadway, with its musical roots in Europe, was giving way to the newer sounds, indigenous to America. The excitement of blue notes and syncopated rhythms was, at that point, the sound of Modernism, and this period, from 1909 to 1915, was a time of trial and error and a period of gestation for musical talents that were to triumph in the following decades.

Lecture Ten
Transition into the Jazz Age (1916–20)

Scope:

To some extent, every period of time represents a breakaway from the period that preceded it, but the years from 1916 to 1920 represent a particularly dramatic breakaway—in clothing styles, in acceptable public behavior, in language, in visual arts, and in the kind of music Americans created and listened to. America, for the first time, made the blues mainstream by turning W. C. Handy's song of 1914, "St. Louis Blues," into a standard over the next few years. Albert Einstein's 1915 publication of his general theory of relativity reformed the educated man's sense of space and time and created a rationale for artistic, social, and moral relativity. The dream world of surrealism allowed the artist to create worlds that defied the logic of everyday life but provoked the viewer into examining his or her inner life. In 1920, prohibition became law, but a few months later, another prohibition was lifted: The 19th Amendment allowed women to vote and, consequently, to possess a new power.

We might tend to ascribe these changes to World War I, but to some extent, the changes were already occurring, and the war, of course, accelerated them. Women shed pounds of clothing and cut their hair in the flapper bob. The new clothing styles, frenetic dances, and informal language appeared shortly after the war was over, as did the jazz- and blues-inspired songs that became the basis for George Gershwin's compositional technique a few years later. As the end of the Vietnam War did, the end of World War I gave us an excuse to kick up our heels and rebel against the past.

Outline

I. On the musical stage, particularly in vaudeville and in the revue, songs of suffrage, both pro and con, were sung in the period 1916–1920. There were several parodies of the old song "Everybody Works but Father" with the gender changed because mother was busy on the picket lines.

    A. At the same time, Hollywood began to challenge the musical theater stage for America's attention. Mary Pickford and Pearl White, both silent film stars, each had vaudeville songs written about them. These two celebrities represented the pre-feminist and post-feminist ideals.

1. Biographer Lester Levy called Pickford "a beautiful girl with golden ringlets, a captivating smile, and innocent blue eyes." She was born Gladys Smith in 1893 in Toronto, Canada, and she came to Hollywood in the days when Los Angeles was mostly adobe haciendas, sand, and sagebrush.

2. In 1917, the magazine *Ladies World* conducted a popularity contest, in which Pickford received 1,147,000 votes, a half million more than her closest competitor. Several years later, Sid Grauman, the owner of Grauman's Chinese Theatre, gave her the title by which she is remembered today, "America's Sweetheart."

3. One of Richard Whiting's first songs was called "Mary Pickford—The Darling of Them All." It became a favorite on the vaudeville stage.

B. In contrast, Pearl White's *Perils of Pauline* films were rugged adventures, and she found her own solutions to problems, rather than waiting to be rescued. Regardless of the danger, Pearl White insisted on doing her own stunts.

1. In April 1916, in New York City, White hung from the roof of a building on Seventh Avenue, and at a height of several hundred feet, using a gas torch, she burned her initials in large letters on the wall, a stunt that made front-page headlines.

2. Immediately after the United States entered World War I, White was lashed to a steel cable being used in the construction of a 20-story building and hauled to the top, throwing down American flags and recruiting circulars during her upward journey. When she was lowered to the ground, she led dozens of young men to an Army recruiting station, where they immediately enlisted.

3. White became fabulously wealthy, her income, at its peak, reaching $10,000 a week, which she spent lavishly. Sadly, she died alone, addicted to gambling and still given to sudden, compulsive adventures.

4. The song "Poor Pauline!" was inspired by her adventure films and was one of the popular songs of the stage during the years immediately before the war.

II. After World War I, jazz had people dancing and singing their way down the road to perdition. Let's take a look at some of the shows of the period from 1916 to 1920.

A. Churning out a new Princess Theatre show as often as every six months, Jerome Kern was honing his craft and, at times, showed glimmers of his greatness yet to come. The Princess was a small theater, and the show's budgets were even smaller; though they generally had short runs, nearly all of Kern's shows made a profit.

    1. *Oh Boy!* was Kern's longest running show before 1920. Premiering at the Princess on February 20, 1917, it ran for 463 performances. Its lyrics were by P. G. Wodehouse and its book was a collaboration between Wodehouse and Guy Bolton.

    2. One lasting song came from the show, "Till the Clouds Roll By." We hear a rare 1917 recording of the song by Anne Wheaton.

B. The *Ziegfeld Follies of 1918* included Marilyn Miller, Eddie Cantor, W. C. Fields, and Will Rogers, among others. This year and the next represent the high points of the Follies.

    1. The first act of the 1918 Follies focused on World War I in most of its sketches, production numbers, and songs. The second act showed women on the home front performing jobs usually done by men. In order not to rankle the audience, who were looking at a stage full of what appeared to be "able-bodied" men, a note in the program stated, "All members of the male chorus were rejected for military service."

    2. For these Follies, Ziegfeld hired bandleader Art Hickman, who wrote an instrumental for the show called "Rose Room," which we listen to. During the big band era, the song became a staple, recorded by Ellington, Lunceford, Artie Shaw, and Benny Goodman, among others.

    3. Few recorded examples exist from the 1918 Follies, but we'll listen to Eddie Cantor singing a song he recorded from the Follies the year before, "That's the Kind of Baby for Me."

III. Eddie Cantor (1892–1964) was one of America's most popular comedian singers and one of Ziegfeld's highest paid stars. In the years after World War I, he became a household name.

A. At around 14, Cantor landed his first job on Broadway with a vaudeville juggling act called Bedini and Arthur. He was originally hired to run errands and to press the jugglers' costumes. Later, after drawing a laugh from the audience during a walk-on, he was billed as part of the act.

B. It was in this show that Gus Edwards saw Cantor and offered him $75 a week to star in his *Kid Kabaret* vaudeville act. In 1916, after appearing in *Kid Kabaret*, Cantor was discovered by Ziegfeld, who made him into a Broadway star. Cantor later starred in *Whoopee*, the biggest show of 1928, in which he introduced the great standard "Makin' Whoopee."

IV. The war was in full swing, and the Harlem Renaissance was also starting to take shape.

A. The Army had promised to open a special officer training school if 200 college-educated African-Americans enlisted; 1,500 did so, including James Reese Europe, who had been Vernon and Irene Castle's band leader and music director. Europe organized an orchestra of African-Americans that played close to the fighting lines in a regiment called the Hell Fighters.

B. By the end of World War I, the Harlem area of New York had become the largest urban black community in the world.

1. The crowded streets of Harlem were alive with different kinds of music and speech. Poets, such as Langston Hughes and Contee Cullen; musicians, including Duke Ellington and Eubie Blake; authors; and actors flocked to Harlem.

2. In the 1930s, new dances, invented in Harlem, swept the nation, including the Jitterbug and the Lindy Hop. After World War I, Harlem's Savoy Ballroom became the home of the earliest big band jazz. By 1927, young Duke Ellington led his band at Harlem's world-famous Cotton Club.

3. In 1917, a Chicagoan named Shelton Brooks wrote music and lyrics to a hit song that would soon bring him to Harlem. The "Darktown Strutters' Ball" was introduced in vaudeville by the white vocal trio of Benny Fields, Jack Salisbury, and Benny Davis, and its catchy tune was immediately recorded by the Original Dixieland Jazz Band. We listen to the song now.

C. During the early 1920s, Spencer Williams brought his Harlem cabaret to Paris with his latest discovery, a teenaged dancer named Josephine Baker. In Paris, in *Charleston Cabaret*, Baker danced wearing only a strategically placed flamingo feather. The opening-night audience went crazy. Baker had shocked the unshockable city. From that point until her death in 1975, Baker was a Parisian and a legendary performer.

V. The *Greenwich Village Follies of 1919*, produced by John Murray Anderson, opened at the Greenwich Village Theatre on July 15, 1919, running for 232 performances and threatening Flo Ziegfeld's supremacy in the production of lavish revues.

A. The show was so successful that the small Greenwich Village Theatre couldn't accommodate the crowds. After six weeks, the show was moved uptown to the larger Nora Bayes Theatre on 44th Street, close enough to Ziegfeld's Winter Garden to further rankle Ziegfeld.

B. The show, which called itself a revusical comedy of New York's Latin Quarter, took satirical aim at all the topics that were destined to dominate the 1920s—free love, prohibition, and modern art, among others. Its distinguishing characteristic was the use of female impersonators.

C. The year 1919 also gave the world Cole Porter's first hit song, which was absolutely abominable but popular nonetheless! It appeared in *Hitchy-Koo of 1919*, produced by Raymond Hitchcock. We listen to the song of the same name.

VI. Though the ubiquitous Cinderella stories of the 1920s seemed as if they'd been around forever, they began, as a popular musical theater genre, in 1919, with the longest running show of that year, *Irene*, with music by Harry Tierney and lyrics by Joseph McCarthy.

A. *Irene* ran at the Vanderbilt Theatre for 670 performances, and its record wasn't broken until 1937's *Pins and Needles*. *Irene* had a fairly believable plot, told about fairly believable people who sang songs that weren't forced into the story but appeared, on the whole, at places where songs might further the story.

B. Irene O'Dare, a poor shop girl from a Lower East Side tenement, is sent on an errand to the Marshalls' elegant estate. The critics loved the set that depicted the fire escape outside the O'Dares' flat. The scene (though not the action) is nearly identical to the balcony scene in *West Side Story*. The Marshalls' son falls in love with Irene and attempts to palm her off on his parents as a debutante.

C. The hit of the show, sung in the first act by Irene, was one of the most popular waltzes of the 20th century. The original Irene, Edith Day, had to leave the cast after the first five months to head the London cast. She was succeeded in the New York run by a series of Irenes that included a real Irene—Irene Dunne, who was at the beginning of her career. We listen to this hit, "Alice Blue Gown."

VII. In 1920, Jerome Kern graduated from the tiny Princess Theatre shows to the spacious New Amsterdam Theatre in a show produced by Flo Ziegfeld, *Sally*. The hit of the show, "Look for the Silver Lining," remains one of Kern's greatest songs.

A. We'll hear a recording of this song in our next lecture when we take a closer look at two Broadway greats, Irving Berlin and Jerome Kern, but we'll listen to just a little of the melody here.

B. In *Sally*, Sally Green first appears as a dishwashing drudge at the Alley Inn in Greenwich Village, dreaming of a better future. The song she sings, "Look for the Silver Lining," is also sung by Judy Garland in MGM's film biography of Jerome Kern, *Till the Clouds Roll By*.

C. Sally is invited by one of the Alley Inn's waiters (played by Leon Errol), who is really the exiled Duke of Cheshogovina, to an elegant uptown ball. Sally goes, pretending to be a celebrated ballerina, Mme. Nookerova. Her true identity is discovered, but in the end, she not only wins the wealthy young tenor but is also signed for the Ziegfeld Follies, where she dances an interpolated "Butterfly Ballet" by Victor Herbert.

D. At 570 performances, *Sally* was the third longest-running musical of the 1920s, coming in close behind number two, Kern's *Show Boat*, and number one, Romberg's operetta of 1924, *The Student Prince*. *Sally* is the first all-Kern show to display consistently that Schubertian lyricism so evident in later Kern songs, such as "Smoke Gets in Your Eyes," "Yesterdays," and "The Way You Look Tonight."

VIII. Finally, we take a look at the George White Scandals of 1919 and 1920. The name alone is a sign of the times to come. Before the war, scandals were to be avoided; after the war, they were to be indulged in and enjoyed.

A. White, who began as a dancer in the Ziegfeld Follies, produced shows that contained well-crafted songs and lively, athletic dances. White's name was not in the title of the first Scandals in 1919, but after the immense success of that first revue, the series became known, from 1920 onward, as the George White Scandals.

B. White (1890–1968), born George Weitz on the Lower East Side, worked his way from being a Bowery saloon hoofer to a solo spot in the Ziegfeld Follies. With Ann Pennington, he choreographed the first edition of the Scandals. Though there was more dancing in the first Scandals than in the Follies, the formula was similar. A stage filled with beautiful girls, beautifully attired, made the Scandals the "must-see" show of Broadway.

IX. A new age was firmly established in 1920. The war was over; the ragtime era was over; the prewar formality and elegance were gone. New ideas and new forms of behavior were coming to be accepted. And a new young composer named George Gershwin was about to give jazz new, and apparently permanent, respect.

A. The country's postwar prosperity gave it a new optimism, tempered by a light-hearted cynicism. During the 1920s, young men and women would turn their backs on "Alice Blue Gown" and dance the Charleston to "Runnin' Wild" and "Yes Sir, That's My Baby."

B. I think it would be appropriate to end this lesson with a hit song from the 1918 Broadway musical *Ladies First*. The show ran through 1919, and on January 29, 1919, the secretary of state announced that prohibition would be the law of the land. Broadway's reaction was a rash of interpolated songs about prohibition.

1. First, we listen to "Jada," a popular World War I song that was converted into a prohibition parody.
2. From *Ladies First*, we hear "Prohibition Blues," sung by Nora Bayes and written by Bayes and the humorist Ring Lardner. The popularity of this interpolation outlasted the show.

Suggested Reading:

Gerald Bordman, *American Musical Theatre: A Chronicle.*

Stanley Green, *The World of Musical Comedy.*

Questions to Consider:

1. What changes in the arts occurred during this period that might be called harbingers of the modernist 1920s?
2. Discuss the relationships between the new music called *jazz* and the Harlem Renaissance that was on the horizon.

Lecture Ten—Transcript
Transition into the Jazz Age (1916–20)

To some extent, every period of time represents a breakaway from the period that preceded it, but the years between 1916 and 1920 represent a particularly dramatic breakaway. A breakaway in clothing styles, in acceptable public behavior, in language, in visual arts, and in the kind of music Americans created and listened to.

America, for the first time, made the blues mainstream by turning W. C. Handy's song of 1914, "St. Louis Blues," into a standard. Albert Einstein's 1915 publication of his general theory of relativity reformed the educated man's sense of space and time, and created a rationale—however specious—for artistic, social, and moral relativity. In 1916, Margaret Sanger founded the first birth control clinic in the United States in Brooklyn, New York; and, with this action, she helped create the possibility of a woman whose fate did not totally depend upon the whims of a man.

Though the surrealist movement was founded by André Breton in France in 1924, the word "surreal" was created in 1917 by the poet Apollinaire. He described Picasso's set designs for the Ballet Russe as "surreal." The dream world of Surrealism allowed the artist to create worlds that defied the logic of everyday life, but which, hopefully, provoked the viewer into examining his own inner life. In 1920, Prohibition became law, but a few months later, another prohibition was lifted—the passage of the 19th Amendment allowed women to vote and, consequently, to possess a new power. Now, we might tend to ascribe these changes to the war—World War I—but to some extent, the changes were already in progress and the war, of course, accelerated them.

Women shed pounds and pounds and pounds of clothing, discarding their bustles, their ostrich-feather hats for the new near naked little-girl look. Even their long hair—the crowning glory of their femininity and of their servitude—was shorn off in favor of the flapper bob. These new clothing styles, the frenetic new dances, and the more informal language appeared shortly after the war. So did the jazz- and blues-inspired songs that became the basis for George Gershwin's compositional technique a few years later. The 1920s may have hatched the jazz age, but—if you'll excuse my word choice—World War I laid the egg. Like the end of the Vietnam War,

 ©2006 The Teaching Company.

the end of World War I gave us an excuse to kick up our heels and rebel against the world of our parents.

On the musical stage—particularly in vaudeville and in the revue—songs of suffrage, both pro and con, were being sung. There were several parodies of the old song "Everybody Works but Father," with the gender changed due to mother's being busy on the picket lines. The suffragettes themselves sang:

> We will ne'er retreat an inch
>
> Until opposition's done
>
> And all the world proclaims to us
>
> That women's rights are won.

Hollywood began to challenge the musical theater stage for America's attention. Mary Pickford and Pearl White, both silent-film stars, each had vaudeville songs written about them. These two celebrities represented the pre-feminist and post-feminist ideals. Biographer Lester Levy called Pickford, and I'm quoting, "a beautiful girl with golden ringlets, a captivating smile, and innocent blue eyes." She was born Gladys Smith in 1893 [sic 1892] in Toronto, Canada, and she came to Hollywood in the days when Los Angeles was mostly adobe haciendas, sand, and sagebrush.

In 1917, the magazine *Ladies World* conducted a popularity contest. Mary Pickford received 1,147,000 votes—a half million more than her closest competitor. Several years later, Sid Grauman, the owner of Grauman's Chinese Theatre, gave her the title by which she is remembered today—America's Sweetheart. At the age of 25, Pickford's silent films were making her a million dollars a year. Through it all, she remained feminine, in the old fashioned sense, and modest.

When she was told one day that she had drawn a crowd larger than any crowd that ever assembled outside the White House to see the President of the United States, she replied: "A white elephant taking a morning stroll would have drawn a bigger crowd than either of us."

One of Richard Whiting's earliest songs was written for Mary Pickford. Richard Whiting was the father of the Big Band singer, Margaret Whiting—wrote a lot of great songs with Johnny Mercer, including "Too Marvelous for Words," but this was one of his earliest songs; it may be the first. It's called "Mary Pickford—The Darling of Them All" and it became a favorite on the vaudeville stage. This is how it goes. *(Plays piano—"Mary Pickford—The Darling of Them All.")*

But Pearl White was a silent star whose film persona was less like that of Mary Pickford than it was like that of Arnold Schwarzenegger. Her *Perils of Pauline* films were rugged adventures and, seldom waiting to be rescued by some Hollywood ham, she found her own solutions to her perilous problems. Regardless of the danger, Pearl White insisted on doing all her own stunts.

In April, 1916, in New York City, she hung from the roof of a building on Seventh Avenue and, at the height of several hundred feet, using a gas torch, she burned her initials, P. W., into the wall in very, very large letters that could be seen from the ground. It was a stunt that made front-page headlines. Immediately after the United States had entered World War I, she was lashed to a steel cable being used in the construction of the 20-story Bush Terminal Building and they hauled her to the top. All the way up and all the way down, she threw down American flags and recruiting circulars. When she was lowered to the ground, she shouted, "I have done my part—now you do yours!" She then marched to an Army recruiting station, followed by dozens and dozens of young men who immediately signed up for the service.

Pearl White became fabulously wealthy; her income—at its peak—was at least $10,000 a week, which she spent lavishly. Among Pearl White's acquisitions were a Park Avenue penthouse, a French maid, $25,000 worth of jewels, a $14,000 Rolls Royce, and a sporty Stutz-Bearcat—which she drove herself. I mention that because most women did not drive cars in those days. Pearl White, as wild in life as on the screen, was far closer to the feminine ideal of the jazz age than was Mary Pickford, who finally cut off her curls, settled down with bandleader Buddy Rogers, and raised two children to live a responsible and peaceful life into contented old age.

Pearl White, on the other hand, retained the wildness of her youth and died alone. A heavy drinker addicted to gambling, still given to sudden compulsive adventures, which bring a younger woman admiration but often bring an older one pity. As the titles in her adventure films so often said. "Poor Pauline!" She lived like a 21st-century rock star. "Poor Pauline," by the way, was one of the popular songs of the stage during the years immediately before the war. It goes like this. *(Plays piano—"Poor Pauline.")*

Before World War I, women were arrested for wearing bathing suits that exposed the arms and the knees. After World War I, the bathing suits that most young women wore exposed both the thighs and even a little bit of the bosom. Jazz and jazz dances had people in public places shimmying parts of the body that would also have brought the paddy wagon around before the war. The country was dancing and singing its way down the road to Perdition. That road was paved during the years from 1916 to 1920. Let's take a look at some of the shows of that era.

Churning out a new Princess Theatre show as often as every six months, Jerome Kern was honing his craft and, at times, showed glimmers of his greatness to come. The Princess was a tiny theater and the show's budgets were even tinier, so the generally short runs of his shows didn't reflect lack of success; nearly all of them made a profit.

Oh, Boy! was Kern's longest-running show before 1920 and was the third longest-running musical by anyone during the decade between 1910 and 1920. Premiering at The Princess on February 20, 1917, it ran for 463 performances. With lyrics by P. G. Wodehouse and the book by a collaboration between Wodehouse and Guy Bolton, two of the show's stars were destined for successful film careers—Edna May Oliver and Marion Davies, who is probably best remembered for being the mistress of William Randolph Hearst.

Now he's the newspaper tycoon whose social life at his California castle, San Simeon, revolved around entertaining America's new royalty, film stars like Douglas Fairbanks, Charlie Chaplin, and our friend, Mary Pickford. Hearst's life inspired the Orson Wells's film *Citizen Kane.*

One lasting song came from *Oh, Boy!* sung by Anne Wheaton. Here's the rare 1917 recording sung by Wheaton exactly as she sang it in the show. By the way, this song title, "Till the Clouds Roll By," became the title of MGM's 1946 film biography of Kern. Here's the song. *(Plays recording—"Till the Clouds Roll By.")* That was the Jerome Kern standard, "Till the Clouds Roll By," as people heard it a long, long time ago.

The *Ziegfeld Follies of 1918*, included Marilyn Miller, Eddie Cantor, W. C. Fields, and Will Rogers, among others; 1918 and 1919 represent the high points of the Follies. The 1918 show put the focus on World War I in most of its sketches, production numbers, and songs. These included a "Yankee Doodle" dance by Marilyn Miller, Will Rogers's topical monologues, a skit with Eddie Cantor playing a rather clumsy would-be aviator in a recruiting office, a parade of showgirls representing the allied nations, and a first-act finale of living statues entitled "Forward Allies."

The second act showed women on the home front performing jobs usually done by men. Now, in order not to rankle the audience, who could have been very upset by this, the audience was looking at a stage full of what appeared to be "able-bodied" men. So, a note in the program stated that, and I'm quoting, "All members of the male chorus were rejected for military service." The rehearsal pianist for this show was a 19-year-old boy named George Gershwin.

For these Follies, Ziegfeld hired bandleader Art Hickman who wrote an instrumental for the Follies called "Rose Room." During the Big Band era, "Rose Room" became a standard, recorded by Ellington, Lunceford, Artie Shaw, and Benny Goodman, among others. Here it is. *(Plays piano—"Rose Room.")*

Few recorded examples exist from the 1918 Follies, so we'll let you hear Eddie Cantor sing the song he recorded from the Follies the year before. This is called "That's the Kind of Baby for Me." *(Plays recording—"That's the Kind of Baby for Me.")* Eddie Cantor.

Eddie Cantor was one of America's most popular comedian singers and one of Ziegfeld's highest paid stars. He deserves a little more of our attention, particularly now, because the years after World War I made him a household name. At around 14, Cantor landed his very first job on Broadway with a vaudeville-juggling act called *Bedini and Arthur*. He was hired not to be an actor or to juggle; he was hired to run to the store for sandwiches and coffee, and to press the jugglers' costumes. But, he fell in love with show business.

One day he was told to come onstage at a signal and hand Bedini a plate. Now, unknown to the jugglers, Eddie Cantor worked for hours and hours on his makeup and costume, and decided to take his time giving Bedini the plate. Eddie had huge, round, expressive eyes; later in his career, he was often called "banjo eyes." So, from offstage, he watched the juggling act. When Bedini gave him the signal to come on, Eddie walked on to the stage. But, instead of just handing over the plate, he looked at Bedini with those big eyes, he looked at Arthur with those big eyes, he looked at the audience with those big eyes, and then finally gave Bedini the plate and walked off. The audience laughed and applauded. From that day on, Eddie Cantor was billed as part of the act.

It was in this capacity that Gus Edwards saw Cantor and offered him $75 a week to star in his *Kid Kabaret* vaudeville act; and it was in 1916, after appearing in *Kid Kabaret*, that Cantor was discovered by Ziegfeld, who turned him into a Broadway star. Eddie Cantor later starred in *Whoopee*, the biggest show of 1928, in which he introduced the great standard:

> Another bride
>
> Another groom
>
> Another sunny honeymoon
>
> Another season
>
> Another reason
>
> For makin' whoopee.

Now, with the war in full swing, the Harlem Renaissance was just around the corner. The Army had said that if 200 college-educated blacks signed up for the army, they would open a special officer training school for blacks. How many signed up? Fifteen-hundred black college men signed up—including James Reese Europe, who had been Vernon and Irene Castle's band director and music director. He organized an orchestra of blacks that played close to the fighting lines. Their regiment was called the Hell Fighters and they were welcomed home with a ticker-tape parade as they marched down 5th Avenue after the Armistice. Returning blacks expected something a little better after the war and what they got was a *little* better.

By the end of World War I, the Harlem area of New York City had become the largest urban black community on the face of the planet Earth. Black people from Jamaica, Haiti, Cuba, Puerto Rico, Africa, and other places mingled with American blacks from the North and from the South. The crowded streets of Harlem were alive with different kinds of music and different kinds of speech. Poets like

Langston Hughes and Contee Cullen, musicians like Duke Ellington and Eubie Blake, authors, and actors flocked to Harlem. It became a black Greenwich Village.

In the 1930s, new dances invented in Harlem swept the nation, including the Jitterbug and the Lindy Hop. After World War I, Harlem's Savoy Ballroom became the home of the earliest Big Band jazz, played by bandleaders like Don Redmond and Chick Webb. By 1927, young Duke Ellington led his band at Harlem's world-famous Cotton Club.

In 1917, a Chicagoan named Shelton Brooks wrote music and lyrics to a hit song that would soon bring him to Harlem. He had already written Sophie Tucker's theme song, "Some of These Days," back in 1910. The year 1917 saw the publication of the song, "The Darktown Strutters Ball." It was introduced in vaudeville by the white vocal trio of Benny Fields, Jack Salisbury, and Benny Davis, and its catchy tune was immediately recorded by the hottest new group in America, the Original Dixieland Jazz Band. The title, by the way, "The Darktown Strutters Ball," referred to an annual social event in San Francisco's black community. Soon, band after band was playing the song. In a relatively short time, the sheet music, published by Leo Feist in New York, sold three million copies. It was even a bestseller in Europe, with French words. This is a song that never goes out of style; a nice little bluesy thing really, "The Darktown Strutters Ball." *(Plays piano—"The Darktown Strutters Ball.")*

During the 1920s, Spencer Williams brought his Harlem cabaret to Paris. Now anybody who's over 50 may remember Spencer Williams from the old *Amos and Andy Show* because he played Andy on that series. That was much, much later in life. At this point, he was a very young man; he was a piano player and a composer. Well he brought his Harlem cabaret to Paris with his latest discovery, a young Harlem dancer named Josephine Baker. In Paris, in Williams's show called *Charleston Cabaret,* Baker danced frenetically, wearing only a strategically placed flamingo feather. The opening-night audience went crazy. Baker had shocked the unshockable city. From that point until her death, Baker was a Parisian and a legendary performer.

Now at the Music Box, a small club on the Rue Pigalle run by West Virginian expatriate Ada "Bricktop" Smith, Baker would eat soul food while Cole Porter and Spencer Williams took turns playing the piano. On and off, Williams remained in Europe until after World

©2006 The Teaching Company.

War II. In 1928, he revisited his old hometown of New Orleans, where he wrote music and lyrics of a great New Orleans standard called "Basin Street Blues." Josephine Baker remained in Paris until her death in 1975.

The *Greenwich Village Follies of 1919*—which was successful enough to run through eight yearly editions—opened at the Greenwich Village Theater on July 15, 1919, running for 232 performances and threatening Flo Ziegfeld's supremacy in the production of lavish revues. As a matter of fact, Ziegfeld tried his best to sue John Murray Anderson, the producer of the show, claiming that Anderson had stolen his title, "The Follies." Anderson proved that a "Follies" had been produced in New York City long before Ziegfeld had begun his own Follies. Consequently, the label "Follies" could not be considered Ziegfeld's private property.

The show became so successful that the small Greenwich Village Theater couldn't accommodate the crowds. So, after six weeks, they moved it uptown to the much larger Nora Bayes Theatre on 44th Street, close enough to Ziegfeld's Winter Garden to further rankle the man.

Now that became the usual procedure for producing the Greenwich Village Follies. You had to start in Greenwich Village because if you didn't, how could you have the nerve to call it The Greenwich Village Follies? Subsequent editions played the mandatory few weeks in the Village before they moved on to a larger house on Broadway. The show, which called itself a "revusical" comedy of New York's Latin Quarter, took satirical aim at all the topics that were destined to dominate the 1920s—free love, Prohibition, modern art, among others. The distinguishing characteristic—something that was never close to Ziegfeld's heart—was the use of female impersonators. Now while Ziegfeld was glorifying the American girl, John Murray Anderson was also glorifying the American girl, even though, in this case, she was really a boy.

The year 1919 gave the world Cole Porter's very first hit song; it's absolutely awful, but it was his first hit! It appeared in *Hitchy-Koo* of 1919, produced by Raymond Hitchcock, hence the title *Hitchy-Koo*. This is that first Cole Porter hit. *(Plays piano—"Old Fashioned Garden.")*

Would you ever believe that was Cole Porter? But a very young Cole Porter. Now how was that song staged? You're going to find this hard to believe, but it's the truth. Two American Indians—Chief Eagle Horse and Princess White Deer—sang and danced this ballad that gives new meaning to the word "schmaltz." The song was a success; the show was not, closing after the first five weeks. It would be five years before another Cole Porter score would be heard on a Broadway stage.

Though the ubiquitous "Cinderella" shows of the 1920s seemed as if they'd been around forever, they began as a popular musical theater genre in 1919, with the longest-running show of that year and of the century up to 1919. The show was *Irene*, with music by Harry Tierney and lyrics by Joseph McCarthy. The show ran at the Vanderbilt Theatre for 670 performances and its record wasn't broken until 1937's *Pins and Needles*.

Irene had a pretty believable plot for the time. It told about pretty believable people who sang attractive songs that weren't totally forced into the story, but appeared, on the whole, at places where songs might actually further the plot. Irene O'Dare, a poor shop girl from the Lower East Side tenement, is sent on an errand to the Marshall's elegant Long Island estate. The critics loved the set that depicted the fire escape outside the O'Dare flat. The scene—though not the action—is nearly identical to the balcony scene in *West Side Story*. The Marshall's son falls in love with Irene and attempts to palm her off on his parents as a debutante.

The hit of the show, sung in the first act by Irene, was one of the most popular waltzes of the 20th century. The original Irene—Edith Day—had to leave the cast after the first five months to head the London cast. She was succeeded in the New York run by a series of Irenes that included a real Irene named Irene Dunne who was at the very beginning of her career. Irene Dunne went on to star in the 1936 film version of *Showboat*. Here's Irene's big song from *Irene*. It's called "Alice Blue Gown." *(Plays piano—"Alice Blue Gown.")*

In 1920, Jerome Kern graduated from the tiny Princess Theatre shows to the spacious New Amsterdam Theatre in a show produced by Flo Ziegfeld called *Sally*. The hit of the show, "Look for the Silver Lining," remains one of Kern's greatest songs. You'll hear the recording in our next lecture when we take a closer look at two Broadway greats—Irving Berlin and Jerome Kern—but for now, let

 ©2006 The Teaching Company.

me just play the melody. *(Plays piano—"Look for the Silver Lining.")*

In 1920's *Sally*, Sally Green first appears as a dishwashing drudge at the Alley Inn in Greenwich Village, dreaming of a better future in a better place. That's when she sings "Look for the Silver Lining." Now if you want to see that number almost exactly as it was originally staged and sung—not by the original star, Marilyn Miller, but by Judy Garland, a far better singer—go to your local video store and take out a copy of *Till the Clouds Roll By*, MGM's film biography of Jerome Kern.

Sally's plot is an exaggerated version of *Irene*'s plot. You see, Sally is invited by one of the Alley Inn's waiters—played by Leon Errol—who is really the exiled Duke of Cheshogovina, to an elegant uptown ball. Now Sally goes to the ball pretending to be the celebrated ballerina, Madame Nookerova. Now in *Irene* fashion, her true identity is, at last, discovered. At the end, she not only wins the wealthy young tenor, but she is also signed for the Ziegfeld Follies, where she dances an interpolated Butterfly Ballet written by Victor Herbert.

At 570 performances, *Sally* ended up being the third longest-running musicals of the 1920s, running close behind number two, Kern's *Showboat*, and number one, Romberg's operetta of 1924, *The Student Prince*. *Sally* is the first all-Kern show to consistently display that Schubertian lyricism so evident in later songs like "Smoke Gets in Your Eyes," "Yesterdays," and "The Way You Look Tonight."

Finally, we have to look at the George White Scandals of 1919 and 1920. The name of the series alone is a sign of the time to come. Before the war, can you imagine a show called the Scandals? Scandals were something to be avoided; after the war, they were something to be indulged in—enjoyed. Newly emancipated women drank and smoked in public; couples lived together without benefit of a marriage license; men strolled the public beaches naked from the waist up. It was a scandal! And it was also fun. And, wasn't it appropriate to call an up-to-the-minute revue the Scandals? Young George Gershwin was soon to write his earliest quality songs for the Scandals, among them "Stairway to Paradise," "Do it Again," and "Somebody Loves Me."

White, who began as a dancer in the Ziegfeld Follies, produced shows that contained well-crafted songs and lively athletic dances. White's name was not in the title of the first Scandals—the 1919 Scandals—but after the immense success of that first show, the series became known, from 1920 onward, as The George White Scandals.

George White, born George Weitz—W-E-I-T-Z—on the Lower East Side, worked his way from being a Bowery Saloon hoofer to a solo spot in the Ziegfeld Follies. With his Follies associate Ann Pennington, he choreographed the first edition of the Scandals. A chorus of shimmying dancers helped keep the Scandals scandalous. Now though there was more dancing in the Scandals than in the Follies, the formula was very similar. A stage filled with beautiful girls, beautifully—and skimpily—attired, made the Scandals the "must-see" show of Broadway.

The year 1920 firmly established the fact that a new age had begun. The war was over, the ragtime era was over; the pre-war formality and elegance was gone. New ideas and new forms of behavior were roaring and rioting. A new young composer named George Gershwin was about to give the jazz age—and, apparently, jazz, itself—new respect.

The country's post-war prosperity gave it a new optimism, tempered by a lighthearted cynicism. "You are all a lost generation," Hemingway had written in *The Sun Also Rises*, quoting Gertrude Stein, who, in turn, was quoting her garage mechanic, who was frustrated with the young jaded World War I veterans who worked for him.

During the 1920s, Sheiks and Shebas would turn their backs on "Alice Blue Gown" and dance the Charleston to "Runnin' Wild" and to "Yes Sir, That's My Baby." The noble experiment would prove to be a noble bust. In frustration, the mayor of New York City said, "It would take a police force of 250,000 to enforce Prohibition. And, it would take another 200,000 to police the police!"

I think it would be appropriate to end this lesson with a hit song from the 1918 Broadway musical *Ladies First*. The show ran through 1919 and on January 29, 1919, the Secretary of State announced that Prohibition would be the law of the land. Broadway's reaction was a rash of interpolated songs about Prohibition. Now here's a popular World War I song that was converted into a Prohibition parody.

©2006 The Teaching Company.

Originally, it was called "Jada," *(Plays piano—"Jada.")* with sort of nonsense lyrics. But, during Prohibition and right before Prohibition, because they were all looking forward to the day that it would be enforced—maybe "looking forward" isn't a good phrase—they sang this song. *(Plays piano.)* Now Nora Bayes, herself, with a little assistance from her friend, humorist Ring Lardner, helped pen an interpolation whose popularity actually outlasted the show. Here's Nora Bayes singing "Prohibition Blues." *(Plays recording— "Prohibition Blues.")*

In the next lecture, we'll contrast two great songwriters—two of the greatest of the 20th century—Irving Berlin and Jerome Kern.

Lecture Eleven
Irving Berlin and Jerome Kern—Contrasts

Scope:

Up to this point, we've thrown out, periodically, the names of some icons of the American musical theater scene—Rodgers and Hammerstein, George Gershwin, Leonard Bernstein, Stephen Sondheim—people who really need no introduction. Two towering icons who've been quite active in our last several lectures also require no introduction, but they make for such an interesting contrast—and have made such a lasting impression—that I think they deserve a more intense focus. In this lecture, we'll learn more about the lives and the music of Irving Berlin and Jerome Kern.

Outline

I. We start with a little bit of a 1915 Billy Murray recording of one of Irving Berlin's earliest hits, "I Love a Piano."

    A. Irving Berlin and Jerome Kern each produced one masterwork for the musical theater. In Berlin's case, the work is *Annie Get Your Gun*; in Kern's, *Show Boat*.

    B. At the same time each composer is diametrically opposite in almost any way we might compare—in musical background, in early environment, in their relationship to their parents, in the way they treated the people around them, and in their general temperaments.

II. We begin with Irving Berlin (1888–1989).

    A. Berlin's childhood was far from privileged. Born in a Russian *shtetl*, he was the youngest of six children. In America, all six children, two parents, and a distant relative lived in three windowless rooms on Cherry Street near the East River. When Irving was 8, his father died, and he left school to help support the family.

    B. The Lower East Side, at the turn of the 20th century, was so exciting to a small boy that poverty might have seemed like a minor inconvenience. People of every race and nationality crowded by the hundreds into every block, and live singing, dancing, and comedy waited at the neighborhood vaudeville house for a nickel's admission.

C. Like all real craftsmen, Berlin created his timeless songs by paying careful attention to small details. For example, there is a vast difference between starting a song with "Heaven! I'm in heaven," as Berlin did in "Cheek to Cheek," rather than just "I'm in heaven."

D. Around 1910, after writing a few modestly successful songs, Berlin bought a unique piano.

    1. He had learned to play the piano by ear, in the key of F#, on the black keys. In his mind, he heard his songs modulating (moving from key to key), but he couldn't play those key changes because his fingers were stuck in F# major.

    2. The new piano had a lever with 12 notches under the keyboard. If Berlin moved the lever one notch to the right, the entire keyboard moved up to the next string. Though Berlin's fingers remained in F#, his tunes could now wander from key to key.

E. In 1911, Berlin wrote "Alexander's Ragtime Band," which was so popular that he was summoned to London to perform the song for the king and queen of England. We hear this hit, performed by vaudevillian and bandleader Ted Lewis.

F. Having finally achieved security, Berlin set a wedding date with his fiancée, Dorothy Goetz. For the honeymoon, he bought two steamship tickets to Havana, not knowing that Cuba was experiencing outbreaks of typhoid fever. A few months after the newlyweds returned to New York, Dorothy Berlin died of the disease. Berlin blamed himself and went into a depression that didn't lift completely until more than 10 years later when he met Ellin Mackay.

G. At the same time, Berlin's songwriting style underwent a dramatic transformation. All his earlier songs are light, most of them broadly comic. But after Dorothy's death, he wrote: "I lost the sunshine and roses. I lost the sky of blue. I lost the gladness that turned into sadness…When I lost you."

III. Berlin's first Broadway musical was written in 1914 for America's most popular dance team, Vernon and Irene Castle.

    A. Berlin united the modern and the antique by having two characters in the show, Algy and Ernesta, sing two songs at once. Nearly 40 years later, the duet became a number-one hit for Bing and Gary Crosby. We hear Sara Achor and Doug Jimmerson singing "Simple Melody."

B. The year after World War I ended, Ziegfeld commissioned Berlin to write a theme song to be used for every subsequent edition of the Follies. We hear tenor John Steel singing "A Pretty Girl is Like a Melody" exactly as he sang it in the *Ziegfeld Follies of 1919*.

1. The chord changes in this song are fairly complicated and would have required Berlin to make good use of his transposing piano.

2. It's hard to believe that Berlin wrote both his melodies and his harmonies when he played everything by ear in the key of F#. But according to Sid Lippman, Berlin's arranger, he did indeed play the harmonies, which were then recorded by Sid.

C. Two years after the war and 10 years after his wife's death, Berlin, with a dark cloud over his head, wrote "All By Myself." That feeling of isolation dissipated when he finally met his second wife-to-be, Ellin Mackay. But, first, the two of them had to overcome a few obstacles, the most formidable of which was Ellin's fabulously wealthy father, Clarence Mackay, who tried desperately to keep the couple apart.

D. As a wedding present to Ellin, Berlin wrote "Always." The song declares his love for her—at least the chorus does—but the verse is more introspective—it's a look at the years of crippling depression Berlin lived through before Ellin Mackay came into his life.

IV. After 15 years of Hollywood scores and a tremendously successful World War II musical called *This Is the Army*, Berlin wrote his masterwork for musical theater, *Annie Get Your Gun*.

A. The strength of this show (aside from Berlin's brilliant score) is its main character. It's a Cinderella story, like *Irene*, *Sally*, and *My Fair Lady*, but Annie Oakley is even earthier than Eliza Doolittle, not only at the beginning of the show but also at the end. She's not a woman driven to imitate the manners and speech of her social superiors; she's a woman determined to be herself in the face of fame, fortune, and adulation.

B. Berlin's *Annie Get Your Gun* racked up 1,147 performances in its initial run at the Imperial Theatre, making it the third longest-running show of the decade.

C. Interestingly, the score of *Annie Get Your Gun* was originally to have been written by Kern, with lyrics by Dorothy Fields. But Kern's sudden death required Rodgers and Hammerstein, the producers of the show, to bring the project to Berlin. The change was probably a boon for musical theater. Kern's aristocratic touch would never have allowed him to craft the simple-minded perfection of "Anything You Can Do I Can Do Better!" or "Doin' What Comes Natur'lly."

D. The score is one of the greatest ever written for musical theater, running the gamut of types, forms, and emotions. "They Say That Falling in Love Is Wonderful" is an exquisite gem of a ballad, while "There's No Business Like Show Business" is a rabble-rousing showstopper. "Moonshine Lullaby" skirts around the blues, with a subtlety previously displayed only by Gershwin and Harold Arlen.

E. In an older composer, whose best days seemed to be behind him, what caused the creative explosion that produced the score of *Annie Get Your Gun*? Mary Ellin Barrett, Berlin's daughter, asked essentially the same question of Berlin's orchestrator, Jay Blackton, in her perceptive book *Irving Berlin: A Daughter's Memoir*. According to Blackton, "I would say Irving Berlin wrote this tremendous score, not just for himself, but for Richard Rodgers. The extra reach, again and again, to show he still had it in him."

F. Though labeled by biographers as one of the top five American songwriters, Berlin is, unquestionably, in a class by himself. Everyone in America knows some Berlin songs: "God Bless America," "White Christmas," "Easter Parade," "There's No Business Like Show Business," and "Oh! How I Hate to Get Up in the Morning."

G. Berlin knew nothing about prosody or music theory, yet he wrote songs as lyrically and musically sophisticated as any of the top five. To quote Berlin's colleague Jerome Kern, "Irving Berlin has no place in America's music; he is America's music."

H. We close the Berlin portion of our lecture with a medley of his early hits, arranged by Berlin himself in 1913 for a performance before the king and queen of England, re-created by Ed Goldstein and company.

V. We now turn to Jerome Kern (1885–1945).

A. We start by hearing "Bill," a song written by Kern and lyricist P. G. Wodehouse for their 1918 show *Oh Lady, Lady!* and resurrected for *Show Boat*.

B. If any great American songwriter could be called the opposite of Irving Berlin, it's Jerome Kern. Where Berlin grew up in poverty, Kern's father owned a legendary emporium in Newark, NJ, where he sold, among other things, inexpensive pianos.

C. Kern's parents showered him with love and encouraged his artistic development by sending him, after high school, to Germany for advanced study in theory and composition.

    1. Not yet 20, Kern acquired the polish of a European gentleman and a writing style patterned on classical European models.

    2. We can hear the European influence in *Show Boat*, in which "Can't Help Lovin' Dat Man" is patterned on the blues and "Old Man River" has the simplicity of a spiritual, but "Why Do I Love You?" and "Make Believe" and "You Are Love" would be perfectly at home in a Viennese operetta.

D. After studying in Europe, Kern returned to America, found little success in American theater, and traveled to England, where he interpolated his songs into English musicals and operettas. We listen to "How'd You Like to Spoon with Me," one of young Kern's songs from his days in London.

E. At about this same time, America's most prominent theatrical producer, Charles Frohman, arrived in London, looking for British talent. When Kern played some of his music for Frohman, the producer said, "I wish our American songwriters could write the way you British do!" and Kern agreed to accompany him to America.

F. Several weeks passed before Kern's New Jersey origins were revealed. Nonetheless, he began writing for Frohman's shows. Shortly after his return, Kern's mother died, followed by his father. Kern became attached to a showgirl named Edie Kelly, who ran through his money before leaving him. In 1909, he returned to England, where he met and proposed to the 19-year-old Eva Leale.

VI. Kern's true style appeared, for the first time, in 1914, in a show Frohman produced in which Kern had been asked to interpolate a few songs. The show was called *The Girl from Utah*; we listen to one of its songs, "They Didn't Believe Me."

    A. In 1915, Kern's partnership with Charles Frohman ended suddenly and tragically. Kern was scheduled to go to Europe with Frohman on the *Lusitania*, but he overslept and missed the ship. As we know, the ship was sunk by the German navy, and Frohman was killed.

    B. After Frohman's death, Kern wrote a series of low-budget, short-running shows for the Princess Theatre, giving him a wonderful chance to experiment and polish his technique. Between 1915 and 1919, Kern's Princess shows included *Nobody Home*, *Very Good Eddie*, *Miss Springtime*, *Oh Boy!*, *Love of Mike*, and *Have a Heart*. The songs were well-crafted, though on the whole not spectacular.

    C. In 1920, Ziegfeld commissioned Kern to write a show at the Ziegfeld Theatre. The result, *Sally*, was the most popular show of 1920, but the simple-minded Cinderella story and the songs were not integrated, as Kern's *Show Boat* would be six years later.

    D. We must also mention Oscar Hammerstein here, who wrote the lyrics and libretto for *Show Boat* and was at least as important to that groundbreaking musical as Kern. For example, Hammerstein was responsible for the song "Old Man River."

    E. We close this lecture with the cast recording of one of Kern's earliest classics, "Look for the Silver Lining," from 1920's *Sally*, sung in our recording by Marilyn Miller, the original Sally.

VII. Because musical theater in the 1920s was dominated by one composer, we will devote the entire next lecture to him. George Gershwin was the personification of his era, and both the stage songs and the concert works he created are "here to stay."

Suggested Reading:

Lawrence Bergreen, *As Thousands Cheer*.

Michael Freedland, *Jerome Kern: A Biography*.

Questions to Consider:

1. How might their different musical backgrounds have affected the marked difference in Berlin's and Kern's musical styles?

2. What qualities made *Show Boat* perhaps the most important musical turning point of the 20th century?

©2006 The Teaching Company.

Lecture Eleven—Transcript
Irving Berlin and Jerome Kern—Contrasts

Up to this point, we've thrown out, periodically, the names of some icons of the American musical theater—Rodgers and Hammerstein, George Gershwin, Leonard Bernstein, Stephen Sondheim—people I feel really need no introduction. Two towering icons who've been quite active in our last several lectures also require no introduction, but they make for such an interesting contrast and have made such a lasting impression that I think they deserve a more intense focus. I'd like to take this lecture to tell you a bit more about the lives and the music of Irving Berlin and Jerome Kern. We'll start with a little bit of a 1915 Billy Murray recording of one of Irving Berlin's earliest hits, "I Love a Piano." *(Plays recording—"I Love a Piano.")*

Ironic that you'll discover how much Irving Berlin loved the piano, one piano in particular—without it, none of Irving Berlin's greatest songs could have been written—but we'll explore that in detail later.

Irving Berlin and Jerome Kern have each produced one masterwork for the musical theater. In Berlin's case, the work is *Annie Get Your Gun*; in Kern's, *Showboat*. Along with a body of beautifully crafted popular songs, each man is likely to be remembered a century or two from now by his theatrical masterpiece. But, aside from that, each is diametrically different in almost any way you might care to compare—in musical background, in early environment, in their relationship to their parents, in the way they treated the people around them, and in their general temperaments. We'll begin with Berlin and end with Kern.

Irving Berlin's childhood was about as far from privileged as it gets. Born in a Russian *shtetl*, he was the youngest of six children. In America, all six children, two parents, and a distant relative lived in three windowless rooms on Cherry Street near the East River. When Irving Berlin was eight, his father died; he left school, forever, and helped support the family. Of his childhood poverty, Berlin shrugged his shoulders and said, "It wasn't so bad. We always had bread, butter, and tea." Well, often, that's about all they had. But, the Lower East Side, at the turn of the 20th century, was so exciting to a small boy that poverty may have seemed like a minor inconvenience. People of every race and nationality crowded by the hundreds into every block, the curbs were cluttered with the pushcarts of sidewalk vendors, and live singing, dancing, and comedy waited at the neighborhood vaudeville house for a nickel's admission. Today's scheduled computer-bound childhood seems deprived in comparison.

Many years ago, journalist Hal Eaton interviewed Irving Berlin and asked, "Mr. Berlin, do you write your songs for posterity?" And Berlin replied, "No, for prosperity." Despite that fact, the artistry in Berlin's best songs has never been surpassed by any other American songwriter. Like all real craftsmen, Berlin created his timeless songs by paying careful attention to small details. If you look at the song he wrote for Fred Astaire, "Cheek to Cheek," it begins, "Heaven / I'm in heaven." Most people would have thought, "Okay, I'll say, 'I'm in heaven, I'm in heaven',", which doesn't work. It's monotonous and by starting with "Heaven!" you're starting with an exclamation; you're also starting on the strong beat. It's much more interesting: "Heaven! I'm in heaven." Now another example of this attention to detail is in his song, "How Deep Is The Ocean." He writes, "How many times a day do I think of you? / How many roses are sprinkled with a dew?" Almost any other lyricist would have written, "How many roses are covered with dew?" which is a nice line, but "sprinkled" gives us an image and "sprinkled" also gives us an internal rhyme with the word "think."

Around 1910, after writing a few modestly successful songs, Berlin bought a unique piano from the Weser Brothers in New York City. Berlin—who never learned to read music—had learned to play the piano by ear, in the key of F#, on the black keys. In his head, he heard his songs modulating—that is, moving from key to key—but he couldn't play those key changes because his fingers were stuck in F# major. The new piano had a lever with 12 notches under the keyboard. If Berlin moved the lever one notch to the right, the entire keyboard moved up to the next string. So, though Berlin's fingers remained in F#, his tunes could now wander from key to key.

In 1911, Irving Berlin wrote not just the most popular song in America, but the most popular song in the world. This song was to 1911, what Bill Haley's "Rock Around the Clock" was to 1955 or what Michael Jackson's "Thriller" was to 1984. Except, that it was bigger than both those songs put together. It was so popular that Berlin was summoned to London to perform the song for, among others, the King and Queen of England. Here is Irving Berlin's hit of 1911, performed by vaudevillian and bandleader Ted Lewis,

"Alexander's Ragtime Band." *(Plays recording- "Alexander's Ragtime Band.")* "Alexander's Ragtime Band."

With real security, Berlin at last set the wedding date with his fiancée, Dorothy Goetz. Planning a surprise honeymoon for his wife-to-be, he bought two steamship tickets to Havana—something he would regret for the rest of his life. Now Cuba was not about to discourage tourist trade by announcing that, in the villages outside the city, there had been outbreaks of typhoid fever. The newlywed Berlins returned to New York City, full of plans for their future together. And a few months after the wedding, Dorothy Berlin died of typhoid fever; and who did Berlin blame? Of course, he blamed himself. He went into a deep depression that didn't lift totally until more than 10 years later when he met Ellin Mackay.

But meanwhile, Berlin's songwriting style underwent a dramatic transformation. All of Berlin's earlier songs are light, most of them broadly comic. Think of the two you've heard so far, "I Love a Piano" and "Alexander's Ragtime Band." But, after Dorothy Goetz's death, he wrote: "I lost the sunshine and roses. I lost the sky of blue. I lost the gladness that turned into sadness…when I lost you."

Irving Berlin's first Broadway musical *Watch Your Step* was written in 1914 for America's most popular dance team, Vernon and Irene Castle. Berlin united the modern and the antique by having two characters in the show—Algy and Ernesta—sing two songs at the same time. Now the fact that Berlin could do this by ear really shows how unique his talent was. Nearly 40 years after he wrote this tune, the duet became a Billboard number-one hit for Bing and Gary Crosby, and it became the number-five song for the entire year of 1950. Here is Sara Achor and Doug Jimmerson singing the song, "Simple Melody." *(Plays recording—"Simple Melody.")* Irving Berlin, 1914, "Simple Melody."

The year after World War I ended, Flo Ziegfeld commissioned Irving Berlin to write a theme song to be used for every subsequent edition of the Follies. Here is the tenor, John Steel, singing Berlin's song exactly as he sang it in the Ziegfeld Follies of 1919. *(Plays recording—"A Pretty Girl Is Like A Melody.")*

That was John Steel singing "A Pretty Girl Is Like A Melody." Let me play a little bit of that song to demonstrate something to you. *(Plays piano.)* Now that was a pretty complicated song and, if you listen to the chord changes *(plays piano)*, Berlin sure had to use that little gadget on his piano several times to get through those.

Now when I first heard that Berlin didn't read music, played everything by ear in the key of F#, and used that transposing piano, I was certain that he only wrote his own melodies, not his harmonies. But, I talked to Sid Lippman, who is now in his 90s—and you might recognize that name because Sid, in 1950, wrote a song for Nat King Cole called "(They Tried To Tell Us We're) Too Young." Sid began as an arranger at Irving Berlin Music and I said to him, "Sid, I can't believe this guy could make up his harmonies; he had no background in music." Sid said, "He would play them, it wouldn't sound too pretty all the time, and then you'd write them down and play them back for him. If you changed one note, he'd know it instantly." And he said, "Sometimes, he would listen and he'd say, 'Well, raise that note' or 'lower that note' and there would be other times, because he didn't know the names of the chords, he'd say, 'Play me every chord you know and I'll tell you which one I like.'"

Two years after World War I and ten years after his wife's death, unable to commit to another woman, but desperately needing to do so—probably thinking of himself as a jinx—Berlin, with a dark cloud over his head, wrote this. And this shows you that at this point in his life, Berlin begins to use these songs almost as diary entries. He wrote: *(plays piano)*

That feeling of isolation dissipated when Berlin finally met his second wife-to-be, Ellin Mackay. But, first, the two of them had to overcome a few obstacles, the most formidable of which was Ellin's fabulously wealthy father, Clarence Mackay, who sent Ellin to Europe to separate Ellin and Berlin. Now if I fill in the blanks with my imagination, the story ended like this. After a long day's walking tour, Ellin climbs the stairs to her hotel, sits on the edge of her bed, kicks off her shoes, and turns on the radio. And the announcer says, "Now we'll play the latest song by Irving Berlin." And she hears, "I'm all alone, by the telephone, wondering where you are and how you are and if you are all alone, too." Immediately after hearing that song, still sitting on the edge of her bed, Ellin Mackay, known for her composure, burst into tears. She picks up the phone and dials her father. At his Harbor Hill estate, Mackay picks up the phone and hears his daughter say, "I'm coming home and I'm going to marry the man!" Mackay says, "You do and I'll disinherit you!" She says,

 ©2006 The Teaching Company.

"I don't care," and slams down the phone. Mackay hangs up the phone and then picks it up again to dial Berlin. When Berlin answers the phone, Mackay says, "We have to talk." Their conversation, a few days later, was chronicled by Alexander Woolcott—writer, radio personality, and Berlin's close friend and confidante during this period. Mackay said, "She's coming back. She wants to marry you, but I'll give you a million dollars to leave my daughter alone!" According to Woolcott, Berlin said, "I'll give you $2 million to leave me alone!"

Then, Berlin went to the dock to meet Ellin's ship, with the sheet music to a song he'd written for her. The song, a wedding present to his wife-to-be, is copyrighted in her name. It's a song declaring his love for her—at least that's what the chorus is about—but the verse is something a little more introspective. It's a look at the years of crippling depression Berlin lived through before Ellin Mackay came into his life. The verse begins, "Everything went wrong and the whole day long, I'd feel so blue." The verse ends with, "Now that my blue days are past, now that I found you at last," and then, the chorus begins with the words "I'll be loving you…always."

Later, after 15 years of Hollywood scores—most of them for Fred Astaire—after a tremendously successful World War II musical called *This Is the Army*, Irving Berlin wrote his masterwork for musical theater, *Annie Get Your Gun*. It premiered at the Imperial Theatre. The greatest strength of this show—aside from Berlin's brilliant score—is its main character. It's a Cinderella story like *Irene,* like *Sally*, and like *My Fair Lady*. But, Annie Oakley is even earthier than Eliza Doolittle, not only at the beginning of the show, but also at the end. She's not a woman driven to imitate the manners and speech of her social superiors; she's a woman determined to be herself in the face of fame, fortune, and adulation, and she succeeds. Berlin's *Annie Get Your Gun* racked up 1,147 performances in its initial run at the Imperial Theatre, making it the third longest-running show of the decade.

Now since we're contrasting Berlin with Kern, you might find it interesting to know that the score of *Annie Get Your Gun* was originally to have been written by Kern, with lyrics by Dorothy Fields. But, Kern's sudden death required Rodgers and Hammerstein—the producers of the show—to bring the project to Berlin. *Annie Get Your Gun*, by the way, is the only Rodgers and

Hammerstein musical production without a Rodgers and Hammerstein score.

It was a break for Berlin and, I think, a break for musical theater. Kern's aristocratic touch would not have allowed him to craft the simple-minded perfection of "Folks are dumb where I come from, doin' a-what comes naturally." Or, "Anything you can do I can do better, yes I can, no you can't, yes I can, no you can't." But those songs work and they work for the characters. It is one of the greatest scores ever written for musical theater, running the gamut of types, of forms, of emotions as skillfully as Lerner and Loewe do in *My Fair Lady*. "They Say That Falling in Love is Wonderful" is an exquisite ballad, while "There's No Business Like Show Business" is a rabble-rouser, a showstopper. "Moonshine Lullaby," one of the lesser-known songs from the show, skirts around with the blues with the subtlety of George Gershwin or Harold Arlen.

In an older composer, whose best days seemed to be behind him, what caused the explosion of creativity that produced the score of *Annie Get Your Gun*? Mary Ellin Barrett, Berlin's daughter, asked herself essentially the same question in her perceptive book, *Irving Berlin: A Daughter's Memoir*. She interviewed Berlin's orchestrator, Jay Blackton, who attempted to answer the question for her. He said this:

Irving Berlin, coming out of retirement, as far as Broadway is concerned…Rodgers and Hammerstein, the new kings of Broadway, with *Oklahoma!* and *Carousel*, both huge hits, setting a new kind of style. Now you know Dick and Irving had the greatest mutual respect. Irving called Dick a musical genius and I remember Dick, one day on stage during a rehearsal, looking at Irving pacing below, saying, "There is America's folk song writer."

Let me pause here and say that I feel Rodgers's comment was both condescending and unwarranted. Berlin's creative process was unquestionably unorthodox—maybe even weird—but the final product of Berlin's labors was far more complex and far more sophisticated than real folk song or even the fake folk songs of a composer like Stephen Foster. Give the man his due!

Now back to Jay Blackton's comments; Blackton says:

I would say Irving Berlin wrote this tremendous score, not just for himself, but for Richard Rodgers. The extra reach, again and again, to show he still had it in him. I think what Berlin's score *is* saying to Rodgers and Hammerstein in essence is, "I'll show them! The old King is not dead!"

Although labeled by biographers as one of the top five American songwriters, Berlin is unquestionably in a class by himself. Everyone in America knows some Irving Berlin songs: "God Bless America," "White Christmas," "Easter Parade," "No Business Like Show Business," "Oh! How I Hate To Get Up In the Morning." Berlin is the only one of the big five to create a body of songs that mirrors events in his life. Berlin lived 101 years, much longer than any of the other big five. He was born poorer than any of them—and died richer. Berlin knew nothing—refused to know anything—about prosody or music theory and, yet, he wrote songs as lyrically and musically sophisticated as any of the five. To quote Berlin's colleague, Jerome Kern, "Irving Berlin has no place in America's music; he is America's music."

Let's end this Berlin portion of our lecture with a medley of his early hits, arranged by Berlin himself in 1913, for a performance before the King and Queen of England. Now this little medley includes a lot of snatches of songs that became famous by this point, by 1913— "Everybody's Doing It," "That Mesmerizing Mendelssohn Rag," "When the Midnight Choo-Choo Leaves for Alabam," "Fiddle Up, Fiddle Up on Your Ragtime Violin," and "Alexander's Ragtime Band." The premise of the little medley is that the singer is addicted to ragtime, so he goes to a doctor to cure him. Here it is, recreated by Ed Goldstein and company. *(Plays recording—"They've Got Me Doin' It Now")*

Now, let's turn to Kern. We'll start by playing a song written by Kern and lyricist P. G. Wodehouse for their 1918 show, *Oh Lady, Lady!* As soon as you hear it, you'll say, "No, wait a minute! That's from *Showboat*." Well actually, it was resurrected for *Showboat*. *(Plays piano)*. Well actually, when that song reached *Showboat*, Hammerstein had to change a few of Wodehouse's lines. For example, the line "I know that Apollo would beat him all hollow," became, "He's not the kind that you would find in a statue."

If any great American songwriter could be called the diametrical opposite of Irving Berlin, it's Jerome Kern. Where Berlin grew up in poverty, Kern's father owned a legendary emporium in Newark, New Jersey where he sold—among other things—inexpensive pianos, the latest status symbol among tenement families. In the 1880s, he also managed to acquire the contract for cleaning all of the 5,800 miles of New York City streets. Michael Freeland begins his 1978 biography of Jerome Kern with the sentence "Jerome David Kern survived the immense handicap of not being born on the Lower East Side." His parents showered their love on him and encouraged his artistic development by sending him after high school, to Germany for advanced study in theory and composition. Teenaged Jerome Kern loved the operettas he saw in Berlin.

Not yet 20, Jerome Kern was acquiring the polish of a European gentleman and a writing style patterned on classical European models. Throughout his life, Jerome Kern had one foot in Europe and the other in America. You can certainly hear that in *Showboat*, where "Can't Help Loving Dat Man" is patterned on the blues and "Old Man River" has the simplicity of a spiritual. But, "Why Do I Love You?," and "Make Believe," and "You Are Love" would be perfectly at home in a Viennese operetta.

After studying in Europe, Jerome Kern returned to America, found little success in American musical theater, and returned, this time, to England—where he interpolated his songs into English musicals and operettas. At the age of 20, he looked as English and sounded as English as the English. Here's one of young Kern's songs from his days in London. It certainly doesn't sound much like later Kern, but here it is. *(Plays piano—"How'd You Like To Spoon with Me?")*

Meanwhile, America's most prominent theatrical producer, Charles Frohman, had arrived in London looking for British talent. When he heard about a 20-year-old composer named Jerome Kern, he just assumed the boy was English. When Kern played some of his music for Frohman, the producer said, "I wish our American songwriters could write the way you British do!" And Kern agreed to accompany him to America. Several weeks passed before Kern had the nerve to reveal his Newark, New Jersey origins. He did this accidentally when the ship reached port. He looked over and paled and moved back, but it was too late. From the dock, he heard a high-school classmate say, "Hey, Jerry Kern, your father still selling them cheap pianos in Jersey?" Nevertheless, Kern, back in the U. S., was now to begin writing for Frohman's shows. Not long after this, Kern's mother died. He was very close to his mother; and then shortly after that, his father died.

©2006 The Teaching Company.

Kern became attached to a redheaded showgirl name Edie Kelly and she took him for almost everything he had, and then left him and married a rich guy. Kern was determined never to let a woman take advantage of him again and P. G. Wodehouse said he saw a marked change in Kern's personality during this period. Well—around 1909—he goes to England again and he stays at Walton-on-Thames. The landlord's daughter, Eva Leale is 19 years old and, by this point, Kern is 29. He proposes; she agrees. She's a rather timid girl—rather fragile—and certainly has not had a lot of experience in the world. When she comes to America, she is just overwhelmed by it and this was just what Kern wants.

The Kern style was waiting to hatch. It appeared for the first time in 1914, in a show Frohman produced in which Kern had been asked to interpolate a few songs. The show was called *The Girl from Utah* and this was the first Kern home run, written after 200 strikeouts. The song is one of his beautiful ballads, "They Didn't Believe Me." *(Plays piano— "They Didn't Believe Me.")*

The year after "They Didn't Believe Me" appeared, 1915, Kern's partnership with Charles Frohman ended suddenly and tragically. Kern was scheduled to go to Europe with Frohman, but he overslept. Eva, who as I mentioned was rather timid and maybe a little browbeaten, didn't know what to do. She thought, "Well, if I wake him up, he's going to be upset. If I don't wake him up, he's going to be upset." By the time she had decided what to do; he'd already missed the ship. The ship was the *Lusitania* and when the German navy sank it, Charles Frohman was killed. If Kern hadn't slept through his alarm clock, he most likely would have shared Charles Frohman's fate and, today, I wouldn't be doing this lecture! Also, songs like "Smoke Gets in Your Eyes," "Yesterdays," and "The Way You Looked Tonight" would never have been written. And, the musical *Showboat* would have been composed, if at all, by someone else.

With Frohman no longer in the picture, Kern wrote a series of low-budget short-running shows for the tiny, 292-seat Princess Theatre. It was a wonderful chance to experiment and polish his technique. Between 1915 and 1919, Kern's Princess shows included *Nobody Home, Very Good Eddie, Miss Springtime, Oh Boy, Love of Mike,* and *Have a Heart*. The songs were well crafted, though on the whole, not spectacular. In 1920, Ziegfeld commissioned Kern to write a spectacular show at the Ziegfeld Theatre. *Sally* was the most popular show of 1920. But the simple-minded Cinderella story and the songs were not as integrated as *Showboat* would be six years later. Musical theater still wasn't musical theater, in the sense that we think of it today.

Now so far, we've been talking Kern, Kern, Kern, but Hammerstein, who wrote the lyrics and the libretto for *Showboat*, is at least as important to that groundbreaking musical as Kern is, if not more important in certain ways. For example, they finished the score in 1926. While Flo Ziegfeld was looking for more money, Hammerstein came up with the idea of "Old Man River." It would otherwise not have been in the show, and it begins with an almost stream-of-consciousness lyric. It almost sounds as if he woke up at the middle of the night:

> Old man river
>
> That old man river
>
> He don't say nothin'
>
> Must know somethin'
>
> That old man river he keeps on rolling along.

Dorothy Hammerstein, his wife, used to tell the story of people who would bump into her and apparently a woman once said to her, "I just loved Jerome Kern's 'Old Man River,'" and she became incensed and said, "Jerome Kern didn't write 'Old Man River,' my husband wrote 'Old Man River'! Jerome Kern wrote 'dum, dum, dum, dum.'"

Paul Robeson's the man that Kern wanted for this show, but he resisted the show and didn't come in until the show was six months in to production, and they wanted a British company. When he met with Kern, Kern showed him the music, and Robeson, an educated man, looked at it and said, "Well, Mr. Kern, excuse me, what's a tater?" Kern says, "Well a tater is a potato." Robeson said, "Well, shouldn't it be 'doesn't plant taters?' And Kern says, "Well don't blame me, I only wrote the music."

We'll end with the cast recording of one of Kern's earliest classics. This is the theme song of Turner Classic Movies, by the way, sung for them by jazz trumpeter Chet Baker; but we're going to hear it

 ©2006 The Teaching Company.

sung by Marilyn Miller, the original Sally in 1920's *Sally*. The song is "Look for the Silver Lining." *(Plays recording—"Look for the Silver Lining.")*

Because, during the 1920s, musical theater, popular song, and the concert stage were dominated by one composer, we're going to devote the entire next lesson to him. George Gershwin was the personification of his age, and both the stage songs and the concert works he created are here to stay. Next: George Gershwin!

Lecture Twelve
George Gershwin's Legacy (1919 to c. 1935)

Scope:

George Gershwin, by incorporating the musical ideas of blues and jazz into his concert and stage works, became a living symbol of the jazz age. With the exception of Jerome Kern, no other theater composer of the 1920s equals Gershwin in importance. Gershwin got his start with the song "Swanee," made famous by Al Jolson and, early in his career, wrote songs for the yearly productions of George White's Scandals. Among these were "Stairway to Paradise" and "Somebody Loves Me." In 1924, George began his collaboration with his brother, Ira, which resulted in such songs as "The Man I Love," "Someone to Watch Over Me," and "I Got Rhythm." In 1935, Gershwin wrote his most important stage work, *Porgy and Bess*; politically incorrect even in its time, the show is nonetheless a masterpiece. Shortly after the production of *Porgy and Bess*, Gershwin moved to Hollywood to write film musicals. After just 15 months there, he died following surgery on a brain tumor at age 38.

Outline

I. We begin this lecture with a rare 1919 recording of Gershwin playing a piano piece he wrote at age 18, "Novelette in Fourths."

    A. In discussing songs, people often ask: "Which came first, the words or the music?" With the Gershwins, the music almost always came first, with one notable exception. In 1937, when the two brothers were writing the score for *Shall We Dance?*, Ira recalled a lesson from an English teacher that prompted him to write the lyrics for "Let's Call the Whole Thing Off."

    B. The Gershwin style influenced the style of every composer on Broadway for the next 20 years. Two of the most important aspects of that style are *repeated notes* and *blue notes*.

        1. In "Embraceable You," the "Come to Papa" section is played all on one note. We hear the same kind of repetition in "They Can't Take That Away from Me" and the Piano Concerto.

 ©2006 The Teaching Company.

2. A blue note is a flatted note that does not belong in the key. For example, we hear "The Man I Love" played with and without the blue note.

C. On December 4, 1926, George Gershwin presented five piano preludes to the public in a recital at the Roosevelt Hotel in New York. Three of the preludes have survived; we don't know what happened to the other two. "Prelude # 1" is full of repeated notes and blue notes, a perfect model of the Gershwin style. We hear it played by Duke Thompson, an internationally acclaimed concert pianist and an acquaintance of Frances Gershwin, George and Ira's sister.

D. We also hear Duke Thompson play "Rialto Ripples," a 1914 ragtime piece that was probably the first thing Gershwin ever wrote. In writing the music, Gershwin was assisted with the orthography by a co-worker at Remick's. The music publishing firm printed the sheet music, but the song wasn't recorded for 40 years.

II. At age 19, with his neighborhood friend Irving Caesar, Gershwin wrote a song about the South using every cliché imaginable, including a quote from the original nostalgic song about the South—Stephen Foster's "Old Folks at Home."

A. A new revue was in rehearsal at the Capitol Theatre, and Gershwin's song seemed perfect for a special production number the theater had planned. On October 24, 1919, "Swanee" was introduced by 60 chorus girls with electric lights in their shoes on a semi-darkened stage. The electric lights were such a hit that nobody noticed the song.

B. Later that year, Gershwin played the piano at a party at which Al Jolson was in attendance. Never shy, the young Gershwin managed to get Jolson's attention and insisted he listen to the song. Jolson loved it.

C. Jolson interpolated "Swanee" into his Broadway show *Sinbad*; it became the hit of the show and one of the biggest hits in Jolson's career. Overnight, Gershwin became the boy wonder of Broadway. We listen to the original recording of Jolson singing "Swanee" in 1919.

D. "Swanee" is usually performed in Jolson's style, but that's not the way that Gershwin played it. The composer loved jazz and was fascinated by jazz musicians' ability to spontaneously create multiple variations on popular songs. We still have Gershwin's concert variation on "Swanee," which brings a little more sophistication to the song. We hear it played by Duke Thompson.

E. From 1920 to 1924, Gershwin wrote songs for the yearly productions of George White's Scandals. These shows produced his first timeless songs, among them "Stairway to Paradise" (1922) and "Somebody Loves Me" (1924).

F. Earlier, we mentioned blue notes; notice that "Somebody Loves Me" uses a blue note on every sustained "who." We hear the song performed by Alan Gephardt, singer and dancer with Goucher College's Choreographie Antique, accompanied by James Harp of the Baltimore Symphony Orchestra and Baltimore Opera Company.

III. George and Ira Gershwin (1896–1983) began their long-term collaboration in 1924 with the show *Lady Be Good.* Two years later, in 1926, the Gershwins mounted a show called *Oh, Kay!*, with Kay played by a frail and not-altogether-confident Gertrude Lawrence. Three decades later, Lawrence would play the female lead in Rodgers and Hammerstein's *The King and I.*

A. Though *Oh, Kay!* was fluff, it produced one of Gershwin's greatest songs, "Someone to Watch Over Me."

1. Lawrence's uncertain delivery of the song almost caused it to be dropped from the show, but Gershwin saved the song by instructing Lawrence to sing it to a sad-looking little doll instead of the audience.

2. We hear "Someone to Watch Over Me," featuring Matt Belzer on tenor sax, James Fitzpatrick on piano, and Sara Achor on the vocal. As we listen, notice the unusually long lyrical verse melody, another characteristic of the Gershwin style.

B. In 1924, the Gershwins wrote *Lady Be Good* for Fred and Adele Astaire, a show that produced "The Man I Love," "Fascinatin' Rhythm," and the title song. In 1927, they wrote another show for the Astaires, originally called *Smarty* but later changed to *Funny Face.* The hit song of the show was "'S Wonderful."

1. "'S Wonderful" is a prime example of Gershwin's less obvious debts to the world of jazz. It's not a lyrical melody like "Someone to Watch Over Me," as we hear in a comparison of the two.

2. "S'Wonderful" is, essentially, a *riff* song. *Riffs* are short musical jazz figures, played over and over, avoiding monotony by changing the harmonies each time the riff is played. Without the harmony changes, a riff tune can be boring.

3. We hear Alan Gephardt, accompanied by James Hart, sing "'S Wonderful."

IV. Gershwin wrote his most important stage work, *Porgy and Bess*, in 1935. Given that both the Gershwins and Dubose Heyward, their collaborator, thought of this show as an opera, why are we discussing it in a course about musical theater?

A. The critics in 1935 were hesitant to call *Porgy and Bess* an opera; it contained too many hit songs, they contended, to be a real opera. But it used recitative and required trained voices, and Gershwin orchestrated every one of *Porgy and Bess*'s hundreds of pages of manuscript. If it premiered today, *Porgy and Bess* would fit neatly into the musical theater niche filled by *Les Miserables* and *Miss Saigon*; conversely, it would be accepted as an opera, too.

B. *Porgy and Bess* was politically incorrect, even in 1935, when it premiered. Many educated blacks were repelled by it. The story showed a side of ghetto life as shocking in 1935 as the tenement world of *West Side Story* in 1957. Porgy, the hero, is handicapped; Bess, the heroine, is a cocaine-sniffing prostitute; and Sportin' Life is a drug dealer. But we're forced to look at them as sympathetic beings.

C. Duke Ellington, who later grew to love the work, attended the premiere and immediately dashed off a letter to *The New York Times*, part of which read: "It is high time we put a stop to George Gershwin's coal black Negro-isms."

D. As for its musical content, the month after *Porgy and Bess* premiered, Virgil Thomson wrote an article in *Modern Music* magazine that began, "Gershwin does not even know what an opera is." True or not, the statement is inconsequential. Whatever it was that Gershwin had written, it was, unquestionably, a masterpiece.

E. Let's listen to a little more of the Gershwin sound. We hear Duke Thompson playing Gershwin's own arrangement of a song we heard earlier, "Somebody Loves Me."

F. A personality as strong as Gershwin's was bound to repel some people as strongly as it attracted others. As thick-skinned as Gershwin may have appeared, stings from the artistic establishment, including Virgil Thomson and the well-known teacher Nadia Boulanger, hurt him, despite the fact that, by this time, he had written, among many other pieces, the timeless song "The Man I Love." We hear Duke Thompson play Gershwin's concert arrangement of that song.

G. In 1935, Gershwin was faced with both the critical rejection and the financial losses of *Porgy and Bess*; nonetheless, the show was changing musical and social history. Black opera singers were performing on Broadway, and African-American social problems were being seriously explored. When the show was performed at the National Theatre in Washington, DC, Gershwin insisted that black theatergoers be allowed to attend performances without the indignity of segregated seating.

V. At the same time, Gershwin's experiences seemed to him like professional defeat. Against Ira's advice, George left New York to write film musicals in Hollywood, but Hollywood did not provide the escape that George anticipated.

A. On Broadway, Gershwin was more than a composer; he had quality control over every aspect of his shows. In Hollywood, where the division of labor was far more rigidly prescribed, he was just another songwriter.

B. Also in Hollywood, Gershwin began to experience the symptoms of the brain tumor that would kill him, although at the time, the tumor went undiagnosed.

C. Gershwin's talents went undiminished. During his approximately 15 months in Hollywood, he wrote some of his best songs, including "A Foggy Day (in London Town)," "Nice Work If You Can Get It," "They Can't Take That Away from Me," and "Love Walked In."

D. As George's condition worsened, Ira called in Dr. Ernest Simmel, a psychiatrist, on the assumption that George's symptoms were psychological, not physical. On July 9, 1937, during one of his daily psychoanalytical sessions with Gershwin, Simmel recognized that his patient was experiencing papilledema and sent him to the hospital.

E. Gershwin underwent brain surgery but never regained consciousness. He died on July 11, 1937, at the age of 38. We conclude this lecture with my own respectful parody of one of Gershwin's songs, composed in his honor and sung by Alan Gephardt.

Suggested Reading:

Joan Peyser, *The Memory of All That: The Life of George Gershwin*.

Deena Rosenberg, *Fascinatin' Rhythm*.

Questions to Consider:

1. Give several reasons for the critics' slow acceptance of George Gershwin's genius.

2. Discuss both the positive social fallout and the negative fallout Gershwin's *Porgy and Bess* has had over the decades.

Lecture Twelve—Transcript
George Gershwin's Legacy (1919 to c. 1935)

George Gershwin was a living symbol of the Jazz Age. With the exception of Jerome Kern, no other theater composer of the 1920s equals Gershwin in importance. Let's begin with a rare 1919 recording of Gershwin playing a piano piece he wrote at age 18, "Novelette in Fourths." (*Plays recording—"Novelette in Fourths."*)

George Gershwin's father was born Morris Gershovitz in a little *shtetl* near St. Petersburg, and he never learned to speak English very well. He often called George's song, "Fascinatin' Rhythm," fashion on the river. Gershwin was not the most modest man in the world; his friend Oscar Levant said that he would sometimes get into taxicabs and say, "Drive carefully, Gershwin's in the back." Levant said the two of them did a two-piano tour of the eastern seaboard in the early '30s, and, on the first night, Levant was relegated to the upper berth. Levant climbed up to the upper berth and if you can remember him from films like *The Bandwagon* and *An American in Paris,* Levant was a very nervous man. When he got up there, he looked down. He said, "George, I'm going to roll over in my sleep and kill myself. I'll fall on the floor. Please, let's switch berths." Gershwin said, "No." Oscar said, "Why?" Gershwin said, "Oscar, that's the difference between talent and genius."

Now people always ask: "Which comes first—the words or the music?" Well with the Gershwins, the music almost always came first and the lyrics came second. Now there's one notable exception. When George and Ira were in Hollywood in 1937 writing the score of *Shall We Dance?* for Fred Astaire and Ginger Rogers, one morning Ira burst into the room where George was playing, put a piece of paper on the piano, and said, "George, write me a melody." Now George was surprised and he said, "Well, what inspired this?" and Ira said, "George, last night I had a dream and, in the dream, I was back at PS 20 in my old 6B English class." He explained that in the dream he remembered something he'd forgotten for years. He remembered that his English teacher, in order to teach the difference between English English and American English, told a story about an American and an Englishman in a saloon arguing over how to pronounce a word. And the American said the word is neither and the Englishman said the word is neither. It went back and forth—neither neither, neither neither, neither neither, neither neither—until, finally, the American in frustration turned to an Irishman three stools down and said, "Who's right?" And the Irishman said, "Neither." Ira used to tell an apocryphal story about this song. He said that a woman walked into a Broadway theater and asked to see the director. When the director was found, she said, "I want to audition for the show." Now the director said, "Well, go on stage and sing me something." So, she got on stage and she sang, "You say either and I say either / You say neither and I say neither / Either, either / Neither, neither." And the director said, "That was fine. Thank you very much, Ms. Levine." And she says, "It's Levine."

The Gershwin style influenced the style of every composer on Broadway for the next 20 years. I want to illustrate what that style sounds like. Two of the most important aspects of that style are repeated notes and blue notes. For example, in "Embraceable You," we have the come-to-papa section all on one note (*plays piano—"Embraceable You"*). In "They Can't Take that Away from Me," (*plays piano—"They Can't Take that Away from Me"*). In the "Piano Concerto," and we have (hums) repeated notes. Now what's a blue note? If I play a C major scale (*plays piano*) without the blue notes, then this is how "The Man I Love Sounds" (*plays piano—"The Man I Love Sounds,"*)…missing something. But the blue note is a flatted note that does not belong in the key, so we're going to flat the seventh note of the scale. Listen to the difference (*plays piano*)— blue notes and repeated notes.

On December 4, 1926, George Gershwin presented five piano preludes to the public in a piano recital at the Roosevelt Hotel in New York City. Three of these preludes have survived; nobody knows what happened to the other two. The first prelude is full of repeated notes and blue notes. It's a perfect model of the Gershwin style. I would like to at this time introduce Duke Thompson, an internationally acclaimed concert pianist and an acquaintance of Francis Gershwin, George's sister, who praised Duke's interpretation of George's work. Here is Duke playing the Gershwin Prelude in B flat major (*Plays piano—"Prelude # 1"*).

Duke, stick around, I'd like you to play one more piece by Gershwin. This is a 1914 piece of ragtime; it's probably the first thing George Gershwin ever wrote. Now he was working at Remick's as a piano demonstrator and he had orthography problems—that is, he could play it, but he couldn't quite get it down on paper. So, an older staff member named Will Donaldson helped him do that and in exchange for that, Gershwin gave him co-credit, but this is really Gershwin's work and first work. Remick's, as a favor to the young boy, decided to print the sheet music, but it wasn't recorded for almost 40 years. You may remember this piece of music as the theme song of the Ernie Kovacs television show in the 1950s *(Plays piano—"Rialto Ripples")*.

At age 19, with his neighborhood friend, Irving Caesar, George Gershwin wrote a song about the south using every cliché in the book, including a quote from the original nostalgic song about the south, Stephen Foster's "I Love the Old Folks at Home."

A new revue was in rehearsal at the Capitol Theatre. George's song seemed perfect for a special production number the theater had planned. On October 24, 1919, "Swanee" was introduced by 60 chorus girls with electric lights in their shoes on a semi-darkened stage. The electric lights were such a hit that nobody noticed the song.

Later that year, he played the piano at a private party at which Al Jolson was in attendance. Never shy, 19-year-old George Gershwin managed to get Jolson's attention and insisted that he listen to the song. Now Jolson loved it and Gershwin, always prepared, pulled a folded copy of "Swanee" out of his pocket and handed it to Jolson.

Jolson interpolated "Swanee" into his Broadway show *Sinbad*, and the song became the hit of the show and one of the biggest hits in Jolson's entire career. Overnight, George Gershwin had become the boy wonder of Broadway. Jolson's recording sold nearly a million copies during that first year, a phenomenal figure for those days. Here's the original recording of Jolson singing "Swanee" in 1919. *(Plays recording—"Swanee.")*

That's "Swanee" the way it's usually performed, but not the way that Gershwin always played it. Gershwin loved jazz and he was fascinated by the jazz musician's ability to create spontaneous variations on popular songs. So, at parties, he'd often create variations on his own songs, then he'd go home and write them down. As a result, we now have written examples of Gershwin's own variations on many of his early songs. Now you'll notice that Gershwin's concert variation on "Swanee" brings a little more sophistication to the song. Here's Duke to play George Gershwin's own piano variation on his song "Swanee" *(Plays piano—"Swanee.")*.

From 1920 to 1924, George Gershwin wrote songs for the yearly production of George White's *Scandals*. These shows produced his first timeless songs, among them "Stairway to Paradise" in 1922, and "Somebody Loves Me" in 1924.

Now we talked about blue notes being part of the style; "Somebody Loves Me" uses a blue note on every sustained "who." For example: *(Plays piano—"Somebody Loves Me")*. George Gershwin's verses were not throwaway verses. Now notice the blue notes in "Somebody Loves Me" as you listen to Alan Gephardt, accompanied by James Harp. James Harp is associated with the Baltimore Symphony Orchestra and with the Baltimore Opera Company; Alan Gephardt is a singer and dancer with Goucher College's Choreographie Antique. Here is "Somebody Loves Me," verse and all *(Plays piano—"Somebody Loves Me")*.

Ira and George began their long-term collaboration in 1924 with the show *Lady Be Good*. Two years later, in 1926, the Gershwins mounted a show called *Oh, Kay!* That's spelled O-H, comma, K-A-Y, exclamation point. Kay was played by a frail and not altogether confident Gertrude Lawrence, whom we'd see on Broadway two decades later as the star of Kurt Weill's *Lady in the Dark* and three decades later as the female lead of Rodgers and Hammerstein's *The King and I*. But in *Oh, Kay!*, Lawrence was in her 20s, inexperienced, and still a little unsure of herself.

When Gertrude Lawrence went out alone on the stage to sing this love song, there was an uncertainty about her delivery that sent a combination of grumbles and yawns through the audience. The backers of the show were convinced the song wouldn't work and wanted it dropped from the show. Then, Gershwin thought of a way to make the song work.

Gershwin went to FAO Schwartz and bought a sad-looking little doll. That evening, as Lawrence was about to go out to sing the song, Gershwin stopped her, handed her the doll, and said, "Don't sing the song to them (the audience); sing it to the doll." She did and it left the audience dewy-eyed and she got a standing ovation, and the flop of the show had became the hit of the show.

This is the song. As you listen to it, notice the unusually long and lyrical verse melody, another characteristic of the Gershwin style. Here it is: (*Plays recording—"Someone To Watch Over Me"*) That is such a nice song.

Well the next year, in 1927, the Gershwins wrote another show for Fred and Adele Astaire. Now their first show for the Astaires was 1924's *Lady Be Good*, which produced "The Man I Love," "Fascinatin' Rhythm," and the title song. The new show—the 1927 show—was originally called *Smarty*. Now it stayed with that title until they got to New Haven and, then, the Gershwins were seated in the audience during the day while Fred and Adele were rehearsing. Fred was a workaholic and a perfectionist. Adele, on the other hand, valued nothing more than her social life. And so, they had done a step that he didn't feel was quite right and she said, "I've got a date, I've got to go. Forget it." He became angry and he had a little name that he called her when he became irritated with her. So, she's about to leave the stage and as she stomps out and says, "I'm leaving," he says, "Cut that out, funny face!" George turned to Ira and they knew they had a new song and a new title for the show; they were going to call it *Cut That Out*. Obviously, they were going to call it *Funny Face*.

One of the most popular songs from *Funny Face* is the song "'S Wonderful;" and "'S Wonderful" is a prime example of Gershwin's less obvious debts to the world of jazz. It's not a lyrical melody like "Someone To Watch Over Me" (*plays piano—"Someone To Watch Over Me"*); instead it's two notes over and over again (*plays piano*).

"'S Wonderful" is essentially a riff song. Riffs are short musical jazz figures, played over and over, but avoiding monotony by changing the harmonies each time the riff is played. Without the harmonic changes, a riff tune can be boring; and certainly, "'S Wonderful" can be, too, but listen to it with the harmonies (*Plays piano—"'S Wonderful."*). Now, here's Alan Gephardt accompanied by James Harp to sing "'S Wonderful," verse and all (*Plays recording—"'S Wonderful."*).

George Gershwin wrote his most important stage work in 1935. *Porgy and Bess* dwarfs everything of Gershwin's that preceded it. The question may arise here that since the Gershwins and Dubose Heyward, their collaborator, thought of this show as an opera, why are we bothering with it in a course about musical theater?

 ©2006 The Teaching Company.

Well, the critics in 1935 were hesitant to call *Porgy and Bess* an opera. They said it contained too many hit songs; it couldn't be an opera. But it used recitative, it required trained voices, and George Gershwin orchestrated every one of *Porgy and Bess*'s hundreds of pages of manuscript. If it premiered today, *Porgy and Bess* would also fit neatly into the musical-theater niche filled by *Les Miserables* and *Miss Saigon*. Conversely, I think it would also be accepted as an opera so the gap, as you can see, is just not as wide as it once was. But, thank goodness, *Porgy and Bess* is already in the standard repertoire because its political incorrectness would not allow it to premier today.

Now *Porgy and Bess* was politically incorrect even in 1935 when it premiered. Many educated blacks were repelled by the show. After all, the story showed a side of ghetto life as shocking in 1935 as the tenement world of *West Side Story* in 1957. Porgy, the hero, is a cripple, Bess, the heroine, is a cocaine-sniffing prostitute, and Sportin' Life is a drug dealer. But, we're forced to look at these people as sympathetic human beings.

Duke Ellington, who later grew to love the work, attended the premiere and immediately dashed off a letter to the *New York Times*, part of which read like this: "It's high time we put a stop to George Gershwin's coal-black Negro-isms."

As far as its musical content is concerned—the month after *Porgy and Bess* premiered—Virgil Thomson wrote an article in *Modern Music* magazine that began, "Gershwin does not even know what an opera is." True or not, that statement is inconsequential. The label on the bottle means nothing; the contents mean everything. Whatever it was that George Gershwin had written it was unquestionably pure Gershwin, 100 percent American, and a masterpiece.

Now let's hear a little more of the Gershwin sound. Here's Duke to play Gershwin's own arrangement of a song you heard earlier. Listen to how different it sounds arranged by Gershwin as a little concert piece; this is "Somebody Loves Me" *(Plays piano—"Somebody Loves Me.")*.

A personality as strong as Gershwin's was bound to repel some people as strongly as it attracted others. Virgil Thomson, who had given *Porgy and Bess* a scathing review, was a small dog with a big bite. He had studied in Paris with Nadia Boulanger, a teacher who later rejected Gershwin when he came to Paris hoping to study with her. That probably delighted Thomson.

And, as thick-skinned as Gershwin may have appeared, these stings from the artistic establishment did hurt him. He often told this story about his trip to Paris to request study with Nadia Boulanger. I'll tell it in the first person, as Gershwin used to tell it. Well, she turned me down, but I said to myself, "I'm not leaving Paris until I find my master teacher." So, I sat down at a little sidewalk café, ordered a glass of wine, and who do I see walking in my direction but Igor Stravinsky. And I say to myself, "there's my master teacher." So I walk over to him, introduce myself—he recognizes the name, of course—and invite Stravinsky to sit for a drink. When Stravinsky's about half finished his drink, I pop the question. Suddenly, Stravinsky stands up, looks at me from head to toe, and says, "Mr. Gershwin, how much money did you make last year?" Now, I'm willing to pay well, but I try to come up with the smallest relatively accurate figure I can say, and I say, "Oh, $250,000." And Stravinsky says, "Can I study with you?" It's a nice story, but after Gershwin's death, Stravinsky swore the meeting with George Gershwin in Paris had never occurred. Gershwin had made up the story to soothe his wounded ego. Nonetheless, it's a good story.

Now I find it hard to believe that Gershwin needed those ego-propping stories, knowing that by that time he had not only written his "Rhapsody" and his "Piano Concerto," but also the timeless classic song, "The Man I Love." It was accepted as a masterpiece of American song around the world. Here's Duke to play Gershwin's lush concert arrangement of that song. *(Plays piano—"The Man I Love.")*

So, now it's 1935, and George Gershwin is faced with yet another rejection. Not just a critical rejection; *Porgy and Bess* lost $70,000, a considerable sum in those days.

If Gershwin were alive, I'd like to tell him that even in the midst of his 1935 failure with *Porgy and Bess*, his opera—or whatever you want to call it—was changing musical and social history. Black opera singers were performing on Broadway and not since *Showboat*, had black social problems been seriously explored in a musical.

            ©2006 The Teaching Company.

When the show left Broadway, it performed at the National Theatre in Washington, D.C. and, at that theater, for the first time in a century, blacks were allowed—at Gershwin's insistence—to attend performances without the indignity of segregated seating.

But, I doubt that these things did much to soften the blow for Gershwin. The summer before *Porgy and Bess*, he had conducted an all-Gershwin concert in a packed Lewisohn Stadium. The summer after *Porgy and Bess*, he conducted another concert at the stadium to a house with hundreds of empty seats. Now, I see no cause and effect relationship between that event and *Porgy and Bess*, but Gershwin probably did. New York must, to him, have looked like the scene of his defeat.

Against Ira and Lee's advice—Lee was Ira's wife—the family left New York City to write film musicals in Hollywood; I guess, in a sense, to escape to Hollywood. But if George thought Hollywood would be an escape from his troubles, it didn't quite work out that way. You see, on Broadway he was more than a composer. When he deemed it necessary, he had quality control over any and every aspect of his shows, as you saw previously.

In Hollywood, where the division of labor was far more rigidly proscribed, George Gershwin was just another songwriter. Sam Goldwyn actually told him, "George, give me the songs, but stay off the sound stage!"

It was there in Hollywood that he began to experience the symptoms. He had a memory loss during a performance at The Hollywood Bowl, but he managed to catch up and finish his performance. When he went backstage, his friend Oscar Levant was waiting for him. Gershwin, who had never muffed a performance in his life, snarled at Oscar and said, "I was thinking you. It was your fault, bastard!"

Later, in a calmer mood, he explained that during the performance he had smelled burning rubber—a classic symptom of a brain tumor. But, strangely, two different examinations by two different physicians failed to suggest that diagnosis.

Now, his talents certainly hadn't diminished. During those approximately 15 months in Hollywood, Gershwin wrote some of his best songs, including "A Foggy Day (In London Town)," "Nice Work If You Can Get It," "They Can't Take That Away From Me," and his final song, "Love Walked In."

As George's condition worsened, Ira called in Dr. Ernest Simmel, a psychiatrist. Simmel, Ira, and Lee all assumed that George's symptoms were not physical, but psychological. Yip Harburg, who was in the process of writing his lyrics for MGM's *The Wizard of Oz*, was leaving his Beverly Hills home to return to New York and turned the house over to Simmel, Simmel's male nurse, and George, where George underwent daily psychoanalysis.

Then, on July 9, a symptom appeared that made it clear to Simmel that George's problems were not psychological. George's eyes bulged to the point that they appeared to be the size of golf balls. Simmel immediately recognized a papilledema.

The surgeon at the hospital, Dr. Carl A. Rand, warned Ira to let him call in Dr. Walter E. Dandy at Johns Hopkins, possibly the best brain surgeon in America at that time. The call was made, but Dandy was cruising somewhere on the Chesapeake Bay on a private yacht. In those days, before cell phones, there was no way to reach him.

The California brain surgeon, Dr. Howard Nafzinger, performed the operation. George had suffered from a cystic degeneration of a tumor on a part of the brain that Dr. Nafzinger could not reach. Shortly after the operation on July 11, 1937, at 10:35 AM, George died without regaining consciousness. He was 38 years old.

Unfortunately, all biographies have the same ending. When I used to do my one-man show called *Gershwin-In-Person*, I always ended it with a little parody of one of Gershwin's songs to help cheer up the audience. We'll finish this lesson by having Alan share that with you *(Plays piano)*.

 ©2006 The Teaching Company.

Lecture Thirteen
Rodgers and Hammerstein Era (1940s)

Scope:

In 1941, four years after his brother's death, Ira Gershwin collaborated with Kurt Weill to write *Lady in the Dark*, a musical about a highly successful businesswoman undergoing psychoanalysis. With this show and the earlier *Pal Joey*, musical theater forged into new territories. On the whole, however, the 1940s belonged to Rodgers and Hammerstein, with the production of *Oklahoma!*, *Carousel*, and *South Pacific*. Other shows included Leonard Bernstein's and Jerome Robbins's *On the Town*, Yip Harburg's and Burton Lane's *Finian's Rainbow*, Lerner and Loewe's *Brigadoon*, and Cole Porter's masterwork, *Kiss Me, Kate*. If 1927's *Show Boat* had represented the beginnings of modern musical theater, the decade of the 1940s saw this art form firmly taking root and declaring the supremacy of the book musical for the rest of the century.

Outline

I. The end of the 1920s aspired to a more serious musical theater with *Show Boat*, but the Depression era that followed *Show Boat* gave us only one lasting show, *Porgy and Bess*.

   A. The only pre-Rodgers and Hammerstein show that was a harbinger of what was to come in the 1940s was written by Rodgers with his earlier colleague, Larry Hart. The show was *Pal Joey*, more serious, more nearly integrated, and more character-centered than most of the previous Rodgers and Hart shows.

   B. But Larry Hart was the anti-Hammerstein. Where Hammerstein's humanity brightens all his shows, we tend, with Hart, to marvel at his pessimistic wit, his impossible rhymes, and his sardonic view of love.

   C. Hart's anti-hero, Pal Joey, is a selfish, shallow opportunist, a far cry from the conventional musical comedy hero. He is a fascinating character, making the audience realize, as women become involved with him, that we often settle for what's available at the moment and regret it later. The chorus of

"Bewitched, Bothered, and Bewildered" is so overloaded with triple rhymes that we know with certainty that the praise for Joey is at least partially tongue-in-cheek.

D. Another serious incursion into integrated musical theater occurred in 1941 with Kurt Weill and Ira Gershwin's *Lady in the Dark*, the first major musical of World War II. A show about psychoanalysis, this Freudian story loses a little impact in today's world. The one aspect of the show that might hold a modern audience's attention is its surreal dream sequences.

II. The 1940s is, in certain ways, a unique decade in the musical's history: It was the first decade to leave substantial documentation in the form of cast recordings. The first such recording was from *Oklahoma!*.

III. The 1940s continued doing what the 1930s had done—that is, producing a large number of undisputed classic songs regularly performed today. Despite the other great teams writing then, however, the 1940s belonged to Rodgers and Hammerstein.

IV. On March 31, 1943, the curtain of the St. James Theatre rose to show a simple scene of the early American western frontier, and from offstage, a voice was heard singing a song so simple that, at first hearing, it might have been mistaken for a folksong.

A. Of course, the show was Rodgers and Hammerstein's first collaboration, *Oklahoma!*, one of the longest-running Broadway shows in history and one that influenced all other musicals from that time on.

B. The success of *Oklahoma!* was at least partially due to the fact that in 1943, America was at war with three fascist powers. *Oklahoma!* was about America's pioneer past, about home and family and love—precisely what we were fighting for.

C. There is, however, a touch of evil in *Oklahoma!*, as there is in almost every Hammerstein show. The evil is embodied in Jud, the farmhand who collects pornographic pictures and who has shown the potential for both murder and rape. But the evil is there to be vanquished by the forces of good, which always triumph in Hammerstein's world.

 ©2006 The Teaching Company.

D. The ballet in *Oklahoma!*, conceived by choreographer Agnes de Mille, introduced a new concept in which dancing became part of the story and character development.

    1. De Mille's ballet in *Oklahoma!* existed as a seamless part of the central plot, and from de Mille onward, the choreographer became a significant, often indispensable, part of musical theater production.

    2. Before de Mille, the term used in musical theater was dance director. De Mille brought prestige and a new label to a job that had previously commanded little attention from critics.

V. The initial run of *Oklahoma!* at the St. James Theatre was 2,212 performances. Its young, unknown cast included Alfred Drake and Celeste Holm. The show has been performed, somewhere in the world, every day since it premiered.

    A. Based on Lynn Rigg's 1931 *Green Grow the Lilacs*, *Oklahoma!* is set in Indian territory soon after the turn of the century. The simple tale is mostly concerned with whether Curly or Jud will take Laurey to the box social. When the show toured before premiering on Broadway, it was called *Away We Go!*. Theresa Helburn of the Theatre Guild is credited with the stroke of genius—the exclamation point—that convinced the creators and producers to change the name to *Oklahoma!*.

    B. As mentioned earlier, *Oklahoma!* contained no rousing opening chorus. As a matter of fact, it contained no chorus at all until midway through the first act. Later in the first act comes the long ballet and other serious overtones, including the inadvertent killing of Jud by Curly. These innovations proved that musical theater could address topics that were previously unheard of in these shows.

    C. Another peculiarity of *Oklahoma!* is that nowhere in the show do the lyrics call attention to the lyric writer's cleverness. The lyrics are beautiful but nearly invisible. This is not the case with such writers as Larry Hart, Ira Gershwin, Cole Porter, or William S. Gilbert.

    D. If Hammerstein's lyrics are more straightforward than Hart's, then so is Rodgers's musical style. He adapts to his lyricist in *Oklahoma!*, showing none of the Gershwin-influenced jazzy style of his 1930s collaborations with Hart. The fact that Hart let Rodgers write the music before the lyrics, while Hammerstein usually wrote the lyrics first, is also a factor in the appearance of the new Rodgers style.

1. The difference between the Rodgers style of Rodgers and Hart and that of Rodgers and Hammerstein was discussed in an interview conducted by radio host Bob Allen with William Hammerstein, Oscar's son.

2. Mary Rodgers, daughter of the composer, is a composer in her own right. We also listen to an interview with her, in which she comments on her father's compositional technique.

E. Before we move on from *Oklahoma!*, let's listen to "Oh, What A Beautiful Mornin'." Ours is the cast recording from the 1979 revival of *Oklahoma!*, featuring Lawrence Guittard.

1. The essential romanticism of the new Rodgers style and of Hammerstein's affinity for bucolic lyrical expression is perfectly encapsulated in this opening song. Curly is heard singing the song as he enters, unaccompanied, natural, and spontaneous. One note, which almost sounds like a wrong note, conveys the emotion under the surface of the song.

2. The combination here—folk-like simplicity with the impression of something deeper—establishes Curly as a potential folk hero. It may seem as if we're reading a great deal into a single flatted note, but we can hear the difference if we listen to the song without it.

F. The weakest part of Hammerstein's lyric is the first verse of the song. Before we examine the reasons for this, we should understand something about the functions of effective lyrics.

1. Lyricists do not have the freedom that poets take for granted. The verse of a lyricist must fit the melody; its accents must coincide with the accents of the melody. The sound of the lyrics must match the melody note-for-note and must "sing" well.

2. Music is the most abstract of the arts; it may create a mood, but no piece of music by itself tells precisely the same story to two different listeners. Lyrics, in contrast, are made up of words, which have both meanings (sense) and sound.

©2006 The Teaching Company.

3. When something has to give in a lyric, sense goes first. No lyric that doesn't sing well will be successful, but many lyrics that make little or no sense have been very successful. Of course, the lyrics of many songs, including "Oh, What A Beautiful Mornin'," are often adapted to fit the requirements of the music.

4. "Oh, What A Beautiful Mornin'" reflects Hammerstein's love of nature; he saw, in nature, the creative force that sustains humans and their fellow creatures. Indeed, Hammerstein's lyrics abound with images from nature.

5. Hammerstein wrote in the rural tradition of Whittier and Frost; in this age of computer realities and lives insulated from nature, his words remain relevant, but it seems unlikely that a lyricist of his ilk will ever appear again.

VI. On December 28, 1944, one year after the premiere of *Oklahoma!*, a young composer mounted a show that has been successfully revived several times since then. In 1944, this composer was totally new to Broadway.

A. At this point in his life, Leonard Bernstein (1918–1990) was living in Greenwich Village and had recently met a young dancer named Jerome Robbins. With Robbins, Bernstein created a ballet, *Fancy Free*, which was later turned into a full-blown musical and performed as *On the Town* at the Adelphi Theatre in 1944. The show garnered rave reviews.

B. Soon Robbins and Bernstein came up with an idea for another musical and gave it the tentative title *East Side Story*. This musical was to be about two tenement dwellers, one Jewish and the other Catholic. Eventually, they discarded the idea because it sounded too much like a mushy hit play of the 1930s, *Abie's Irish Rose*.

C. The year following the premiere of *On the Town* saw the production of a second Rodgers and Hammerstein musical. *Carousel* premiered at the Majestic Theatre on August 19, 1946. With *Carousel*, Rodgers and Hammerstein solidified their position as the dominant creators of musical theater in the 1940s.

1. This production transported playwright Molnar's 1921 fantasy from Budapest to a New England fishing village

to make the 19th-century story more relevant to an American audience.

2. Billy Bigelow, a swaggering carnival barker, meets Julie Jordan, a local factory worker, and in their soaring duet "If I Loved You," they reveal their feelings for each other. They marry, Julie becomes pregnant, and Billy, desperate for money to support his family, is killed in an attempted robbery.

3. Later, however, he is allowed to return to Earth to do one good deed. This is accomplished when he shows up at his daughter's high school graduation and encourages the girl to have confidence in herself by singing "You'll Never Walk Alone."

4. Bigelow was played by John Raitt; Julie by Jan Clayton; and the daughter by Bambi Lynn, whose dancing had been featured in the *Oklahoma!* ballet. Again, Agnes de Mille did the choreography.

VII. In 1947, Yip Harburg wrote lyrics and libretto to a score by Burton Lane for *Finian's Rainbow*, a show whose secondary theme paralleled the theme of racial intolerance in Kern and Hammerstein's *Show Boat*.

A. In *Finian's Rainbow*, the bigoted white senator Billboard Rawkins wakes up one day to discover that, overnight, he has become black. For the first time in his life, his tension-fraught encounters with whites instill in the man some empathy for his black brothers.

B. The songs from the show include "How Are Things in Glocca Morra?," "If This Isn't Love," and "Look to the Rainbow." Of course, the show includes a pot of gold, stolen from and pursued by Og the leprechaun, whose magic results in Senator Rawkins's waking up to a surprise when he looks in the mirror.

C. One of Harburg's lyrics for *Finian's Rainbow* was a rewrite of an earlier song originally written for Gene Kelly's first film, *For Me and My Gal*. The song is "Old Devil Moon"; we listen to the lyrics as originally written and later changed.

VIII. The year 1947 also brought to Broadway the first successful collaboration between Fritz Loewe (1904–1988) and Alan Jay Lerner (1918–1986). The show, of course, was *Brigadoon*, which ran at the Ziegfeld Theatre for 581 performances. Agnes de Mille, a hot commodity in the 1940s, again was the choreographer, and the stars were David Brooke and Sharon Bell.

A. *Brigadoon* is a story about two American tourists in Scotland, Tommy Albright and Jeff Douglas, who stumble upon a mist-clouded town that, they eventually discover, reawakens only one day every 100 years.

B. Tommy falls in love with Fiona, one of the town's residents, and at the end, he makes the ultimate romantic sacrifice, giving up his earthly existence to spend one day every 100 years with the woman he loves. "Almost Like Being in Love," sung by Tommy to Fiona, was one of the most recorded and most popular songs of 1947 and 1948.

IX. We can't leave the 1940s without mentioning one of the most cleverly integrated shows in musical theater history, Cole Porter's masterwork, *Kiss Me, Kate*.

A. Again, we can see how *Oklahoma!* set the pace for the decade. The star of *Oklahoma!*, Alfred Drake, also co-starred in *Kiss Me, Kate*, along with Patricia Morrison. The dances are by another choreographer from the world of ballet, Hanya Holm, who would later choreograph *My Fair Lady*. The show premiered at the New Century Theatre and, in its initial incarnation, ran for 1,070 performances.

B. After a long period of depression (the aftereffect of a crippling horseback-riding incident in 1937), Porter emerged triumphant in 1947, with one of the greatest musicals in the history of Broadway. It begins with "Another Opening, Another Show."

C. *Kiss Me, Kate* is two stories, one within the other, brilliantly written by Bella and Samuel Spewack. Drake and Morrison played a divorced couple brought back together after they've been cast in a tour of *The Taming of the Shrew*.

D. "So in Love" is the timeless love ballad of the show, more direct than most of Porter's love songs, more intense, and not the least bit ironic.

E. The tour after the Broadway run played two years, and the London company racked up 400 more performances. Cole

Porter was back on top again, more on top than he'd ever been before.

X. We come full circle in this lecture; we started with Rodgers and Hammerstein, and we end with them.

A. The greatest musical about World War II, *South Pacific*, appeared four years after the war had ended, and again, it was a blockbuster. Adapted from James Michener's *Tales of the South Pacific*, it was set in Micronesia. The book had an Oscar Hammerstein kind of message—we need to be tolerant and to treat people as we'd want them to treat us.

B. The show opened at the Majestic Theatre and, in its initial production, ran for 1,925 performances. It starred Ezio Pinza and Mary Martin and was beautifully orchestrated by Robert Russell Bennett. Dance was a somewhat less important part of the show than in *Oklahoma!* and *Carousel* probably because director Joshua Logan also choreographed the show, and Logan was not a dancer.

C. The show is a romance involving nurse Nellie Forbush and French planter Emile de Becque, who has two children by a native island woman, now dead. As had earlier shows, *South Pacific* made its case for racial tolerance within the escapist world of musical comedy.

D. In the show, Bloody Mary, a large Polynesian woman, tacitly breaks away from stereotypes by singing the most beautiful song in the show, "Bali Hai."

E. In addition to thunderous praise for Mary Martin and Ezio Pinza, reviewers were rapturous about *South Pacific* itself. Brooks Atkinson's opening night review in *The New York Times* was exultant: "This is a tenderly beautiful idyll of genuine people inexplicably tossed together in a strange corner of the world; and the music, lyrics, singing, and acting [all] contribute to the mood."

F. The phrase "genuine people" is a significant one. From *Show Boat* onward, the musicals that have lasted have created memorable and believable characters.

    1. The Faustian lead in 1866's *The Black Crook*, for example, was a stock character, not a breathing soul. Magnolia, Ravenal, and Julie in *Show Boat*, however, approach reality, and with Curly and Laurey in

Oklahoma!, we meet two real, if somewhat simple-minded, people.

2. In *South Pacific*, the two leads are mature and complex. What makes *South Pacific* a little dated today is that, though racism certainly hasn't vanished, the variety of it shown in Nellie Forbush is far less prevalent than during World War II.

G. At the end of *South Pacific*, de Becque's two children sing "Dites-Moi." Nellie joins in the song, and Emile answers her singing. The show ends on a quiet note, unthinkable in earlier musical comedy, with Nellie and Emile looking into each other's eyes.

H. Earlier in the show, Nellie sings a rousing waltz, "I'm in Love with a Wonderful Guy."

1. Rodgers's career is filled with updated waltzes, including "Hello Young Lovers" from *The King and I*, "The Most Beautiful Girl in the World" from *Jumbo*, "Falling in Love with Love" from *The Boys from Syracuse*, and others.

2. In Nellie's song, the repetition of "I'm in love" reminds us of what Bernstein and Sondheim did eight years later in *West Side Story*, with Tony showing his joy by singing the name *Maria* over and over. In closing, we hear a bit of "I'm in Love with a Wonderful Guy."

Suggested Reading:

William G. Hylands, *Richard Rodgers*.

Mark Steyn, *Broadway Babies Say Goodnight: Musicals Then and Now*.

Questions to Consider:

1. Explain in detail how *Oklahoma!* broke with tradition, musically, dramatically, and in terms of its use of dance.

2. Name several 1940s musicals and explain what each owed to an earlier show.

Lecture Thirteen—Transcript
Rodgers and Hammerstein Era (1940s)

The '40s and, to a lesser extent, the '50s are the Rodgers and Hammerstein era. The end of the 1920s aspired to a more serious musical theater with *Showboat*, but it turns *Showboat* was a spark in the darkness. The Depression Era that followed *Showboat* gave us great songs—possibly the best we've ever had—but with the exception of *Porgy & Bess*—really an opera—lasting shows are not part of its legacy.

In any case, the only pre-Rodgers-and-Hammerstein show that was really a harbinger of what was to come in the 1940s was written by Rodgers in his previous incarnation as half of the team of Rodgers and Hart. The show was 1940's *Pal Joey*, more serious, more nearly integrated, and more character-centered than most of the previous Rodgers and Hart shows.

But, Larry Hart was the anti-Hammerstein. Where Hammerstein's humanity brightens all his shows, where we walk away from Hammerstein's lyrics feeling enlightened and ennobled, we tend instead with Hart to marvel at his pessimistic wit, his impossible rhymes, and his sardonic view of love. Hart wrote, "This can't be love because I feel so well."

Hart's anti-hero, Pal Joey, is a selfish, shallow opportunist, a far cry from the conventional musical comedy hero. This show, in many ways, is more 1960s than 1940s or 1950s. I sometimes think that Joey may provide some of the inspiration for the decadent master of ceremonies in 1967's *Cabaret*. Now, though *Cabaret*'s emcee made Joey look wholesome in comparison, Joey too was a leering emcee in a sleazy nightclub.

Joey is a fascinating character in that we realize, as women become involved with this pseudo-talented sleaze ball, that we often settle for what's available and regret it later. The chorus of "Bewitched, Bothered and Bewildered" is so overloaded with triple rhymes— "I'm wild again, beguiled again, a-whimpering, simpering child again"—that we know with certainty that the praise for Joey in this chorus is at least partially tongue-in-cheek. In the verse of "Bewitched, Bothered and Bewildered," Vivienne Segal sings, "He's a fool and don't I know it, but a fool can have his charms." In the second chorus, she sings, "I'm vexed again, perplexed again, Thank God I can be oversexed again!"

Hammerstein never allowed his references to be so sexually blatant. Ado Annie, the girl who can't say no in *Oklahoma!*, would never use the word sex—though her song makes it clear that the fact that she wouldn't say it doesn't mean she wouldn't do it. Hammerstein is a little stuffier than Hart, a little more moral in the 19th-century sense of that word. If Hart can be caustic, Hammerstein can be sweet. Nonetheless, no lyricist in the 20th century has created a more finely crafted musical theater than Oscar Hammerstein.

Another serious incursion into integrated musical theater occurred in 1941 with Kurt Weil and Ira Gershwin's *Lady in the Dark*. This was Ira Gershwin's first major project after his brother George's death in 1937. A musical about psychoanalysis, this Freudian story loses a little impact in today's world where psychoanalysis has all but been replaced by quick fixes and drugs like Valium and Prozac. The one aspect of the show that might hold on a modern audience's attention is the dream sequences in which the kinds of surreal vision that dominates MTV today, dominates those dream sequences. *Lady in the Dark* is the first major musical of World War II.

The '40s is, in certain ways, a unique decade in the musical's history. It was the first decade to leave a substantial documentation in the form of cast recordings. Now true, there had been recordings of show songs in the previous decades—you've heard quite a few of them— but *Oklahoma!*'s Decca recording was the first to do the entire score of a show—six heavy 78 RPM discs in one cardboard binder. And, it sold a million copies its first year—that's six million records! Half the score ended up being heard on "Lucky Hart Strike Hit Parade"— each week they played the Billboard top ten bestsellers for that week. Show music was mainstream in those days. It continued to be that way into the late '50s. It is not that way today and probably never will be again.

The '40s continued doing what the '30s had done—producing a large number of undisputed classic songs regularly performed today. They continued adding pages to "The Great American Songbook." But, despite the other great teams writing during the '40s, that decade belonged to Rodgers and Hammerstein.

On March 31, 1943, the curtain of the St. James Theatre rose to disclose a simple scene of the early American Western frontier and, from offstage, a voice entered singing a song so simple that, at first hearing, it might have been mistaken for a folk song. Of course, the show was Rodgers and Hammerstein's first collaboration, *Oklahoma!*. One of the longest running Broadway shows in history and one that influenced every Broadway musical from that time on. The fabulous success of *Oklahoma!* was at least partially due to the fact that, in 1943, America was at war with three fascist powers. *Oklahoma!* was about America's pioneer past, about home, and family, and love. These were precisely what we were fighting for. Thank goodness *Oklahoma!* is already a classic because if it were to premiere today, its wholesomeness would probably make it a box-office disaster!

Now there is a touch of evil in *Oklahoma!*—as there is in almost every Oscar Hammerstein show. The evil is embodied in Jud, the farmhand who collects pornographic pictures and who has shown the potential for both murder and rape. But, the evil is there to be vanquished by the forces of good. That's the sole purpose for its existence in the show. In Hammerstein's world—because man is good at his core—good eventually triumphs. That is one of the primary differences between Oscar Hammerstein and the worldview in later shows like *West Side Story*, *Sweeney Todd*, *Miss Saigon*, and *Chicago*.

Oklahoma!'s ballet, conceived by choreographer Agnes de Mille—de Mille, by the way, was the niece of film director Cecil B. DeMille—*Oklahoma!*'s ballet introduced a new concept, where dancing became part of the story and part of the character development. Now to a lesser extent, this had been done in the 1936 Rodgers and Hart show, *On Your Toes*, starring Ray Bolger. But, Rodgers's Gershwinesque "Slaughter on Tenth Avenue" from that show was not a part of a larger story—it was a story within a story. Agnes de Mille's ballets, on the other hand, existed as a seamless part of the central plot. From Agnes de Mille onward, the choreographer became a significant, often indispensable part of musical theater production. Before de Mille, the term in musical theater was not choreographer—a Greek word that comes from classical ballet—the term was dance director. De Mille brought prestige and a new label to a job previously commanding little attention from the critics.

©2006 The Teaching Company.

The year before *Oklahoma!*, De Mille had choreographed Aaron Copland's ballet music "Rodeo." It was her work in "Rodeo" that convinced Rodgers and Hammerstein that she was the right person for *Oklahoma!*. The prairie dresses and the austere un-Broadway look of the dances supposedly prompted Walter Winchell's secretary to send him a now infamous telegram after she had seen the out-of-town tryouts in New Haven. The telegram read, "No legs! No jokes! No chance!"

The initial run of *Oklahoma!* at the St. James Theatre was 2,212 performances. Its young, unknown cast included Alfred Drake and Celeste Holm. The show has been performed, somewhere in the world, every day since it premiered. Based on Lynn Rigg's 1931 *Green Grow the Lilacs*, *Oklahoma!* is set in Indian Territory soon after the turn of the century. The simple tale is mostly concerned with whether Curly (Alfred Drake) or the menacing Jud (Howard Da Silva) will take Laurey (Joan Roberts) to the box social.

Knowing the play had been a box-office flop, the musical version had to go by another name. As it toured before Broadway, it was called—believe it or not—*Away We Go!* Now, that comes from the square dancing directions, "Dosey-do and away we go!" By the time the show reached the Colonial Theatre in Boston, one faction among its creators and producers wanted to call it *Oklahoma!*, but the majority said in essence, "That's ridiculous! That's like calling a show "New Jersey." Theresa Helburn of the Theater Guild came up with a stroke of genius that convinced everyone to call it *Oklahoma!* after all. At the end of the word she placed an exclamation point. That convinced them!

As we said earlier, *Oklahoma!* contained no rousing opening chorus. As a matter of fact, it contained no chorus at all until midway through the first act. Then, later in the first act, we have this long ballet and other serious overtones, including the inadvertent killing of Jud by Curly. Your know if the show had flopped, we would have referred to these things as *Oklahoma!*'s faults. But, since it did the opposite of flop, we now refer to them as *Oklahoma!*'s innovations. It proved we could do things in musical theater we previously thought we couldn't.

Another peculiarity of *Oklahoma!* is that nowhere in the show do the lyrics call your attention to the lyric writer's cleverness. The lyrics are beautiful, but as you take in the show, they're nearly invisible.

Now that's not the case with Larry Hart who, along with Ira Gershwin, Cole Porter, and Yip Harburg, learned his craft from William S. Gilbert, the better half of William S. Gilbert and Sullivan—history's greatest master of the triple rhyme. Gilbert wrote "Let's indulge in the felicity … of unbounded domesticity." In other words, "let's get married."

If Hammerstein's lyrics are more straightforward than Hart's and Gilbert's—and they are—then so is Richard Rodgers's musical style. He adapts to his lyricist in *Oklahoma!*, showing absolutely none of the George Gershwin-influenced jazzy style of the 1930s collaborations with Larry Hart. The difference between the Richard Rodgers style of Rodgers and Hart and the Richard Rodgers style of Rodgers and Hammerstein was discussed during radio host Bob Allen's interview show with William Hammerstein, Oscar's son. Here's what he had to say. (Plays recording of interview):

> **Bob Allen**: Rodgers began his 17-year partnership with Oscar Hammerstein in 1943, after working for 25 years exclusively with Larry Hart. With Hart, Rodgers produced biting, sometimes bitter love songs like, "Spring Is Here. Glad To Be Unhappy." With Hammerstein, happy soaring melodies became the norm. Oscar Hammerstein's son, Bill, told me that he was aware of that difference when I met with him at his office in Manhattan:

> **William Hammerstein**: Yes, I always thought that and I once mentioned it to Dick, who looked at me quizzically, as if he didn't believe that that was so. Now, I don't know. I didn't go into it; I was afraid to consider the conversation because I thought it would be embarrassing. But I don't know whether he really believed that he didn't change his music. I tend to think he knew that he change it because Mary, his daughter, tells about how he began to take piano lessons when he started working on *Oklahoma!* to presumably increase the dimension of what he was writing. And so, I think he must have known, but it was quite different.

Bob Allen also interviewed Mary Rodgers, Richard Rodgers's daughter, on the same topic. Mary Rodgers is a composer in her own right. Her show, *Once Upon a Mattress*, introduced Carol Burnett to

©2006 The Teaching Company.

Broadway in the 1960s. Here's Mary Rodgers talking about her father's work: (Plays recording of interview):

> **Bob Allen**: Mary Rodgers thinks she knows the reason for the difference and talked to me about it when I visited with her at her country home on Eastern Long Island.
>
> **Mary Rodgers**: As you know, he wrote the music after the lyrics when he worked with Oscar and I think that gave them both considerably more freedom. It was an expanded style, the 32-bar song really wasn't functioning or they didn't use it as much as it had been used. It was just a traditional obvious way to write a song in the old days and you could begin to see things like "Lonely Room,"—which I think is one of the most beautiful pieces he ever wrote—is an entirely different kind of Brahmsian rich, sort of sound that he didn't get into. Obviously, he would have had a very chameleon-like musical personality. He could adapt to Larry or to Oscar or, when he wrote his own lyrics, to himself.
>
> **Bob Allen**: And he had the ability to write a song *(snaps)* like that, didn't he?
>
> **Mary Rodgers**: Yes, although I think there was a lot of subliminal thought going on because he had the lyric ahead of time, and he and Oscar had discussed every song in infinite detail—they knew who was gonna sing it, and they knew what rhythm it was gonna be in, and whether it was going to be happy or sad, and slow and fast and exactly where it belonged in the scene. And, when you have all that information—and then your creative genius on top of it—it's when you sit down to actually put your fingers on the keys—if that's the way you write—there's a lot of it that's there, bubbling around in your head ahead of time. So, when he is at the piano and out came "Bali Hai" in no time at all, in fact, there were countless several hours going on ahead of time, probably.

Before we move on from *Oklahoma!*, let's hear that opening song, whose lyric—part of it at least—was lifted from Lynn Rigg's stage directions, which say something like, "There was a golden haze on the meadow." After we hear this familiar song, we'll talk about the lyrical problems Oscar Hammerstein had to solve in order to make the lyric work and why Richard Rodgers's melody is not nearly as simple as it sounds. Here's Laurence Guittard singing "Oh, What a Beautiful Mornin'" from the cast recording of the 1979 revival on Broadway *(Plays recording—"Oh, What a Beautiful Mornin'.")*.

The essential romanticism of the new Richard Rodgers's style and of Oscar Hammerstein's affinity for bucolic lyrical expression is perfectly capsulized in this opening song. With no one else but Auntie Eller onstage churning butter, Curly is heard singing the song on his way to the stage—unaccompanied, natural, and spontaneous. The orchestra in the original production doesn't come in until the second verse. One note conveys the emotion under the surface as Curly sings the song, *(plays piano)* and it's that note *(plays piano)*; it almost sounds like a wrong note. The combination here, folk-like simplicity along with the impression of something deeper, establishes Curly, from the top, as someone consequential—a potential folk hero. Now, that may sound like I'm reading a lot into that single flatted note, but look at it again *(plays piano)*. The note is not part of the chords—an F chord, which has three notes, F, A, C— *(plays piano)* and that B flat dies to lower itself to the A, *(plays piano)*, to complete the chord. And, if I play the song without it *(plays piano)*, it's like French fries without salt.

The weakest part of Oscar Hammerstein's lyric is the first verse of the song. Before we examine the reasons for this, we should understand something about the functions of effective lyrics. Lyricists do not have the freedom that poets take for granted. The verse of a lyricist must fit the melody; its accents must coincide with the accents of the melody. The sound of the lyrics must not only match the melody note-for-note, but they also must sing well. Now here long notes occur, certain vowels sustain better than others. "O" is a beautiful example, but "E" becomes a little tedious.

Music means nothing. It is the most abstract and the most evanescent of the arts. It may create a mood, but no piece of music by itself tells precisely the same story to two different listeners. Without the original narration, *Peter and the Wolf* is not about a boy named Peter or about a wolf; we could just as easily write a program for this music about a man on a bicycle.

Lyrics, on the other hand, are made of words, which have dictionary meanings. They also, like music, have sounds. So, lyrics contain sound and sense. Now, when something has to give in a lyric, which

 ©2006 The Teaching Company.

do you think gives first—sound or sense? If you said sense, you're right. A lyric must sing well. No lyric that doesn't sing well will be successful; however, a lot of lyrics that make little or no sense have been very successful. And, I'm not just talking about nonsense lyrics.

In the mid-19th century, Stephen Foster was working on a song and he had a line that went, "Way down upon the Pee Dee River." "Pee Dee" did not sing well. He called in his brother, Morrison. Morrison said, "What do you think of the Yazoo River?" Well, the "Z" in Yazoo, for some reason, had a humorous effect and that wasn't what he wanted. So, they looked on the map and they found a river in Florida called the Suwannee; however, he had too many syllables, so he chopped off a syllable and turned it into the "Swanee River." Today, because of the popularity of that song, the people down south also call it the Swanee River.

There's a famous song from early in the 20th century that goes, "There's Pappy, Mammy, down in Alabamy, down on the levee, waiting for the Robert E. Lee." Now, the man who wrote that song—a very popular song, by the way—didn't even know that there are no levees in Alabama. One of the most popular songs of the '40s began "Pennies on a string, falling leaves of sycamore, moonlight in Vermont." Now, the man who wrote the song did not realize that there were no sycamores in Vermont. It's too cold up there for sycamores. But, that became the unofficial state song of Vermont and, as a result, the chambers of commerce hauled in sycamores all over the place and a few survived, though they're rather spindly.

We talk about art imitating life, but as you can see, sometimes life imitates art. There's a very beautiful song from the '30s, with lyrics by Yip Harburg, that goes, "April in Paris, chestnuts in blossom, holiday tables under the stars, I never knew the charm of spring until April in Paris." Well a friend of Harbor's went to Paris in April and it rained every single day and it was icy cold at night and the sun didn't shine once. He came back, saw Yip Harburg at a nightclub, grabbed him by the lapels, shook him, and explained what happened. Harburg said, "Well, you know, May is a much better month, but we needed a two-syllable word."

And now, to Oscar Hammerstein's problem with the lyric for "Oh, What a Beautiful Mornin'." He originally wrote, "There's a golden haze on the meadow," and then followed that with, "The corn is as high as a cow pony's eye." Now the problem with that is this—the song is in 3/4 time with the accent on the first beat. With "cow pony," we end up with a stronger accent on the first syllable of "pony," which throws the accent off the first beat onto the second beat. It won't work. But, "elephant" sounds beautiful, so Oscar Hammerstein put an elephant in the cornfield and it's been there ever since.

Hart, great lyricist that he was, could never attempt to write a lyric like "Oh, What a Beautiful Mornin'" without being disastrously clever. Hart was as urban as Times Square, and to him, the countryside was fantasyland. But, Oscar Hammerstein lived as at ease on the farm, as he did on Broadway; he owned a working farm in Bucks County. Long before the fancy word "ecology" replaced the simple Anglo-Saxon word "nature," Oscar Hammerstein felt an urgency to retain the balance of nature into the future, and he saw, in nature, the creative force that sustains man and all his fellow creatures. Larry Hart was far too self-absorbed and far too much an urban sophisticate to see the world in these terms. In Hart, we find a handful—maybe not quite a handful, even—of nature images. But, Hammerstein's lyrics abound with them. "I'm as restless as a spider spinning daydreams"—"The hills are alive with the sound of music"—"Ray, a drop of golden sun"—"I'm as corny as Kansas in August." At times, Oscar Hammerstein writes in the rural tradition of Whittier and Frost; in this age of computer realities and lives insulated from nature, Oscar Hammerstein's words remain relevant, but it seems unlikely that a lyricist of his ilk will ever appear again.

Remember, we talked earlier about how when Hammerstein worked and lounged on the farm, he always kept a little notebook and a pencil stub in his back pocket. When lyric ideas came to him, he'd whip out the notebook and write them down. Nearly 10 years before *Oklahoma!*, he had looked out at the pasture on his farm from the front porch, noticed something, reached into his pocket, and wrote down what he saw. What he had seen was this. This was the image he put in his notebook: "All the cattle are standing like statues..." This became the second verse of "Oh, What a Beautiful Mornin'." Oscar Hammerstein was born to write *Oklahoma!*.

Rodgers and Hammerstein continued to mount new musicals throughout the '40s. On December 28, 1944,—one year after *Oklahoma!*'s premiere—a very young composer mounted a show successfully revived several times since then. In 1944, the composer was totally new to Broadway. At this point in his life, Leonard

Bernstein was sharing a small apartment in Greenwich Village with a childhood friend, Adolphe Green. Around this time, he also met a young dancer named Jerry Robbins. With Robbins, Leonard Bernstein created a ballet called *Fancy Free*, which was performed a few times and that might have been that.

Fancy Free was about three sailors on 24-hour leave in New York City, but Adolphe Green, Bernstein's roommate, had an idea. He and his friend, Betty Comden, worked with a group called "The Reviewers" at a small theater in the Village. It was a little like today's "Forbidden Broadway," which does satirical take-offs on current Broadway musicals. Green and Comden thought they could turn Bernstein's ballet into a full-blown musical, and on December 28, 1944, at the Adelphi Theatre, the show, *On the Town*, premiered to rave notices. The show was revived on Broadway in 1959, in 1971, and again in 1998. In 1949, MGM produced a successful film version of the show starring Gene Kelly, Vera Ellen, Frank Sinatra, and Betty Garrett.

Meanwhile, Jerome Robbins and Leonard Bernstein came up with an idea for another musical; they even gave it a tentative title. The musical was to be about two tenement dwellers, one Jewish and the other Catholic. Eventually, they discarded the idea because it sounded too much like *Abie's Irish Rose*. The tentative title for this discarded musical was—are you ready for this?—*East Side Story*, more during a later lesson, about how this idea was transformed into one of the greatest musicals of the 20th century.

The year following the premier of *On the Town* saw the production of a second Rodgers and Hammerstein musical. *Carousel* premiered at the Majestic Theatre on August 19, 1946. With *Carousel*, Rodgers and Hammerstein solidified their position as the dominant creators of musical theater in the '40s. This production transported playwright Molnar's 1921 fantasy from Budapest to a New England fishing village to make the 19th-century story seem more relevant to an American audience.

Billy Bigelow, a swaggering carnival barker, meets Julie Jordan, a local factory worker; and in their soaring duet, *If I Loved You,* they reveal their feelings for each other. They marry, Julie becomes pregnant, and Billy, desperate for money, does something he shouldn't do, and he is killed in an attempted robbery. Later he is, however, allowed to return to Earth to do one good deed. This is accomplished when he shows up at his daughter's high school graduation and encourages the girl to have confidence in herself by singing, "You'll Never Walk Alone."

Bigelow was played by John Raitt, Julie by Jan Clayton, and the daughter by Bambi Lynn, whose dancing had been featured in the *Oklahoma!* ballets. *Oklahoma!* was still running at this time, so Rodgers and Hammerstein had two hit shows running simultaneously on Broadway. Again, the choreography was done by Agnes de Mille.

In 1947, Yip Harburg wrote lyrics and libretto to a score by Burton Lane for a show whose secondary theme paralleled the secondary theme of Kern and Hammerstein's *Showboat*. That theme, of course, is racial intolerance. While Joe's singing about white people playing and black people working on the river in "Old Man River" in *Showboat* disturbs us, Harburg engages our sympathy with humor. The bigoted white senator, Billboard Rawkins, wakes up one day to discover that, overnight, he's become black. For the first time in his life, his tension-fraught encounters with whites instill in the man some empathy for his black brothers.

The songs from the show include "How Are Things in Glocca Morra?," "If This Isn't Love," and "Look to the Rainbow." *Finian's Rainbow*, that's the title—Harburg had a fascination with rainbows and that led him to inject a rainbow into his book and lyrics for MGM's *The Wizard of Oz* with Judy Garland. There was no mention of a rainbow in Frank L. Baum's original book, *The Wizard of Oz*. In *Finian's Rainbow*, the rainbow's end contains a pot of gold, stolen from and pursued by Og, the leprechaun, whose magic results in Senator Rawkins waking up to a surprise when he looks in the mirror.

One of Harburg's lyrics for *Finian's Rainbow* was a total rewrite of an earlier song originally written for Gene Kelly's first film, *For Me and My Gal*. This is how it went then:

> I came to give you back that ring
>
> Came to drop the whole darned thing
>
> And to take it on the wing

The song was dropped from the film and later rewritten for *Finian's Rainbow*; these lines became:

 ©2006 The Teaching Company.

I looked at you and suddenly

Something in your eyes I see

Soon begins bewitching me

It's that old devil moon

The hit song of *Finian's Rainbow*.

The year 1947 also brought to Broadway the first successful collaboration between Fritz Loewe and Alan Jay Lerner. The show, of course, was *Brigadoon*, which ran at the Ziegfeld Theatre for 581 performances—a run that doesn't reflect the high quality of the show. Agnes de Mille again was the choreographer and the stars were David Brooke and Sharon Bell.

You can see that, during the '40s, de Mille's choreography dominated Broadway in the way that Susan Stroman's did in the '90s. A hot commodity, de Mille choreographed—in addition to the shows we've already mentioned—*Bloomer Girl*, *One Touch of Venus*, *Paint Your Wagon*, Rodgers and Hammerstein's *Allegro*, and Jule Styne's *Gentlemen Prefer Blondes*.

Brigadoon is a story about two American tourists in Scotland, Tommy Albright and Jeff Douglas, who stumble upon a mist-clouded town, they eventually discover reawakens only one day every hundred years. Tommy falls in love with Fiona, one of the town's residents, and at the end, he makes the ultimate sacrifice. Tommy Albright gives up his earthly existence in order to spend one day every 100 years with the woman he loves. "Almost Like Being in Love," sung by Tommy to Fiona, ended up being one of the most recorded and most popular songs of 1947 and 1948.

We can't leave the 1940s without mentioning one of the most cleverly integrated shows in musical theater history, Cole Porter's masterwork, *Kiss Me, Kate*. Again, we can see how *Oklahoma!* set the pace for the decade. The star of *Oklahoma!*, Alfred Drake, also costars in *Kiss Me, Kate*, along with Patricia Morrison. The dances are by another choreographer from the world of ballet, Hanya Holm—who would later do the choreography for *My Fair Lady*. The show *Kiss Me, Kate* premiered at the New Century Theatre and, in its initial incarnation, ran for 1,070 performances.

After a long period of understandable depression—the aftereffect of a crippling horseback riding incident in 1937—Porter emerged, in 1947, more triumphant than anyone could have predicted with one of the greatest musicals in the history of Broadway. It begins with:

> Another Op'nin', another Show
>
> In Philly, Boston, or Buffalo.
>
> A chance for show folk to say "Hello"
>
> Another op'nin' of another show!

Kiss Me, Kate is two stories, one within the other, brilliantly written by Bella and Samuel Spewack. Alfred Drake and Patricia Morrison play a divorced couple brought back together after they've been cast in a tour of *The Taming of The Shrew*. "So in Love" is the timeless love ballad of the show, more direct than most of Porter's love songs, not humorous and more intense, and not the least bit ironic. One can't help wondering if the song wasn't, in some sense, payback to Linda, his wife, for the sacrifices she'd made for him—accepting his homosexual dalliances, and nursing him and encouraging him through his most pain-ridden and, simultaneously, most creative 20 years.

The tour after Broadway played 2 years and the London Company racked up 400 more performances. Cole Porter was back on top again, more on top than he'd ever been before.

Now, we come full circle—we started with Rodgers and Hammerstein and we end the decade with Rodgers and Hammerstein. The greatest musical about World War II appeared four years after the war had ended and, again, it was a blockbuster. The show, of course, was *South Pacific*. Adapted from James Michener's *Tales of the South Pacific*, it was a chronicle of Michener's observations while stationed in Micronesia during World War II. It was a book with a message—Oscar Hammerstein's kind of message—we need to be tolerant and to treat people as we'd want them to treat us.

The show opened at the Majestic Theatre and, in its initial production, it ran for 1,925 performances. It starred Ezio Pinza and Mary Martin and was beautifully orchestrated by Robert Russell Bennett. The dance, the dance in this was less important than it had been in *Oklahoma!* and *Carousel*, and that may have been due to the fact that director Joshua Logan also choreographed the show and

©2006 The Teaching Company.

Logan was not a dancer. Rodgers and Hammerstein had produced Irving Berlin's *Annie Get Your Gun* two years previously and had employed Logan to stage that show. Actually, it was Logan, at a cocktail party, who had suggested to Rodgers and Hammerstein the idea of turning Michener's stories into a musical.

The show is a romance involving nurse Nellie Forbush and French planter Emile de Becque who has two children by a native island woman, now dead. As with Kern and Hammerstein's *Showboat* and Harburg and Lane's *Finian's Rainbow*, *South Pacific* made its case for racial tolerance within the escapist world of musical comedy.

Now we know Broadway is only entertainment, but that's like saying "It's only Rock 'n' Roll." Actually, both mediums are formed by and, in turn, help to form our values and our attitudes. I honestly think that certain films and certain Broadway shows helped us, in small ways, to learn to accept our differences. I know that Oscar Hammerstein thought that.

In the show, Bloody Mary—a very large, very dark, Polynesian character—tacitly breaks away from the stereotype by singing the most hauntingly beautiful song in the show, "Bali Hai."

In addition to thunderous praise for Mary Martin and Ezio Pinza, reviewers were rapturous about *South Pacific* itself. Brooks Atkinson's opening night review in the *New York Times* was exultant. It said: "A magnificent musical drama! This is a tenderly beautiful idyll of genuine people inexplicably tossed together in a strange corner of the world; and the music, lyrics, singing, and acting all contribute to the mood."

The phrase "genuine people" is a significant one. From *Showboat* onward, the musicals that have lasted have created memorable and believable characters. The Faustian lead in 1866's *The Black Crook* was a stock character, not a breathing soul. Gilbert and Sullivan survive on their lightning-bright and lightning-fast wit; their characters, however, are pasteboard caricatures. But, Magnolia, Ravenal, and Julie in *Showboat* approach reality. With Curly and Laurey in *Oklahoma*, we meet two real, if somewhat simpleminded, people. But in *South Pacific*, the two leads are mature, they're complex, they are in contact with their inner selves and, at the same time, in conflict with their inner selves. What may make *South Pacific* a little dated today is that, though racism certainly has not vanished, the variety of it shown in Nellie Forbush is far less prevalent than during World War II. Mixed race children are seen in every shopping mall and almost nobody these days finds the sight worth a second glance.

At the end of *South Pacific*, de Becque's two children sing "Dites-Moi," the little minuet the children sing in the first scene of the show. Here's our ubiquitous A-B-A form again, not in a single song, but in the broad structure of an entire show. It begins and ends with "Dites-Moi." The children have to keep helping Nellie out when she gets stuck. Her French is limited. Emile crosses between the children; Nellie faces front.

Nellie sings the song; Emile answers her singing, leaning forward to look at Nellie. The music quietly continues. Nellie hands a bowl of soup to Emile. He puts it down and thrusts his hand forward. Nellie clasps it. Looking into each other's eyes, they hold this pose as the curtain falls—a quiet, thoughtful ending, unthinkable in earlier musical comedy.

Earlier in the show, Nellie sings a rousing waltz. Rodgers's career is loaded with up-to-date, old-fashioned waltzes. There's "Hello, Young Lovers" in *The King and I*; "The Most Beautiful Girl in the World" in *Jumbo*; "Falling in Love with Love" in *The Boys From Syracuse*; "Oh, What a Beautiful Mornin'" from *Oklahoma!*; "It's a Grand Night for Singing" from *State Fair*; "Edelweiss" from *The Sound of Music*; and, of course, the haunting "Carousel Waltz."

Earlier in the show, *South Pacific*, Nellie sings the most exuberant song in the show, "I'm in love, I'm in love, I'm in love, I'm in love, I'm in love with a wonderful guy!" The repetition of "I'm in love" may remind you of what Bernstein and Sondheim do eight years later in *West Side Story* with Tony showing his joy by singing the name "Maria, Maria, Maria!" over and over and over.

I'm going to play a little of "I'm in Love with a Wonderful Guy." *(Plays piano—"I'm in Love with a Wonderful Guy.")*

At the end of the '40s, musical theater seemed to have reached its peak. But, since you haven't seen the 1950s, as Al Jolson used to say, "You ain't seen nothing yet!"

Lecture Fourteen
Golden Age of Musical Theater (1950s)

Scope:

If the 1940s belonged to Rodgers and Hammerstein, the 1950s belonged to Rodgers and Hammerstein, Lerner and Loewe, Leonard Bernstein, and Frank Loesser. Many observers of the Broadway scene consider this period the golden age of the Broadway musical. The list of tuneful hits introduced during this decade reads like a music buff's dream, and the librettos, in many cases, were as strong as the scores. Lerner and Loewe set new standards for adapting difficult material to perfection, turning Shaw's 1911 play *Pygmalion* into *My Fair Lady*. Rodgers and Hammerstein checked in with *The King and I*, *Flower Drum Song*, and *The Sound of Music*. Frank Loesser gave us *Guys and Dolls* and *The Most Happy Fella*.

Outline

I. Frank Loesser (1910–1969) began as a lyricist in the 1930s, penning mostly Tin Pan Alley hits, such as "I Don't Want to Walk Without You," "Two Sleepy People," and "A Slow Boat to China."

   A. With a limited musical background, Loesser progressed to writing lyrics and music and mounted his first complete show, *Where's Charley?*, in 1948. Then, thinking of himself as a composer-lyricist for the first time, he studied piano and composition and emerged as a formidable talent. *Where's Charley?* had a competent score, but two years later, *Guys and Dolls* had a score as varied and complex as any ever written.

   B. Loesser's first stab at writing a complete song (music and lyrics) occurred on December 8, 1941, the day after Pearl Harbor. In the newspapers, Loesser read that Father MacGuire, the Catholic chaplain on Pearl Harbor, had responded to the Japanese attack by telling the men to "Praise the Lord and pass the ammunition!" MacGuire later denied ever having made that statement, but it nonetheless inspired Loesser's song.

C. The cast of *Guys and Dolls* was outstanding, including Robert Alda (Alan Alda's father) and Vivian Blaine, and the show was choreographed by Michael Kidd. Stubby Kaye, who played Nicely-Nicely Johnson, sang "Sit Down, You're Rockin' the Boat," a showstopper that demanded encores at every performance. "I've Never Been in Love Before," "If I Were a Bell," and "Bushel and a Peck" all ended up on the Hit Parade radio program week after week.

D. Curiously, after *Oklahoma!*, many shows, including *Carousel*, *Bloomer Girl*, *Up in Central Park*, *Annie Get Your Gun*, and *High Button Shoes*, turned for their subject matter to the American past. But *Guys and Dolls* turned its back on serious themes and social significance and set itself in the almost contemporary Damon Runyon world of blithe shenanigans.

E. The setting for *Guys and Dolls* is around a Times Square that never quite existed, with no ugliness and no overt violence. Jo Mielziner's sets were an almost cartoon-like stylization of Broadway that would suggest familiar landmarks but also disguise and glorify them.

F. A list of the characters' names reads a little like 1940s excerpts from the "Dick Tracy" comic strip: Harry the Horse, Nathan Detroit, Angie the Ox, Big Jule, and Benny South Street. The opening song establishes the brash, garish pace of the show and introduces a cross-section of Times Square types: police, chorus girls, prostitutes, gamblers, sightseers, photographers, and sidewalk vendors.

G. On opening night on Broadway, Brooks Atkinson of *The New York Times* wrote: "A work of art…gutsy and uproarious!" The frenetic pace, the incredible vitality, help make this show a kind of reverse *West Side Story*.

H. We listen to Susan Loesser talking about her father's work on the show in an interview with Bob Allen.

II. The next year, 1951, saw the production of one of Rodgers and Hammerstein's greatest musicals, *The King and I*. Opening at the St. James Theatre on March 29, this production ran 1,246 performances and saw repeated revivals over the next four decades, most of them with the original star, Yul Brynner.

 ©2006 The Teaching Company.

A. The show was not written for Brynner but for his co-star, the English actress Gertrude Lawrence. Lawrence had read Margaret Landon's book *Anna and the King of Siam* and suggested the idea of turning the book into a musical, first to Cole Porter, then to Rodgers and Hammerstein.

B. Unfortunately for Lawrence, although she had commissioned a vehicle to show off her own talents, in the end, it was her young, unknown co-star who stole the show.

C. Richard Rodgers described his first meeting with Yul Brynner, in which Brynner "projected a feeling of controlled ferocity!" Rodgers knew he had found his king.

D. Lawrence died in September of 1952 and was succeeded by a series of Annas, including Celeste Holm and Patricia Morrison. Though Brynner was originally billed below the title, that changed after he won a Tony as Outstanding Featured Actor. In 1956, when he appeared opposite Deborah Kerr in the Twentieth-Century Fox film version of the show, he won the Oscar for Best Leading Actor.

E. Jerome Robbins's choreography used a highly stylized pseudo-Siamese movement that was spellbinding to Western audiences. The contrast between these faux-Asian movements and the rousing polka "Shall We Dance" with Anna and the king was extreme.

F. In the film, Deborah Kerr was dubbed on the songs by Marni Nixon, an amazing singer whose work, 50 years later, continues to be first-rate. Most dubbing is observable to the focused listener, but Nixon's dubbing never is. Her singing voice sounds exactly like the speaking voice of Deborah Kerr in *The King and I*.

III. On May 7, 1953, at the Shubert Theatre, Cole Porter mounted a new show, *Can-Can*, set in Paris in the late 1890s. The can-can, in which the chorus girls would show their panties, caused outrage in Paris and, of course, made the dance all the rage. The story of the show involves a puritanical magistrate out to ban the can-can; he ends up falling in love with the sexy owner of the nightclub where the dance is performed.

A. The 1953 production was stolen by the ingénue, Gwen Verdon. On opening night, Verdon received such a tremendous ovation performing Michael Kidd's choreography that she stopped the show—twice.

B. Despite this, critics gave the songs a lukewarm reception, saying that Porter's melodies were not up to his usual standards. Nonetheless, "C'est Magnifique," "Allez-Vous En," "It's All Right with Me," and "I Love Paris" remained on the *Billboard* Top Ten for weeks.

IV. In December 1953, a highly original musical with totally unoriginal music—*Kismet*—began playing to packed houses on Broadway.

A. This show used the melodies of the Russian composer Alexander Borodin. The music for the show was adapted and lyrics written by Robert Wright and George Forrest. The story was based on a 1911 play by Edward Knoblock; the setting was ancient Baghdad. The musical starred Alfred Drake and Doretta Morrow. We hear Wright and Forrest talking to Bob Allen about the creation of *Kismet*.

B. A contributing factor to the show's success was the Hit Parade status of several of the songs. We hear the influence of Borodin in "Baubles, Bangles, and Beads" (String Quartet in D, second movement), "This Is My Beloved" (String Quartet in D, third movement), and "Stranger in Paradise" (Polovetzian Dances).

V. On the tail of *Kismet*, on May 13, 1954, *Pajama Game* opened at the St. James Theatre. It has the distinction of being the first entire show choreographed by Bob Fosse. One song from the show became a *Billboard* number-one hit for Rosemary Clooney, "Hey There."

A. With music and lyrics by Richard Adler and Jerry Ross, *Pajama Game* is the story of a pajama factory union organizer and her supervisor, set during a strike. It was based on Richard Bissel's novel *7½ Cents*. Bissel himself wrote the libretto, assisted by George Abbot, the show's director. The stars were John Raitt, Janis Paige, and Carol Haney.

B. Frank Loesser was approached to do the score but turned it down and recommended Adler and Ross, two unknown writers in their early 20s. Director George Abbott decided to take a chance on the team. Jerome Robbins co-directed the show with Abbott but left the choreography entirely up to Bob Fosse.

C. One of Fosse's dancers in the show was a young woman named Shirley MacLaine. During the run of the show, when Carol Haney hurt her ankle, MacLaine went on in her place, got spotted by Hollywood producer Hal Wallis, and was signed for a lead role in Alfred Hitchcock's *The Trouble with Harry*.

D. The *Pajama Game* showstoppers were "Hey There" and Fosse's inventive dance number "Steam Heat," a template for all the ultra-cool Fosse to follow over the coming years. In "Steam Heat," Haney and her male chorus, dressed in derbies, white gloves, and black suits, snapped their fingers to music that was punctuated by the sound of escaping steam from an old-fashioned radiator.

VI. Fosse's next show, *Damn Yankees*, starred Gwen Verdon, who was not yet his wife. With the same songwriting team and director, this show would solidify Fosse's position as the hottest young choreographer on Broadway.

A. *Damn Yankees* was derived from a novel called *The Year the Yankees Lost the Pennant*. It was Douglas Wallop's fantastic takeoff on the Faust legend, in which a disgruntled baseball fan agrees to sell his soul to the devil in order to pitch for his beloved Washington Senators. He takes them to the World Series, defeating the accursed Yankees. The devil's representative is Lola, a temptress, played by Gwen Verdon.

B. Incidentally, no other baseball musical or straight play has ever been a hit on Broadway. In 1984, Harold Prince directed *Diamonds*, a review about the national pastime, which died after about 10 weeks. Another failed baseball musical was *The First*, based on the life of Jackie Robinson. It ran for only a few weeks in 1982.

VII. The year after *Damn Yankees* appeared at the 46th Street Theatre, a musical opened that eclipsed all previous musicals, *My Fair Lady*. At 2,717 performances, it more than doubled the number of performances of any other show of the 1950s. But it was a show that, several times, seemed destined never to materialize.

A. Having written *Pygmalion* in 1911, George Bernard Shaw later saw another of his masterpieces, *Arms and the Man*, made by Oscar Strauss into an operetta called *The Chocolate Soldier*. Shaw despised it and vowed never again to allow one of his plays to be destroyed by turning it into a musical.

B. In 1950, Shaw died. His close friend Gabriel Pascal served as the executor of his estate. Pascal had promised Shaw that he would not allow *Pygmalion* to be turned into a musical, but a few months after Shaw's death, he offered it to Rodgers and Hammerstein, who turned it down.

C. Eventually, after Pascal's death, Allen Jay Lerner bought the rights to *Pygmalion*. Now the question was what to do with the play; after all, Henry Higgins seemed incapable of falling in love, as most leads in musicals must.

D. Fritz Loewe's music for *My Fair Lady* was as good as show music gets, but it was Lerner's Shaw-centered libretto and his ability to "channel" Shaw in his lyrics that controlled the production's creative flow. Lerner's subtle changes in language, depending on who is singing, make the songs an extension of the characters.

E. Lerner played the Pygmalion character himself and chose the 19-year-old Julie Andrews for Eliza. At the time, Andrews was playing on Broadway in the British musical *The Boy Friend*. Lerner saw the show, hired the ingénue, and wrote a new song for her, "All I Want Is a Room Somewhere," that was eerily similar to one she'd sung in *The Boy Friend*.

VIII. The year after *My Fair Lady*, two musicals, both vying against each other for Tonys, both now classics, appeared on Broadway. The first was *West Side Story*; the second was *The Music Man*. The Tony for Best Musical was won by *The Music Man*, despite the fact that it premiered in December of 1957, just weeks before the Tony selections were made.

A. Despite its reputation with critics as "traditional," *Music Man* was one of the most innovative shows of the century. In it, we hear the kind of melodic transformation more commonplace in the works of Wagner or Strauss than on the musical stage.

    1. The tune for the gentle waltz "Goodnight, My Someone" transforms itself in the rousing march "76 Trombones."

©2006 The Teaching Company.

2. The barbershop quartet sings "Lida Rose" in lush four-part harmony as the ladies of the town "pick-a-little, talk-a-little, cheep-cheep-cheep," making them sound like a flock of hens.

3. "The Piano Lesson" is sung to the notes of an ascending major scale and is later heard against a counter-melody.

4. In "Rock Island," Meredith Willson, the composer/lyricist of *Music Man*, has a group of traveling salesmen on a train, standing and holding onto the straps that hang from the ceiling, *talking* in a half-dozen different rhythms simultaneously. The effect simulates the cacophony one might hear on a crowded train, yet it all works together with precision.

5. Willson's book, music, and lyrics create a nostalgic slice of small-town history without becoming maudlin and without sacrificing the music's quality.

B. Ultimately, however, *West Side Story* was the more influential show, a turning point in the history of musical theater.

C. *West Side Story* was disconcerting for critics because it offended their sense of morality. It made audiences feel uneasy and unsafe. And instead of condemning the perpetrators of vulgarity and violence, it showed them with sympathy. This radically new approach was about to change Broadway forever.

D. *West Side Story* was mounted at the Winter Garden Theatre on September 26, 1957. It ran for 732 performances and tempted some students of the Broadway theater to call it a musical tragedy.

E. The spirit of *West Side Story* drifts through the remaining decades of the 20th century. There could have been no *Cabaret*, no *Sweeney Todd*, no *Les Miserables*, *Chicago*, or *Chorus Line* without *West Side Story*.

F. United Artists ultimately brought the show to the screen. The film, co-directed by Robert Wise and Jerome Robbins, used a real tenement neighborhood that had been condemned to make way for what is now Lincoln Center. Parts of the gang fights were brilliantly photographed from above, and Marni Nixon's dubbing of Natalie Wood's songs was flawless. The film won a record 11 Academy Awards, including the Oscar for Best Picture.

IX. The decade of the 1950s ended with yet another Rodgers and Hammerstein show, one of the most beloved of all time and one of the few that not only didn't suffer in its transformation to the screen but actually improved! Of course, the show is *The Sound of Music.*

  A. Let me precede my praise of this show by noting that Hammerstein's lyrics always hovered on the border between sentiment and sentimentality and tread a fine line in this show.

    1. Further, the problem was not strictly Hammerstein's. In a song such as "How Do You Solve a Problem Like Maria?" Rodgers set the already cutesy lyrics to a saccharine melody.

    2. Elsewhere, Rodgers's music elevates the potentially pedestrian "Do-Re-Me." Based on the ascending major scale, the song deviates from the scale and from the chords of the scale just enough to make it interesting.

  B. *The Sound of Music* opened on November 16, 1959, at the Lunt-Fontanne Theatre and ran for 1,442 performances. The novice-turned-nanny, Maria, was played by Mary Martin, and her employer was played by Theodore Bikel. The show was nominated for nine Tony awards and won four. In the film, Bikel was replaced, competently, by Christopher Plummer, and Mary Martin was replaced by one of the finest voices ever to appear on Broadway or in films—Julie Andrews.

  C. The film, directed by Robert Wise, begins with absolute silence as we gaze at the vastness of the Austrian Alps. Far away, on the ground, we detect a speck of life and hear a flute and a distant French horn. As the camera pans down into the endless valley of grass between snow-capped mountains, the speck reveals itself as Julie Andrews. How can we not believe in some higher power in the midst of such magnificence?

  D. Edelweiss, a tiny flower that dots the mountainsides and grassy valleys of Austria in the spring, lends its name to one of the best-loved songs from the musical. Because it is relatively unique to the area, it has long been a symbol of Austrian independence.

1. The Austrian folksong called "Edelweiss" is quite different from the song Rodgers and Hammerstein wrote for *The Sound of Music*. As we listen, I think you will understand why they decided not to use it in the show.

2. As he did with "Oh, What A Beautiful Mornin'" in *Oklahoma!*, Rodgers created a song with a folksy feeling that is a little more complex than a real folksong.

3. One of the ways in which he creates this complexity is by using a descending bass line. The scale tones run down chromatically, moving from, for example, A flat to G to G flat to F.

4. The more lyrical Rodgers and Hammerstein's "Edelweiss" became so popular that the Austrians have almost forgotten the original folksong and made Rodgers and Hammerstein's "Edelweiss" the unofficial anthem of their country.

5. We listen to Theodore Bikel singing "Edelweiss" from a 1959 recording of the original production of *The Sound of Music*.

X. The end of the 1950s left us with two visions—one bright (*The Sound of Music*), and the other dark (*West Side Story*); one hopeful, the other hopeless. Oscar Hammerstein was no fool—he knew what the world was like, but he gave us something to aspire to.

Suggested Reading:

William G. Hylands, *Richard Rodgers*.

Richard Maltby, ed., *Passing Parade: A History of Popular Culture in the 20th Century*.

Questions to Consider:

1. Explain why the 1950s is often referred to as the golden age of musical theater.

2. Compare the Broadway version and the film version of *The Sound of Music*.

Lecture Fourteen—Transcript
Golden Age of Musical Theater (1950s)

If the '40s belonged to Rodgers and Hammerstein, the '50s belonged to Rodgers and Hammerstein, Lerner and Loewe, Leonard Bernstein, Frank Loesser, and a few others. There are quite a few observers of the Broadway scene who consider this period the golden age of the Broadway musical. The list of tuneful hits introduced during this decade reads like a music buff's dream and the librettos, in many cases, were as strong as the scores. Lerner and Loewe set new standards for adapting difficult material to perfection, turning Shaw's 1911 play *Pygmalion* into *My Fair Lady*. Rodgers and Hammerstein checked in with *The King and I* and *Flower Drum Song* and *The Sound of Music*. Frank Loesser gave us *Guys and Dolls* and *The Most Happy Fella*.

Loesser began strictly as a lyricist in the 1930s, penning mostly Tin Pan Alley hits like "I Don't Want to Walk without You, Baby," "Two Sleepy People," and "A Slow Boat to China." With a limited musical background—you see, he didn't want to compete with his concert pianist brother, Arthur Loesser—Frank progressed to writing lyrics and music eventually and finally mounted his first complete show, *Where's Charley*, in 1948. Then, thinking of himself as a composer-lyricist for the first time, he took off a little time to do some serious study of piano and composition, and emerged as a formidable talent. *Where's Charley* had a competent score with "Once in Love with Amy" standing out, but, two years later, *Guys and Dolls* had a score as varied and complex as any ever written.

Frank Loesser's first stab at writing a complete song—that is, music and lyrics—occurred on December 8, 1941, the day after Pearl Harbor. In the newspapers, Loesser read that Father MacGuire, the Catholic chaplain on Pearl Harbor, had responded to the Japanese attack by telling the men to "Praise the Lord and pass the ammunition!" MacGuire later denied ever having made that statement and claimed that what he'd actually said was probably "God, help us!," but because of Loesser's song, the strident misquote haunted MacGuire for the rest of his life.

As for that first complete Loesser song—words and music, "Praise the Lord and Pass the Ammunition"—it wasn't half as good as Irving Berlin on a bad day. The melody and lyrics were predictable, monotonous, and unimaginative, but they were created in the right place at the right time; however, *Guys and Dolls* was another matter.

The show had an outstanding cast, including Robert Alda—Alan Alda's father—and Vivian Blaine. It was choreographed by Michael Kidd in a moderately demanding, but quite effective style. After all, 300-pound Stubby Kaye, who played Nicely-Nicely Johnson, wasn't about to leap across the stage. Kaye's song "Sit Down, You're Rockin' the Boat" was a showstopper that demanded encores at every performance. "I've Never Been in Love Before," "If I Were a Bell," and "Bushel and a Peck" all ended up on the Hit Parade radio program week after week after week. When *Guys and Dolls* was performed on Broadway again in 1992, it won the Tony for "Best Revival."

Curiously, after *Oklahoma!*, so many shows—including *Carousel, Bloomer Girl, Up in Central Park, Annie Get Your Gun, High Button Shoes*—so many shows turned for their subject matter to the American past. But, *Guys and Dolls*, turning its back on serious themes and social significance, set itself in the almost contemporary Damon Runyon world of blithe shenanigans.

The setting for *Guys and Dolls* is around a Times Square that never quite existed, quirkily different from the real place—no ugliness, no overt violence. Jo Mielziner's sets were an almost cartoon-like stylization of Broadway that would suggest familiar landmarks, but also disguise and glorify them into something fabulous. Actually, that is the subtitle of *Guys and Dolls*, "A Musical Fable of Broadway."

A listing of the characters' names reads a little like 1940s excerpts from the "Dick Tracy" comic strip. There's Harry the Horse, Nathan Detroit, Angie the Ox, Big Jule, and Benny South Street. The opening song establishes, instantly, the brash, garish pace of the show. Part pantomime and part frenetic dance, it introduces a cross section of Times Square types—police, chorus girls, prostitutes, gamblers, sightseers, photographers, sidewalk vendors—one of which rushes in with a baby carriage that converts into a sales counter. The music behind all this is breezy and fast.

Now everything new is based on something old and, for years, I felt that I had seen the scene of that opening number somewhere else. Then, I realized that at least part of a number in Warner Brothers's

Gold Diggers of 1935 is choreographed in precisely the same way. Michael Kidd and Frank Loesser, I'm certain, were inspired by Busby Berkeley's film choreography for the song "Lullaby of Broadway." Look at the film and you'll see what I mean.

The gamblers in *Guys and Dolls* introduce themselves in the opening song, "A Fugue for Tin Horns." This is a gentle pun, since we're dealing with tinhorn gamblers. "I got the horse right here. His name is Paul Revere. Can do. Can do. This guy says the horse can do."

On opening night on Broadway, Brooks Atkinson of *The New York Times* wrote this: "A work of art ... gutsy and uproarious!" In *The Evening Post,* Richard Watts called it "Big, brash and bountiful ... tremendously funny—Broadway music at its best and most hilarious." The frenetic pace, the incredible vitality help make this show a kind of reverse *West Side Story*. Both drew on the energy of Manhattan—*West Side Story* chose to select the dark elements; *Guys and Dolls* chose the light elements.

Here's Susan Loesser, talking about her father's work in the show, to radio host Bob Allen: (Plays recording of interview:)

> **Bob Allen**: Frank Loesser was born in New York City 85 years ago last week on June 29, 1910. He was the son of a tough, Prussian Jewish father and a German Jewish mother. His family got along better with Frank's older half-brother, the classical musician, than they did with him. As a result, says Susan Loesser, her father drew away from his family.
>
> **Susan Loesser**: He had different tastes. He always loved popular music and from a very young age, was kind of, was writing lyrics and poems and even music, although he always felt so inferior about that and he did for so long that he didn't until "Praise the Lord and Pass the Ammunition," he never ventured his own tunes. But, clearly he wanted to be different and I think he wanted to irritate, too, because, you know, he was,—I say in my book—he was like a peacock springing out of a swan's nest, you know. They were so genteel and he was just so not genteel.

The next year, 1951, saw the production of one of Rodgers and Hammerstein's greatest musicals, *The King and I*. Opening at the St. James Theatre on March 29, this production ran 1,246 performances and saw repeated revivals over the next four decades, most of them with the original star, Yul Brynner. This show was to Yul Brynner what *My Fair Lady* was to Rex Harrison.

The show was not written for Brynner, though; it was written for his costar, the English actress Gertrude Lawrence. She had been a part of the Broadway scene since her 1926 appearance in George Gershwin's *Oh, Kay!* It was in that show that her disarmingly frail voice introduced one of Gershwin's greatest standards, "Someone To Watch Over Me."

Not having starred in a Broadway musical since her 1940 triumph in Kurt Weil and Ira Gershwin's *Lady in the Dark*, Gertrude Lawrence had read Margaret Landon's book, *Anna and the King of Siam*. She suggested the idea of turning the book into a musical, starring her, to Cole Porter, who turned her down. When she brought the idea, on the rebound, to Rodgers and Hammerstein, initially, they more enthusiastic about the story than they were about the star. Lawrence was a magnificent actress who had made a name for herself in musicals, despite her thin voice, limited range, and a tendency to sing slightly flat.

Rodgers and Hammerstein wrote for real singers—think of Alfred Drake in *Oklahoma!*, John Raitt in *Carousel*, Mary Martin in *South Pacific*, and Julie Andrews in *Cinderella*. But, they knew that Lawrence's name could sell a show, and finally, her enthusiasm about the project won them over. In the end, her character was so believable that, like Rex Harrison four years later in *My Fair Lady*, her limited singing ability in no way hindered the effectiveness of her performance.

But poor Gertrude Lawrence! She had commissioned a vehicle to show off her not-inconsiderable talents, but, in the end, it was not Lawrence but her young totally unknown costar who was destined to make the audiences and the critics sit up.

Richard Rodgers described his first meeting with Yul Brynner, as it occurred on the afternoon of Brynner's audition for the show. Now, Brynner, Russian-born, had been a circus acrobat and a nightclub entertainer. At the time of his audition, he was working at CBS as a director in a relatively new medium called TV. This is what Rodgers had to say:

> When Brynner entered the theater, he scowled in our direction, sat down on the stage, and crossed his legs tailor

fashion, then plunked a whacking chord on his guitar and began to howl in a strange language that no one could understand. He looked savage, he sounded savage, and there was no denying that he projected a feeling of controlled ferocity!

Rogers knew he had found his King.

Lawrence died in September of 1952 and was succeeded by a series of Annas, including Celeste Holm and Patricia Morrison. Though Brynner was originally billed below the title—because Lawrence's name was above it—that changed after he won a Tony as "Outstanding Featured Actor." This overly confident upstart was suddenly a major star. In 1956, when he appeared opposite Deborah Kerr in the Twentieth Century Fox film version of the show, he won the Oscar for "Best Leading Actor."

Jerome Robbin's choreography for both the stage musical and for the film used a highly stylized pseudo-Siamese movement that, at least to Western audiences, was spellbinding. The contrast between these faux Asian movements and the rousing polka, "Shall We Dance," with Anna and the King was extreme; only Brynner and his dance partner could somehow make a polka look erotic.

In the film, Deborah Kerr was dubbed on the songs by Marni Nixon, an absolutely amazing singer whose work, 50 years later, continues to be first-rate. During the 1990s, she appeared on Broadway in Sondheim's *Follies*.

Most dubbing is observable to the focused listener; Marni Nixon's dubbing never is. Her singing voice sounds exactly like the speaking voice of Deborah Kerr in *The King and I*. It also sounds exactly like the speaking voice of Natalie Wood in *West Side Story*, and exactly like the speaking voice in Warner Brothers's *My Fair Lady* when Audrey Hepburn sings. One of her most amazing dubs was the singing voice of the child-actress Margaret O'Brien in the film, *The Secret Garden*.

One additional thought about Yul Brynner. In 1985, Brynner was given a special Tony Award for playing the King in *The King and I* 4,525 times. That statistic remains unbroken in the Guinness *Book of World Records*.

 ©2006 The Teaching Company.

On May 7, 1953, at the Shubert Theatre, Cole Porter mounted a new show set in Paris in the late 1890s—the show was *Can-Can*. The can-can, in which the chorus girls would bare their panties and then some, was the 1890s version of *Dirty Dancing*. Irate citizens from protest groups with names like "The League Against Licentiousness" lobbied the government to have the dance prohibited. Of course, that made it all the more popular and it became the rage of Paris. The story of the show involved a puritanical magistrate out to ban the can-can; he ends up falling in love with the sexy owner of the nightclub where the dance is performed.

In *Can-Can* in 1953, the show ended up being stolen by the ingénue, Gwen Verdon. On opening night, Gwen Verdon received such a tremendous ovation performing Michael Kidd's choreography that she stopped the show—twice. At the conclusion of one number, Verdon left the stage, went to her dressing room, and changed into her bathrobe. The audience was still applauding and would not let the performance continue until Verdon took another bow, which she did, still dressed in her bathrobe.

Despite this, the critics gave the songs a lukewarm reception, saying Porter's melodies were "not up to his usual standards," which for many of the songs may have been right on the button. "C'est Magnifique" and "Allez-Vous En" are more like Porter's more predictable pre-1928 songs; however, those songs, along with the more innovative "It's All Right with Me" and "I Love Paris" remained on the Billboard top ten and the Lucky Strike Hit Parade Top Ten for weeks and weeks—a situation unimaginable in this age when show music and top 40 coexist in total isolation.

In December 1953, a highly original musical with totally unoriginal score began playing to packed houses on Broadway. This 1953 show used the melodies of the Russian composer Alexander Borodin. This new show was *Kismet*, with music adapted and lyrics written by Robert Wright and George Forrest. The story was based on a 1911 play by Edward Knoblock; the setting was ancient Baghdad. The musical starred our friend from *Oklahoma!* and from *Kiss Me, Kate*, Alfred Drake; and it costarred Doretta Morrow.

Here are Wright and Forrest talking to Bob Allen about the creation of *Kismet*: (Plays recording of interview):

Bob Allen: Bob Wright and George Forrest, who adapted Borodin's music and wrote the lyrics said Frank was not the original choice to star. In fact, Bob tells us that after their first Broadway success in the mid-1940s, adapting the music of Edvard Grieg in *Song of Norway*, he and his partner were enticed into the *Kismet* project when producer, Edwin Lester, told them who was going to be the star.

Robert Wright and **George Forrest**: Mr. Lester said I have Ezio Pinza under personal contract. He said, I used to have Laurence Sebid under personal contract to do *Kismet,* but he said that never came about so I now have Pinza. So, he said, "Will you do it?" and he said, "I want to use the music of Tchaikovsky." And we said. "Well, we wouldn't commit to using the music of Tchaikovsky. That was too big a commitment to make," because we didn't really believe that Tchaikovsky should be done for the Broadway theater, not unless it was a ballet story. But I said, "We'll certainly commit to do it with somebody's music, we don't know what." So that was the start. That was 1945 or 44; it was a long, intervening story of what happened to Pinza, according to Mr. Lester, had to yield Pinza to Rodgers and Hammerstein in an attempt, I suppose you know from one percent of the groups, which amounted to quite a few. <Laughter>

Crimes of *South Pacific.*

Of *South Pacific* and so, we lost Mr. Pinza but we put that on, or he put it on the shelf until he could find the right man for it. But then, in '53, we were in Florida for the winter and Mr. Lester called. We were sitting on the water in a seafood restaurant. He called and said, "I have Alfred Drake. Will you do it now?" And we said, "When do you want us?" and he said, "Tomorrow." <Laughter> And I said, "Well we leave the day after" and I said, "Who's the composer?" And he said, "Well." He started again with Tchaikovsky and we said, "No, no, no, no, no, it's not right." And he mentioned Rimsky Korsakov again. And he said, "Any of the others?" and I said, "Well, now we don't know the others that intimately. How much could we do? Does anyone know, you

 ©2006 The Teaching Company.

know?" As a matter of fact, how much Borodin does anyone really know at that time in 1953?

A contributing factor to *Kismet*'s success was the Hit Parade status of several of the songs. Let me show you a little bit. All of them come from *(plays piano)* Borodin's concert works. And, from his "String Quartet in D" comes this, in the second movement: *(plays piano)*. Of course, that became "Baubles, Bangles, and Beads." From the third movement of the same work came this theme: *(plays piano)*, and of course, that became "This Is My Beloved." The biggest hit in the show came from Borodin's "Polotsvian Dances." Wright and Forrest added a bridge to this melody, but I'll just play the part that Borodin wrote. *(Plays piano—"Polotsvian Dances.")* Of course, that was a huge hit for Tony Bennett.

On the tail of *Kismet*, on May 13, 1954, *Pajama Game* opened at the St. James Theatre. It has the distinction of being the first entire show choreographed by Bob Fosse. One song from that show became a billboard top-40 number one hit for Rosemary Clooney, "Hey There."

With music and lyrics by the young team of Richard Adler and Jerry Ross, *Pajama Game* is the story of a pajama factory union organizer and her supervisor, set during a strike. It was based on Richard Bissel's novel *7 1/2 Cents*. Bissel himself wrote the libretto, assisted by George Abbot, the show's director. The stars were John Raitt, Janis Paige, and Carol Haney.

Originally, Frank Loesser was approached to do the score for the show, but turned it down and recommended two totally unknown writers in their early twenties named Richard Adler and Jerry Ross. The only thing in the world that they had to their credit was a hit song they'd written for Tony Bennett called "Rags to Riches."

Director George Abbott decided to take a chance on the team. Jerome Robbins co-directed this show with George Abbott, but left the choreography entirely up to young Bob Fosse.

One of Fosse's dancers in the show was a young woman named Shirley MacLaine. During the run of the show, when Carol Haney hurt her ankle, MacLaine went on in her place, got spotted by Hollywood producer Hal Wallis, and was signed for a lead role in Alfred Hitchcock's *The Trouble with Harry*. This was her turning point. She went on to star in *The Apartment, Irma La Douce, Sweet*

Charity, Terms of Endearment, Postcards from the Edge, and *Steel Magnolias*. MacLaine has proven herself to be one of the most enduring and versatile performers in film.

The *Pajama Game* showstoppers were "Hey There," and Fosse's inventive dance number "Steam Heat," a template for all the ultra-cool Fosse to follow over the coming decades. In "Steam Heat," Haney and her male chorus, dressed in derbies, white gloves, black suits, snapping their fingers to music, which was punctuated by the sound of escaping steam from an old-fashioned radiator. The head drops were there and the shoulder drops, and the patented hip thrusts. The Fosse of legend was born in *Pajama Game*.

Carol Haney and Bob Fosse had met and danced together for the first time in 1952, when they both had small parts in the MGM film version of Cole Porter's *Kiss Me, Kate*. After *Pajama Game*, when Bob Fosse married Gwen Verdon, the couple became the king and queen of Broadway, for a while.

Fosse's next show starred Gwen Verdon—not yet Fosse's wife. Same songwriting team, same director, *Damn Yankees* would solidify Fosse's position as the hottest young choreographer on Broadway.

Damn Yankees was derived from a novel called *The Year the Yankees Lost the Pennant*. It was Douglas Wallop's fantastic takeoff on the Faust legend, in which a disgruntled baseball fan agrees to sell his soul to the Devil in order to pitch for his beloved Washington Senators. He takes them to the World Series, defeating the accursed Yankees. The Devil's representative is Lola, a sexy temptress, played by Gwen Verdon.

Incidentally, no other baseball musical or baseball straight play has ever been a hit on Broadway. In 1984, Harold Prince directed *Diamonds*, a review about the "national pastime" that died after about 10 weeks. Another failed baseball musical was *The First*, based on the life of Jackie Robinson. It ran for a few weeks in 1982. Which shows that when a topic works, if you want to create a hit show, choose a different topic.

The year after *Damn Yankees* appeared at the 46th Street Theatre, a musical opened that practically eclipsed all the previous musicals of the decade, not to mention the century—*My Fair Lady*. At 2,717 performances, it more than doubled the number of performances of any other show of the 1950s. It tripled the run of *West Side Story* and quadrupled the run of *Kismet*. It was a sun so big that its shadow seemed to eclipse everything else, but it was a show that, several times, seemed destined never to happen.

It all began, of course, with the most irascible and wittiest playwright of the 20th century, George Bernard Shaw. Having written *Pygmalion* in 1911—the basis for *My Fair Lady*—he later saw another of his masterpieces, *Arms and the Man*, made by Oscar Strauss into an operetta called *The Chocolate Soldier*. Shaw despised it and vowed never again to allow one of his plays to be destroyed by turning it into a musical. In 1950, Shaw died. If he had lived to see the premier of *My Fair Lady*, I think he would have been surprised—pleasantly.

Shaw's close friend and executor of his estate was a man named Gabriel Pascal, a Hungarian scoundrel who was the model for Zoltan Karpathy, the blackmailing linguist in *My Fair Lady*. Pascal promised Shaw that he would not let them destroy *Pygmalion* by turning it into a musical. A few months after Shaw's death, Pascal was offering it to Rodgers and Hammerstein, who turned it down, respecting Shaw's wishes. Besides, they probably thought, who would come to see a musical about the relationship between speech patterns and social class?

Eventually, after Pascal's death, Allen Jay Lerner bought the rights to *Pygmalion* from the Chase Manhattan Bank, which had taken over the estate. Now the question is: What to do with the play? Musicals, with very few exceptions, are love stories and Henry Higgins was incapable of loving anyone, except maybe himself. He was an over-confident, self-centered, caustically witty man with a mind that combined the best qualities of Shaw and Sherlock Holmes. There is no love song for the lead in the show; there is just a reluctant, understated, tepid admission—"I've grown accustomed to her face," not exactly the height of passion, but perfect for Higgins! Lerner's original choice for Eliza Doolittle was Mary Martin. Luckily, for Lerner and the world, she turned him down, telling her husband after she'd heard what there was of the score at that point: "Those dear boys have lost their talent!"

Fritz Loewe's music for *My Fair Lady* was as good as show music gets, but it was Lerner's Shaw-centered libretto and Lerner's ability to "channel" Shaw into his lyrics that controlled this production's creative flow. The line "I've grown accustomed to her face" comes from the play. Lerner's subtle changes in language—depending upon who was doing the singing— make the songs an extension of the character. The Eliza early in the play, the Eliza of "oh so loverly sittin' abso-bloomin'-lutely still," is not the Eliza who later sings, "I could have spread my wings and done a thousand things I've never done before." Higgins singing "Why Can't the English Learn to Speak English" sounds like Shaw himself.

Alan Jay Lerner, in retaliation against the number one box office star on Broadway—Mary Martin—decided to play *Pygmalion* himself and he decided turn a 19-year-old novice into a star that would outshine Mary Martin. Julie Andrews was playing on Broadway at the time in the British musical called *The Boyfriend*. Lerner saw the show, hired this ingénue, and wrote a new song for her that was eerily similar to one she'd sung in *The Boyfriend*.

Lerner deserves credit for writing a better song than the one he'd stolen from. In *The Boyfriend*, Andrews sings a song that begins "All I want is a room…in Bloomsbury." The song Lerner writes for her begins, "All I want is a room … somewhere, far away from the cold night air." Andrews, of course, did justice to both songs.

The year after *My Fair Lady*, two musicals, both vying against each other for Tony's, both now classics, appeared on Broadway. The first was *West Side Story*; the second was *The Music Man*. The Tony for Best Musical was won by *The Music Man*, despite the fact that it premiered in December of 1957, just a few weeks before the Tony selections were made. Critics tend today to say, disparagingly, that the 1957 Tony went to *Music Man* because, unlike *West Side Story*, it was a traditional musical. But, that's not true at all!

Music Man was one of the most innovative shows of the 20th century. In it, we have the kind of melodic transformation more common in the works of Wagner, Schumann, or Richard Strauss than on the musical stage. The tune for the gentle waltz "Goodnight, My Someone" transforms itself in the rousing march "76 Trombones." The barbershop quartet sings "Lida Rose" in lush four-part harmony as the ladies of the town "pick-a-little, talk-a-little, cheep-cheep-cheep," making them sound like a flock of hens. "The Piano Lesson" is sung to the notes of an ascending major scale and later heard against a countermelody. Thirty-plus years before the age of hip-hop, Meredith Willson, the composer and lyricist of *Music Man,* has a group of traveling salesmen on a train, standing and holding onto the straps, which hang from ceiling, talking in a half-dozen different rhythms simultaneously, simulating the cacophony one might hear on a crowded train, yet making it all work together with the precision of a troupe of African drummers. Willson's book, music, and lyrics, creates a nostalgic slice of small-town history, without becoming maudlin and without sacrificing the music's quality.

But, *West Side Story* was ultimately much more influential, a definite turning point in the history of musical theater—as were *Showboat* and as was *Oklahoma!* We can't say that about *Music Man*, but the Tony went to *Music Man*—not because it was traditional—it wasn't, it was a one-of-kind show—but because it was wholesome.

West Side Story disconcerted the critics because it offended their sense of morality. It made them feel uneasy and unsafe; and instead of condemning the perpetrators of the vulgarity and violence in this show, it showed them sympathy. We don't walk out of the theater after *West Side Story* whistling and tapping our toes; we walk out numb, but, the experience is cathartic and the experience was something radically new on Broadway that was about to change Broadway forever.

So let's look at *West Side Story*. It was mounted at the Winter Garden Theatre on September 26, 1957, and it ran for 732 performances and tempted some students of the Broadway theater to call it a musical tragedy. Actually, it's less tragic than the Shakespearean play on which it's based, *Romeo and Juliet*. In that play, both leads die violently; in this one, we're left with Tony's gunned-down corpse and Maria sobbing over it. Here are a few excerpts from the opening night reviews. Frank Aston of the *New York World Telegram* wrote "*West Side Story* comes right out of urban America, out of the venom generated between races jammed festeringly together…"

Walter Kerr, from the *Herald Tribune*, wrote a complex analysis of this production. Kerr says:

> The radioactive fallout from *West Side Story* must still be descending on Broadway this morning. Jerome Robbins has put together and then blasted apart, the most savage, restless, electrifying dance patterns we've been exposed to in a dozen seasons. A sneer, a hiss, a tempting and tantalizing thrust of

arm, and then—with a powerhouse downbeat from the orchestra pit—the sorry and meaningless frenzy is on…

[Kerr goes on to write,] Apart from the spine-tingling velocity of the dances, it is almost never emotionally affecting. Perhaps these teenagers are too ferocious, too tawdry to interest us compassionately for two and one-half hours. [He concludes his review by saying that in this musical,] Don't look for laughter…or tears.

Oh, come on, Walter! Have you ever witnessed the end of *West Side Story* without seeing half the audience reaching for their Kleenexes?

The spirit of *West Side Story* drifts through the remaining decades of the 20th century. There could have been no *Cabaret*, no *Sweeney Todd*, no *Les Miserables*, no *Chicago*, no *Chorus Line* without *West Side Story* to darken the way.

As mentioned earlier, *Music Man* won the Tony in 1957; it also won the Drama Circle Critics' Award. But, Bernstein was vindicated when United Artists brought the show to the screen. The film, co-directed by Robert Wise and Jerome Robbins, used a real tenement neighborhood that had been condemned to make way for what is now Lincoln Center. Parts of the gang fights were brilliantly photographed from above and Marni Nixon's dubbing of Natalie Wood's songs was flawless. The film won a record 11 Academy Awards, including the Oscar for "Best Picture."

The decade of the 1950s ended with yet another Rodgers and Hammerstein show, one of the most beloved of all time and one of the few that not only didn't suffer in its transformation to the screen—it actually improved! Of course, the show is *The Sound of Music*.

Now before I heap high praise on Rodgers and Hammerstein's final effort—Hammerstein died shortly after the show opened. Anyway, let me precede praise with problems.

Hammerstein always hovered on the border between sentiment and sentimentality—a very dangerous territory. One slip and you could plummet into a raging sea of sugar water. I think he does plummet in "How Do You Solve a Problem Like Maria?" And then, there's Maria's song "Raindrops on roses and whiskers on kittens…bright copper kettles and warm woolen mittens…" These are not a few of

©2006 The Teaching Company.

my favorite things, but I think, maybe to be fair, they might be Maria's and they do sing well.

Elsewhere, Rodgers's music elevates the potentially pedestrian do-re-mi, based on the ascending major scale, because it deviates from the scale here and there and from the chords of that scale just enough to keep the melody interesting.

The Sound of Music opened on November 16, 1959, at the Lunt-Fontaine Theatre and ran for 1,442 performances. The novice-turned-nanny, Maria, was played by Mary Martin and her employer—soon-to-be-husband—was played by Theodore Bikel. *The Sound of Music* was nominated for nine Tony awards and it won four of them.

In the film, Bikel was replaced competently by Christopher Plummer and Mary Martin was replaced by one of the finest voices ever to appear on Broadway or in film, Julie Andrews. If in these final minutes spent on 1950s Broadway, I focus mostly on a film musical, it's because Twentieth Century Fox's *The Sound of Music* was, for decades, the most-viewed film on the planet Earth.

Charmian Carr's Viking Press book, *Forever Liesl*, claims—are you ready for this?—how many people do you think have seen the film? One billion. Carr writes, "It's a story about family and love, standing up for what you believe in…it represents the world, as people want it to be."

Hammerstein, had he lived, would have smiled. That was the artistic goal of all his work. In a dark, dangerous, cynical world, this good man stood above it all, writing in *South Pacific*, "You gotta have a dream. If you don't have a dream, how you gonna make a dream come true?" Despair has an exorbitant price, but hope costs nothing.

The film, directed by Robert Wise, begins with absolute silence as we gaze at the vastness of the Austrian Alps, filmed from a silent and unseen helicopter. Far away, on the ground, we detect a speck of life and hear, first a flute, then a distant French horn. As the camera pans down into the endless valley of grass between snow-capped mountains, the speck reveals itself as Julie Andrews who is singing the same lyrics Mary Martin sang, "The hills are alive with the sound of music." These are some hills! What a voice! What a place! How can we not believe in some higher power in the midst of such magnificence?

A flower lends its name to one of the best-loved songs from the musical. The edelweiss is a tiny flower that dots the mountainsides and grassy valleys of Austria in the spring. Because it is relatively unique to this area, it has long been a symbol of Austrian independence. The original Austrian folk song called "Edelweiss" is quite different from the song Rodgers and Hammerstein wrote for *The Sound of Music*. When you hear it, I think you'll understand why they chose not to use it in the film. Here's the Austrian folk song, "Edelweiss," that goes back to the 19th century. *(Plays recording— "Edelweiss.")*

As he did with "Oh, What a Beautiful Mornin'" in *Oklahoma!*, Richard Rodgers created a song with a folksy feeling that is a little more complex than a real folk song. One of the ways in which he creates this complexity is by using a descending bass line. Instead of running on the scale tones *(plays piano)* of the key—and the key is B flat—they run down dramatically, which means we move from A flat, to G, to G flat, and to F in one portion. Listen to that as you hear it in the song. *(Plays piano—"Edelweiss.")*

The more lyrical Rodgers and Hammerstein "Edelweiss" became so popular that the Austrians have pretty much forgotten the original folk song and have made Rodgers and Hammerstein's "Edelweiss" the unofficial anthem of their country. Every Austrian knows it with German words. I'd like to play for you Theodore Bikel in the original production of *The Sound of Music* singing the song himself and accompanying himself on the guitar. *(Plays recording— "Edelweiss.")*

The end of the 1950s left us with two visions—one bright, the other dark; one hopeful, the other pessimistic. Oscar Hammerstein was no fool. He knew what the world was like, but he gave us something to aspire to.

Next, we'll look at the 1960s and the rest of the 20th century.

Lecture Fifteen
Rock 'n' Roll Reaches Broadway (1960s)

Scope:

The 1960s on Broadway began with *Bye Bye Birdie* and ended with *Hair*, the former a spoof of rock 'n' roll and the latter an homage to it. In between came a number of shows that offered greater variety in musical theater, reflecting the experimental spirit that pervaded the 1960s but hinting at darker themes to come. The decade saw several milestones, including the opening of the longest-running musical in the history of theater, *The Fantasticks*. Musicals of the 1960s also brought theatergoers more serious themes, with such shows as *Fiddler on the Roof*, *Man of La Mancha*, and *Cabaret*. As we'll see in this lecture, some of the trends introduced in the 1960s would dominate musical theater for the remainder of the 20th century.

Outline

I. We start by listening to a chord progression that should be familiar; it was used in hundreds of early rock 'n' roll songs, and it's called the 1-6-2-5 progression because the chords are based on the first, sixth, second, and fifth tones of the scale.

   A. The triplets we hear were also used in many early rock 'n' roll recordings without the 1-6-2-5 progression.

   B. In this lecture, we'll see how these sounds worked their way into musical theater in 1960.

II. The year 1960 brought us a Rodgers-and-Hammerstein-type integrated musical—comic, satirical, fast-paced, and full of fun. The show, intended to be a spoof of rock 'n' roll, was *Bye Bye Birdie*. Though there was great fun in *Bye Bye Birdie*, time has proven that you really can't spoof rock 'n' roll.

   A. Spoof involves parody, and rock 'n' roll is already a parody of the somewhat subtler rhythm and blues. Nevertheless, *Bye Bye Birdie* had great appeal for sophisticated playgoers, who savored a chance to make fun of rock 'n' roll, and the songs appealed to young rock fans. Not only did the cast album make the bestseller lists, but individual songs, such as "One More Kiss" and "Sincere," made the *Billboard* charts.

B. The character of Birdie himself is a peculiar parody of two different entertainers, and the name *Conrad Birdie* is a takeoff on the name of a third person, country singer Conway Twitty. Of course, we know that Elvis Presley is caricatured by Birdie, and his bellowing also brings to mind Marlon Brando in *A Streetcar Named Desire.*

C. Broadway historians often point to *Hair* as the first rock musical, but it wasn't—*Bye Bye Birdie* was. Paradoxically, *Bye Bye Birdie* was both a rock musical and an anti-rock musical, depending on the audience and its mindset.

D. With a score by composer Charles Strouse and lyricist Lee Adams, *Birdie* opened at the Martin Beck Theatre on April 14, 1960, running for 607 performances. It is faced-paced and filled with variety.

   1. We have wonderful rock 'n' roll spoofs, such as "One Last Kiss" and "One Boy," a sendoff on the 1-6-2-5 progressions used in songs by schmaltzy girl vocal groups.

   2. Paul Lynde, who played teenaged Kim's father, places a curse on the rock 'n' roll generation in "Kids," a song wittily set to a Charleston beat, to show how old-fashioned he is.

   3. Maintaining the Rodgers and Hammerstein tradition, Chita Rivera, Albert's secretary, is showcased in two ballets. The first is entitled "How to Kill a Man," in which she vents her frustration with her husband-to-be, Albert, played by Dick Van Dyke. The second involves her in a comic near-orgy at a Shriner's convention.

E. *Bye Bye Birdie* is a show that leaves audiences dancing out of the theater and whistling down the street. The epidemic of revivals during the beginning of the 21st century seems to indicate that such shows are back!

III. On May 3, 1960, the longest-running musical in the history of theater opened at the tiny 150-seat Sullivan Street Playhouse in Greenwich Village, remaining there for 40 years.

A. *The Fantasticks* did not make the kind of money that such productions as *South Pacific* or *My Fair Lady* had made, primarily because it was performed in such a minuscule house.

B. Everything about *The Fantasticks* is intimate—the orchestra consists of a harp and a piano, and the cast has usually remained at eight people. The story is based on Edmond Rostand's play of 1894, *Les Romanesques*, which in turn, was based on *Romeo and Juliet*, considerably lightened up by not killing off the leads.

   1. In this variation, the neighboring fathers pretend to be bitter enemies to make sure that their children will rebel against them by falling in love with each other.

   2. The fathers hire an actor, a monosyllabic American Indian, and a masked swordsman to pretend to abduct Luisa so that Matt can prove his valor.

C. Although the characters are "types," the show doesn't deal in cliché. Its partly-in-verse scripts are full of delightful wordplay and more than a little bizarre. Unquestionably, it's an "artsy" show, but when the house lights come down, it's delightful, easy to enjoy, and funny.

D. Some of the songs were popular outside the show. Ed Ames scored a top-10 hit with "Try to Remember," and Barbra Streisand made a moving recording of "Soon It's Gonna Rain."

IV. On December 3, 1960, John F. Kennedy's favorite musical appeared on Broadway, Lerner and Loewe's *Camelot*.

A. T. H. White based his novel *The Once and Future King* on Thomas Mallory's centuries-old book *Le Morte D'Arthur* (*The Death of Arthur*). White saw the central theme of Mallory's book as a quest to find an antidote to war—a perfect theme for the Cold War era.

B. The show ran for 873 performances at the Majestic Theatre. It starred Richard Burton and Julie Andrews as Arthur and Guinevere and Roddy McDowell as a delightfully evil Mordred. Robert Goulet's arrogant, egotistical Lancelot stole the show when he sang "C'est Moi!"

C. Having succeeded so well with a non-singing singer in *My Fair Lady*, Lerner and Loewe repeated the triumph with Richard Burton, whose resonant speaking voice and rhythmic subtlety made even a schmaltzy, anti-feminist song, such as "How to Handle a Woman," bowl over his audiences.

D. Guinevere's songs—the ironic "Simple Joys of Maidenhood" and the suggestive "Lusty Month of May"—showed that *My Fair Lady* had taught Lerner and Loewe how to show off one of the theater's greatest voices to its best advantage. Julie Andrews never sounded better.

E. In the story, Arthur attempts to bring the various warring factions in medieval England together in Camelot. The *Pax Anglica* imposed by Arthur is destroyed by a love triangle. Guinevere, Arthur's wife, has an affair with a handsome, young knight, Lancelot. The affair and Mordred's scheming result in the destruction of Camelot.

F. The show was larger than life, with 56 in the cast and 33 in the orchestra; it was produced for around a half million dollars. To put that figure in perspective, even *The King and I*, an extremely lavish musical, didn't reach $400,000.

V. On May 8, 1962, at the Alvin Theatre, a show appeared that proved Stephen Sondheim was more than a lyricist.

A. *A Funny Thing Happened on the Way to the Forum* ran for 964 performances and contained Sondheim's most tuneful score to date. The book was written by Burt Shevelove and Larry Gelbart, the team who created *M*A*S*H*.

B. In this show, ancient Roman farce is combined with shtick from a 1930s burlesque show. This begins with the title itself—a typical opener by a moldy second banana. The characters, too, are right out of an ancient Roman burlesque show, had there been such a thing.

VI. The hit of the decade and the show that broke *My Fair Lady*'s record was *Hello, Dolly!*. With music and lyrics by Jerry Herman, it opened at the St. James Theatre and ran for 2,844 performances.

A. In 1938, Thornton Wilder had written a play called *The Merchant of Yonkers*; 17 years later, he rewrote it, giving Dolly Levi a larger part and calling it *The Matchmaker*. That title is all we need to know about the plot of the play on which this musical is based.

B. What set this show apart from everything else on Broadway during this decade was Gower Champion's staging, choreography, and direction. Even if we include Champion's final work for *42nd Street*, *Hello, Dolly!* stands out as his best.

C. Recall Dolly's famous restaurant sequence that starts with "The Waiter's Gallop," conducted with pomp by the haughty headwaiter and broken into by scenes among the restaurant's clientele. All this eventually leads to the title song; in the Gilbert and Sullivan manner, Dolly sings the song to the chorus and the chorus sings back to her.

D. Before we leave *Hello, Dolly!*, we listen to an interview that Jerry Herman gave in 1996, looking back on the incredible success of his first Broadway show.

VII. *Fiddler on the Roof* from 1964 is a milestone in musical theater, and not just because it racked up 3,242 performances at the Imperial Theatre.

A. Set in 1905, in the Jewish village of Anatevka, Russia, this show deals mainly with the efforts of Tevye, a milkman played by Zero Mostel; Tevye's wife, Golde; and their five daughters to cope with their impoverished but proud existence. They do not know, nor does the audience, that the pogroms are about to bring the Cossacks to do away with Anatevka's way of life.

B. The plot summary sounds dreary, but the show is certainly not; the characters remained undefeated, and regardless of the subject matter, the treatment is comic. Tevye and Anatevka, after all, are the creations of Sholom Aleichem, Russia's greatest comic writer during the early years of the 20th century.

C. The show was directed and choreographed by Jerome Robbins; the dancing isn't as difficult and athletic as Robbins's work for *West Side Story*, but it is just as unique and memorable.

D. *Fiddler on the Roof* does not have a "No Business Like Show Business" finale. On the emptying stage, the people we have come to know look at each other, then march off in different directions. Of course, that's exactly what the early-20th-century Russian Jews did in real life, including Sholom Aleichem himself.

E. In *Fiddler*'s quiet finale, Tevye and his family are the last to leave. As Tevye pushes his wagon off stage, the Fiddler appears magically from behind Tevye's wagon. We know now that he is the symbol of tradition.

VIII. No show could be more unlike *Fiddler* than 1965's blockbuster *Man of La Mancha*. Premiering at the Washington Square Theatre in Greenwich Village on November 22, it ran for 2,328 performances, the third longest-running musical of the 1960s.

A. With a score by Mitch Leigh and lyrics by Dale Wasserman, the show starred Richard Kiley and Joan Dennier. It is almost as dark as Sondheim's 1979 musical creep show, *Sweeney Todd*.

B. Kiley played both Cervantes, the Spanish Inquisition–era writer of *Don Quixote*, and Don Quixote himself. Not only is the story dark, but even the stage is. Howard Bay's brilliantly used lighting creates pockets of visibility among the depressing, dark stone in the dungeon. The costumes are extremely important because the drab set never changes, and there is almost no choreography.

C. Set during the Inquisition, the show is about the totalitarian oppression of individuals. *Man of La Mancha*'s protagonist is Cervantes himself, using his imprisonment to enact the story of his novel, *Don Quixote*. Terror looms above the prisoners in the form of the lowering drawbridge, heard when a prisoner is dragged off to his death.

D. The shadowy prison is the show's setting; the scenes from the adventures of Cervantes's fictional character Don Quixote are the show's decoration. The show's content involves Cervantes's ability to stand up to the tortures of the Inquisition.

E. Another innovation in this show is that it's played in real time, without an intermission. Cervantes's two hours on stage equal his two hours in prison, during which he undergoes a mock trial by his fellow prisoners. His defense is drawn from short scenes excerpted from his great novel.

F. What does all this tilting at windmills mean? As Oscar Hammerstein once said in a far lighter vein, "You gotta have a dream…." The Enchanter (or the truth teller) in this story strips Quixote of his pretensions and makes him see himself as he is, a bloated, old nobody. We despise the truth teller and feel sympathy for Quixote's need to believe that he is

©2006 The Teaching Company.

more than he is. Quixote's delusion, or faith, sustains him and helps Cervantes survive the Inquisition.

G. With no choreography of note, little in the way of costumes or scenery, and a dark, depressing story, only the songs can bring a spark to this show, and they do.

    1. *Man of La Mancha* requires real singers if the music is to bring some light into the dungeon. "The Impossible Dream" requires power and range. "Dulcinea" requires both these things combined with tenderness. And "Little Bird, Little Bird" requires a flamenco singer's brassy vocal cords.

    2. If the bolero beat of "Impossible Dream" or the flamenco beat of "Little Bird" is closer in style to 20th-century Spain than to the Spain of the Inquisition, we can easily forgive Mitch Leigh. These songs make the story more accessible to a modern audience.

    3. We listen to an interview with Mitch Leigh, talking about why he decided to create a more contemporary Spanish sound for *Man of La Mancha*.

IX. The year 1966 brought us Kander and Ebb's *Cabaret*, a show that ran at the Broadhurst Theatre for 1,165 performances and has undergone several revivals.

A. The transvestites, the homosexuality, the strange makeup on Joel Grey's emcee, the general decadence, and the sense that Nazi Germany has triumphed make this show the most complete break with the Rodgers and Hammerstein tradition to date. Entering the cabaret, we find ourselves in a repulsive place, a place where, under the surface frivolity, lie utter degradation and hopelessness.

B. On Broadway, Jill Hayworth played Sally, and Joel Grey played the epicene Master of Ceremonies, opening the show with "*Wilkommen.*" In the opening, the song is a lively, Kurt-Weill-type, European 1920s pseudo-jazz number; at the show's finale, "*Wilkommen*" is transformed into a cacophony of dissonance. The world is falling apart, and the audience has entered a nightmare.

C. In 1957, critics were disturbed by *West Side Story*'s unwholesomeness, but the songs of *Cabaret* made *West Side Story* look like *Leave It to Beaver*.

1. "Tomorrow Belongs to Me" uses a hymn-like melody by John Kander, but the lyrics lead us to the tomorrow of triumphant Nazi Germany.

2. "Money, Money" repeats the word *money* so often that we find ourselves irritated by the machine-gun rhythm and the blaring declaration of selfishness; we inwardly rebel against this song of greed—which is exactly what the songwriters want us to do.

3. "If You Could See Her" is so subtly ironic that, if you miss the final six words, you lose the point. Those words are, "she wouldn't look Jewish at all!"

D. The original *Cabaret* ended with the Nazi takeover of Germany. The audience knew that the decadence would be replaced by savagery and cruelty. In the 1999 Broadway revival, the ending is even more chilling: In the final moments, as the cabaret dissolves into chaos, the emcee appears in striped prison pajamas, with the Star of David on his chest. From the back of the stage is heard the hiss of the gas chamber as the emcee walks toward it.

X. The fact that the 1960s began with *Bye Bye Birdie* and ended with *Hair* is a reflection of America's shift in values. The former makes light of rock 'n' roll; the latter deifies it.

A. Less dark than *Cabaret* but just as raunchy, *Hair* racked up 1,750 performances at Broadway's Biltmore Theatre. During a period when deluded youth thought that a brave new world of peace, love, and benevolent anarchy might possibly be around the corner, *Hair* seemed liberating and hopeful. Now, *Hair* seems like one of the most dated shows of the second half of the 20th century.

B. In the 1960s, however, *Hair* was the show to see, drawing in huge audiences. "Good Morning Starshine" was full of drippy lyrics, but these un-hip, pseudo-bop syllables were sung as though they weren't the least bit square. "Let the Sunshine In" was so simple that teenagers repeated it endlessly.

C. The show had a stage full of young performers labeling themselves as "hippies," smoking grass and being "free," which meant taking off their clothing and interacting with the audience.

 ©2006 The Teaching Company.

D. Galt MacDermot wrote the music, and Jerome Ragni and James Rado wrote the lyrics and the book. There were genuine protest songs, staged with humor. At the close of the song "Air," for example, everybody on stage coughs. The song "Initials" brings together LBJ and LSD. "Colored Spade" criticizes racist epithets by using them, as comedian Lenny Bruce had done a few years earlier.

E. The beat is a rock beat, but is this a rock musical? I think it is, though the lyrics are far cleverer than most rock lyrics, and the music is a little less ear-shattering. Because the writers want us to listen to what they have to say, they write in a relatively literate manner and mute their primal screams.

F. *Hair* grew out of the emotional turmoil of the Vietnam War years, with their strong antiestablishment, drug-influenced, sex-obsessed ethos. With a barely discernable story line, the show celebrates the lifestyles of "flower children" who welcome the Age of Aquarius by opposing the work ethos, conventional standards of behavior and dress, and the draft.

G. The audience at *Hair* (most of it) responded as a unit, writhing along with the cast. In its small way, *Hair* may have helped end the war, but unfortunately, I think it also helped created a divisiveness, a laxness, and a self-destructiveness that plague our society to this day.

Suggested Reading:

Gerald Bordman, *American Musical Theatre: A Chronicle*.

Kurt Gänzl, *Song/Dance*.

Questions to Consider:

1. How did the Vietnam War affect the musical theater of the 1960s?

2. Compare the "darker" and "lighter" shows of the 1960s.

Lecture Fifteen—Transcript
Rock 'n' Roll Reaches Broadway (1960s)

(Plays piano.) Does that sound familiar? It should. The chord progression was used in hundreds and hundreds of early rock 'n' roll songs. I'm going to play it again. *(Plays piano.)* It's called the "one-six-two-five progression" because the chords are based on the first, the sixth, the second, and the fifth tones of the scale. Let me demonstrate that: *(Plays piano).* Here's the one chord *(plays piano)*, here's the sixth *(plays piano)*—one, two, three, four, five, six— *(plays piano).* Here's the two chord *(plays piano).* Here's the five chord *(plays piano).* The triplets you heard *(plays piano)* were also used in hundreds of early rock 'n' roll recordings with and without the one-six-two-five chord progression. In a few minutes, we'll see how these sounds work their way into musical theater in 1960. But first, let's take a look at a trend that started in the '40s.

Oddly, from the 1940s onward, each decade seemed to produce more flops than the previous decade. As the economy changed, the cost of creating a Broadway musical kept rising; shows had to run much longer if they were going to pay off their investment. In the early 1940s, a lavish musical could be produced for $175,000 and, with good attendance, could begin to pay off its investors within four months. By the late '50s, that same show would cost over $250,000 and would require at least eight months to begin paying off its investors. In the early 1960s, the cost jumped to $400,000, and payoff time might run to more than a year. As the century wore on, the situation accelerated, so hit shows had to be measured in years instead of months. It's only those shows that we'll have space enough to discuss during this lesson.

The year 1960 brought us a Rodgers-and-Hammerstein-type integrated musical comedy full of satire, it was fast-paced, and loaded with of contemporary fun. The show, intended to be a spoof of rock 'n' roll, was *Bye Bye Birdie*. Though there was great fun in *Bye Bye Birdie*, time has proven that you really can't spoof rock 'n' roll.

Spoof involves parody, exaggeration, and rock 'n' roll is already an exaggeration of somewhat subtler rhythm and blues. The rock 'n' roller lets it all out with maximum emotional effect. He grunts, he screams, sings only in superlatives and turns the volume up to the max. He takes the suggestive gyrations of past dances up several notches so that if any audience member might otherwise not get it, they get it now in spades. Now, how do you parody something like this? You can't get louder, you can't get more suggestive, you can't get more repetitious. What irony you might create will be taken by young rock fans not as irony, but simply as more good raunchy rockin'.

That fact was not a detriment to *Bye Bye Birdie*; it was an asset. The show had tremendous appeal for sophisticated playgoers who savored a chance to make fun of rock 'n' roll. But, the songs in *Bye Bye Birdie* had tremendous appeal to the audiences that just didn't get it, too, the young rock 'n' roll fans. Not only did the cast album make the bestseller lists, but individual songs like "One More Kiss" and "Sincere" ended up on the Billboard rock 'n' roll charts.

The character of Birdie himself is a peculiar parody of two different entertainers, simultaneously. And, the name, Conrad Birdie, is a takeoff on the name of a third person who has just about nothing to do with rock 'n' roll all—the country singer, Conway Twitty. Since a bird "twitters," we create the central character's name by changing "Twitty" to "Birdie."

As to who is caricatured by Birdie, as soon as you see him walk on the stage, you know it's Elvis Presley. But, there's something wrong here because he doesn't have Elvis's civility—"Thank you very much"—and without his respect for other people you know this character is Presley plus something else. What is it? Conrad Birdie is a total slob, opening beer cans so they gush all over his host's kitchen floor and discarding them wherever. When Conrad doesn't get what he wants, he bellows like a baritone baby having a tantrum or he whines in this piercing falsetto. "More beer!!" That part of Birdie is not Elvis Presley; it's Marlon Brando in *A Streetcar Named Desire*. And to complete the picture—now you've got to get it— Birdie wears a copy of Brando's motorcycle jacket from *The Wild One*. His language is also not rock 'n' roll jargon; it's Brando's from the pre-rock days when rebellion was symbolized not by rock 'n' roll, but by modern jazz and the be-bop language of certain modern jazz aficionados.

Broadway historians often point to *Hair* as the first rock musical, but it wasn't; *Bye Bye Birdie* was. Now, paradoxically, *Bye Bye Birdie* was both a rock musical and an anti-rock musical, depending upon the audience and its mindset.

With a score by composer Charles Strouse and lyricist Lee Adams, *Birdie* opened at the Martin Beck Theatre on April 14, 1960. There, it ran for 607 performances; its road companies played the rest of the country for years and years. The leads were played by a young Dick Van Dyke as Albert Peterson; Chita Rivera as his secretary, Rose; Paul Lynde as teenaged Kim's exasperated father; Kay Medford as Albert's overbearing mother, and brilliant comedian Dick Shaun as rock 'n' roll idol, Conrad Birdie.

This show contains so much variety and such a fast pace that no one could fall asleep—easily—during a performance. We have wonderful rock 'n' roll spoofs that use those one-six-two-five chord progressions—"One Last Kiss" *(sings)* and "One Boy" with all the triplets all over the place that mimic those one-six-two-five chords with typical girl vocal groups of the '50s.

Now, we have Paul Lynde, the father, and here comes another kind of music—all this is rock 'n' roll—but the father is placing a curse upon the rock 'n' roll generation in his song "Kids," a song wittily set not to a rock 'n' roll beat, but to a Charleston beat to show how old fashioned the old man is. *(Sings.)* Now, during the brief rests between lyrics, Lynde utters verbal assaults on his children's generation like, "Why don't they lower the draft age to around 11?"

Maintaining the Rodgers and Hammerstein tradition, Chita Rivera is showcased in two ballets. The first is entitled "How to Kill a Man." She vents her frustration with her husband-to-be, Dick Van Dyke. The second involves her in a comic near-orgy at a Shriner's convention.

When old grouches say, "Why can't they write tunes you can remember any more? Why can't musicals lift you up the way they used to?" "Well, back in the old days, we used to dance out of the theater and whistle down the street. Whatever happened to those shows?"

Well, *Birdie* is one of those shows and the epidemic of revivals during the beginning of the 21st century seems to indicate that what happened is—they're back!

The month after *Birdie* opened—May 3, 1960, to be exact—the longest running musical in the history of theater opened at the tiny 150-seat Sullivan Street Playhouse in Greenwich Village, remaining there for 40 years. Now *The Fantasticks* did not make the kind of

 ©2006 The Teaching Company.

money that productions like *South Pacific* or *My Fair Lady* had made, primarily because it was performed in such a tiny house. The Greenwich Village Follies, as you remember, had moved up to Broadway, but *The Fantasticks*, a show that depended on intimacy, would have been destroyed by a move uptown. As a matter of fact, that intimacy was so important that the 1980s Joel Grey film of the show, moving the story from a bare stage to large outdoor and indoor sets, proved so far off the mark that it wasn't even released until 20 years later and then only in video format.

Everything about *The Fantasticks* is intimate—the orchestra consists of a harp and a piano, and the cast has usually remained at eight people. The story is based on Edmond Rostand's play of 1894, "Les Romanesques," which, in turn, was based on "Romeo and Juliet," considerably lightened up by not killing off the leads. In this variation, the neighboring fathers pretend to be bitter enemies to make sure that their children will rebel against them by falling in love with each other. The fathers hire a John Barrymore-ish actor, a monosyllabic American Indian, and a masked Zorro-type swordsman, named El Gallo, to pretend to abduct Luisa so that Matt can prove his valor by sending them off.

Performed properly, this story delights its audience, though I'm aware that, in synopsis, the plot seems unbelievably stupid. Let's make it clear that though the characters are "types," the show doesn't deal in cliché. Its partly-in-verse scripts are full of delightful wordplay and more than a little bizarre. Unquestionably, it's an "artsy" show, but when the house lights come down, it's delightful, easy to enjoy, and funny—honest! The original El Gallo, by the way, was Jerry Orbach of "Law and Order" fame.

Some of the songs were popular outside the show. Ed Ames scored a top-ten hit with "Try to Remember" and Barbra Streisand made a moving recording of "Soon It's Gonna Rain."

On December 3, that same year—a lot of good shows came out in 1960—on December 3, 1960, John F. Kennedy's favorite musical appeared on Broadway, Lerner and Loewe's *Camelot*. The show was so identified with JFK that writers have come to refer to the Kennedy White House as Camelot, a brief buoyant period ending in tragedy. Knowing this, the cocktail pianists in certain Manhattan restaurants would, years after the assassination, play *Camelot* whenever they saw Jackie coming. She usually asked them to switch to something else.

T.H. White based his novel, *The Once and Future King,* on Thomas Mallory's centuries-old book, *Le Morte D'Arthur, (The Death of Arthur).* White saw, as the central theme of Mallory's book, a quest to find an antidote to war. What a perfect theme for the cold war era.

The show ran for 873 performances at the Majestic Theatre. It starred Richard Burton and Julie Andrews as Arthur and Guinevere, and Roddy McDowell playing a delightfully evil Mordred. How could you not be evil with a name like Mordred? And Robert Goulet's arrogant, egotistical, self-possessed Lancelot stole the show when he sang "C'est Moi!"—It's Me!—or, if we want to be grammatically correct, It's I.

Having succeeded so well with a non-singing singer in *My Fair Lady*, Lerner and Lowe repeated the triumph with Richard Burton, whose resonant speaking voice and rhythmic subtly made even a schmaltzy, anti-feminist song like "How to Handle a Woman" bowl over his audiences. "How to handle a woman: love her, love her, love her, love her." It's a somewhat simplistic answer to a complex question, but, in the show, it works.

Guinevere's songs—the ironic "Simple Joys of Maidenhood" and the suggestive "Lusty Month of May"—showed that *My Fair Lady* had taught Lerner and Lowe how to show off one of the theater's greatest voices to its best advantage. Julie Andrews never sounded better.

Though we probably all know the story by now, for those who slept through English 102, we'll review the fact that Arthur—whose historical existence has never been proven—Arthur attempted to bring the various warring factions in medieval England together in Camelot where they met at a round table. Unlike the traditional rectangular table, no one sat at its head and all present were given equal voice.

The *Pax Anglica* imposed by Arthur is destroyed by a love triangle. Guinevere, Arthur's wife, has an affair with a handsome young knight, Lancelot. The affair—and Mordred's scheming—results in the destruction of Camelot.

The show had 56 in the cast and 33 in the orchestra; this was the anti-*Fantasticks*, not intimate, but larger than life, produced for

©2006 The Teaching Company.

around a half million dollars—an astounding sum at the time. To give one a perspective here, even *The King and I*, which was extremely lavish, didn't even reach $400,000. But, *Camelot* appeared on the heels of the Lerner and Lowe show one reviewer had called "The greatest musical of the 20th century." Of course, that was *My Fair Lady*, so the money was found.

On May 8, 1962, at the Alvin Theatre, a show appeared that proved Stephen Sondheim was more than a lyricist. *A Funny Thing Happened on the Way to the Forum* ran for 964 performances and contained Sondheim's most tuneful scores to date. Wonderful characters, clever plot twists, singable songs, and a laugh a minute—not just a laugh, but a howl—the book was written by Burt Shevelove and Larry Gelbart—the team who created *M*A*S*H*. Nobody ever had a better grasp of thinking-man's slapstick.

What they did here was to combine ancient Roman farce with shtick right out of a 1930s burlesque show. This begins with the title itself—a typical opener, you know, by the second banana: "Hey Folks, a funny thing happened on the way to the…" On the way to the what? "On the way to the forum!" The characters, too, are right out of an ancient Roman burlesque show, if there was such a thing—the nagging harridan of a wife, the randy husband, the obliviously naïve son, the braggart soldier, the running gag—in this case, the running gag was the old man who is told to cure himself by walking seven times around the circumference of Rome; he shows up during the show at totally unexpected moments, passing by and keeping tally—"that's five"—and he exits. The show opens by announcing its intentions in song: "Tragedy tomorrow; comedy tonight!" And, that's what you get in this show.

The hit of the decade and the show that broke *My Fair Lady*'s record was *Hello, Dolly!* With music and lyrics by Jerry Herman, it opened at the St. James—the same theater that had housed *Oklahoma!* Maybe that gave it luck. The show ran for 2,844 performances.

Why, you might ask. Was it the score? Well Herman's score was a good score and everybody in America seemed to be singing "Hello, Dolly!" and almost everybody in America seemed to be recording it. Louis Armstrong's recording actually knocked The Beatles off the charts for a while.

"Hello, Dolly!" is a simple, but remarkable catchy tune. Mark David sued Herman over a resemblance between "Hello, Dolly!" and David's 1948 song "Sunflower." Herman reportedly settled for $25,000. Now, the resemblance is there, for sure, but the two songs, of the two songs, "Dolly!" is, by far, the more interesting.

In 1938, Thornton Wilder had written a play called *The Merchant of Yonkers*. Seventeen years later, he rewrote it, giving Dolly Levi a larger part and calling it *The Matchmaker*. That title is about all we need to know about the plot. The play is the basis for the musical.

Now what set this show apart from everything else on Broadway during this decade was not just the music, but it was Gower Champion's wonderful staging, choreography, and direction. That's what made the stage version electric and the lack of it is what made the film version pedestrian. That and the fact that Barbra Streisand and Walter Matthau should never, ever, appear on the stage together—either one, but not both, please. They had—I don't think there's a word for this—is there's a word for the opposite of "chemistry"? If there is, that's the word we should use to describe them together.

Now even if we include Champion's final work for *42nd Street*, *Dolly!* stands out, I believe, as his best. Remember, Dolly's famous restaurant sequence that starts with "The Waiters Gallop" conducted with a symphonic pomp by the haughty headwaiter and broken into by scenes among the restaurant's clientele. All this eventually leads up to the title song, "Hello, Dolly!," and, in the Gilbert and Sullivan manner, Dolly sings the song to the chorus and the chorus sings back to Dolly.

Before we leave *Hello, Dolly!* I'd like to share an interview that Jerry Herman gave on July 30, 1996, looking back on the incredible success of his very first Broadway show. *(Plays recording of Jerry Herman Interview):*

> **Bob Allen**: Jerry Herman remembers that it ran for over 2,800 performances the first time around more than three decades ago.
>
> **Jerry Herman**: *Hello, Dolly!* was a phenomenal experience for me because I was very young and not prepared for what was about to happen. When, we opened in Detroit, it was not received well. Now very few people know that, but it wasn't

received well. It was too long and too complicated and it needed a lot of weeding out and the kind of work people do out of town. We did it. We did all the work. I wrote "Before the Parade Passes By" in a hotel room in Detroit and we really fixed that show. And, when it came to New York, I was so exhausted from the out-of-town experience that I didn't know that we had a mega-hit. I was just relieved that it was working well. And the next morning, the reviews were so extraordinary that David Merrick called me and said, "I don't care what you're doing. Get your clothes on and come to 44th Street because you will never see anything like this again in your lifetime." And there were people lined up for an entire block and he was serving coffee to them. It was in the beginning of the winter. And I'll never forget that, the feeling of getting out of that cab and seeing thousands of people all wanting to buy tickets <laughter> to my show. So *Dolly!* was quite an experience for a young kid, especially.

The year 1964's *Fiddler on the Roof* is a milestone in musical theater, and not just because it broke *Dolly!*'s record by racking up 3,242 performances at the Imperial Theatre. *Fiddler*'s record, by the way was broken by *Grease* in 1979, a show nowhere near *Fiddler* in quality. And, *Grease*'s record was broken in the 1990s by *Miss Saigon*, a first-rate musical tragedy—the score of which, I believe, Bernstein would have admired if he could have seen the show. Let's make it clear that attendance records attest to a show's popularity, but not necessarily to its quality. *West Side Story* broke no attendance records, but it remains a classic and one of musical theater's turning points. Nineteen-thirty-eight's raucous Olsen and Johnson show, *Hellzapoppin!*, ran for a then record-breaking 1,404 performances, doing what? Well, it used gimmicks like dancing in the aisles and occasionally spraying someone in the audience with seltzer water. It is not one of the high points of musical theater.

Ah, but *Fiddler*, set in 1905 in the Jewish village of Anatevka, Russia, it deals mainly with the efforts of Tevye, Zero Mostel, a milkman, Tevye's wife, Golde, and their five daughters, to cope with their impoverished, but proud existence. They do not know that the pogroms are about to bring the pillaging Cossacks to do away forever with Anatevka's way of life. Even the audience doesn't know for certain until near the end of the show and, by this time, the audience has learned to care about the residents of Anatevka, so the destruction of the village affects the audience almost as deeply as it affects Tevye and the rest.

Summarizing the plot, we end up with a pretty dreary picture, but the show is anything but dreary and the characters remain undefeated and, regardless of the subject matter, the treatment is comic. Tevye and Anatevka, after all, are the creations of Sholom Aleichem, Russia's greatest comic writer during the early years of the 20th century.

When Sholom Aleichem arrived in the United States, he was met by an American admirer named Mark Twain—a pretty good humorist himself. Twain said he had read the man's stories in translation and told him that he'd been called "the American Sholom Aleichem." "Funny," Sholom Aleichem said, "because I've been called the Jewish Mark Twain."

The show was directed and choreographed by Jerome Robbins and, if the dancing isn't as incredibly difficult and athletic as his work for *West Side Story*, it is just as unique and just as memorable.

No one who's seen the show will forget the young men of the village dancing while they balance wine bottles on their heads, a tour-de-force not unlike Gower Champion's galloping waiters in *Hello, Dolly!* But, on the whole, the dances in *Fiddler* are a seamless part of the story that deliberately refrain from calling attention to themselves. Rodgers and Hammerstein's ideal of the integrated musical is achieved here with as much skill as it had been in *The King and I* or *South Pacific*. Only a few of the hundreds and hundreds of shows that play Broadway end up as part of the timeless standard repertoire of musical theater, *Fiddler* is unquestionably one of these shows.

Fiddler on the Roof does not have a "No Business Like Show Business" finale. It ends where the story begins. On the emptying stage, the people we have come to know look at each other; they march off in different directions. And of course, that's exactly what these early 20th-century Russian Jews did in real life; some marched off to other European countries, a few to Israel, and many—like Sholom Aleichem himself—found their way to the tenements of New York City.

In *Fiddler*'s quiet finale, Tevye and his family are the last to leave. As Tevye pushes his wagon off stage, the Fiddler appears magically from behind Tevye's wagon. We know now that he is the symbol of tradition, because where they go, tradition goes.

No show could be more unlike *Fiddler* than 1965's blockbuster *Man of La Mancha*. Premiering at the Washington Square Theatre in Greenwich Village on November 22, it ran for 2,328 performances. The off-Broadway theater, in which it opened on West 4th Street, was torn down in early 1968 so the show did its final run uptown at the Martin Beck Theatre. After this musical was first performed at the Goodspeed Opera House in Connecticut, it was considered so radically different from anything that had ever appeared on Broadway that they decided to unveil it as far from the theater district as you could get without ending up in New Jersey; and yet, to their shock, it turned out to be the third longest running musical of the 1960s.

With a score by Mitch Leigh and lyrics by Dale Wasserman, the show starred Richard Kiley and Joan Dennier. What the producers hadn't counted on was the fact that the mood first set by *West Side Story* on Broadway had become masochistically appealing to Broadway audiences. This show is darker than *West Side Story* and almost as dark as Sondheim's 1979 musical creep show, *Sweeney Todd*. Todd, with a single "d," is the German word for "death" or "dead" and not even *Hamlet* equals *Sweeney Todd*'s ability to litter the stage with corpses. Of course, in *Todd*, they're fed into the sausage machine. Now, back to *La Mancha*.

Kiley plays Cervantes, the Spanish Inquisition era writer of *Don Quixote*, and he also plays Don Quixote himself. Not only is the story dark, even the stage is dark, dark as a dungeon. For good reason, that's what it is; it's a dungeon. Howard Bay's brilliantly used lighting creates pockets of light among the depressing dark stone. The ragged costumes, by Bay and Pat Campbell, and the "imagined" costumes are extremely important since the drab set never changes and there is almost no choreography. In this show, we don't even have an orchestra pit; the instrumentalists are seated on two places on stage, upstage left and right.

Being set during the Inquisition, the show, essentially, is about the totalitarian oppression of individuals. *Man of La Mancha*'s protagonist is Cervantes himself, using his imprisonment to enact the story of Cervantes's novel, *Don Quixote*. Terror looms above the prisoners; we hear the drawbridge being lowered, three times—once at the very start of the show; once in the middle, to drag away some unknown prisoner; and once at the very end of the show, to drag away Cervantes to his death.

The shadowy prison is the show's setting; the scenes from the adventures of Cervantes's fictional character, Don Quixote, are the show's decoration. Is Cervantes Don Quixote? Well, if he weren't, to some extent at least, he wouldn't have gotten himself in this mess. The show's content involves Cervantes's abilities to stand up to the tortures of the Inquisition.

Another innovation in this show—excluding the Don Quixote episodes—is that it's played in real time, without an intermission. Cervantes's two hours on stage equal his two hours in prison, during which he undergoes a mock trial by his fellow prisoners. His defense is drawn from short scenes excerpted from his great novel.

Now what does all this tilting your lance at windmills mean? What does imagining the kitchen drudge, Aldonza, as the fair Dulcinea mean? It means, I think—as Oscar Hammerstein once said—"you gotta have a dream…" In the end, even the blousy Aldonza believes she is the fair Dulcinea. The Enchanter—or the truth teller—in this story strips Quixote of his pretensions and makes him see himself as he is, a bloated old nobody. We despise the truth teller and feel sympathy for Quixote's need to believe that he is more than he is. Call it delusion, call it faith—whatever it is—it sustains Don Quixote and it helps Cervantes survive the Inquisition.

Now, with no choreography of note, little in the way of costumes or scenery, and a dark depressing story, only the songs can bring a spark to this show, and they do. This show requires real singers, if the music is to bring some light into the dungeon. *Hello, Dolly!* can be sung by anyone; even I can sing it. But, "The Impossible Dream" requires power and range. "Dulcinea" requires both these things, combined with tenderness. And "Little Bird, Little Bird" requires a flamenco singer's brassy vocal cords. This score does what it needs to do and if the bolero beat of "Impossible Dream" or the flamenco beat of "Little Bird" is closer in style to 20th-century Spain than to the Spain of the Inquisition, we can easily forgive Mitch Leigh.

Now here's Mitch Leigh, himself, talking about why he decided to create a more contemporary Spanish sound for this musical: (Plays recording of Mitch Leigh interview):

©2006 The Teaching Company.

Bob Allen: Mitch says that Joe Darion handed him *a* complete lyric before he began writing the music for "The Impossible Dream." Music, he says, that he researched thoroughly and discovered was totally wrong for the time of Cervantes.

Mitch Leigh: I was closer to Yale in those days and had to do a lot of research. And the music of the period in Spain was, I mean, the most popular thing was the bagpipe. So your liner notes would have to say, "I know, you think it's Scotland, but this is where..." Who cares? So that was out of the question. The flamenco seemed the right thing even though it was anachronistic and it turned out to be. I came and I apologized to my collaborators and said, "I have a song, which I will make fit the fabric, but it's more Italian than it is *Spanish* and I'll sing it for you and you'll see." Well, they went crazy. They thought it was the most wildest thing, couldn't care a fig of the stylistic, you know, inconsistency, which they didn't know anything about. I knew about it and it was interesting because it never came up again because what I did was just color it in Spanish cloth and colors and it was, because it really is a bravura Neapolitan song.

Bob Allen: "The Impossible Dream" may be the most popular song from *Man of La Mancha*, but it isn't composer's Mitch Leigh's favorite.

Mitch Leigh: I think the best song in the show is one that's seldom heard unless you see it. And it's badly recorded because we had to change words. In those days, you couldn't have dirty words, so, we had to, and that's unfortunate. If I do it again, I want to do it with the original thing, it was "Aldonza," which is, I think, the best combination of lyrics and music. Those lyrics are magnificent and I treated them, I think, as well as I've done anything in my life. It's not anything that anybody did, but it's a terrific, very powerful, very moving thing, to me, even now. "The Quest" works all the time so it's easy. Everybody I know gets up and sings it at a bar mitzvah or a wedding and says, "You've gotta hear my cousin; she sings this better, or he sings this better." And so on. But that's the *pretty daughter*. But the one with depth, the one with substance, very few people ask *out*, and her name is "Aldonza."

Now let's stay with the dark side of the musical. The year 1966 brought us Kander and Ebb's *Cabaret*, a show that ran at the Broadhurst for 1,165 performances and has undergone several revivals over the decades.

The transvestites, the homosexuality, the strange white make-up and bright red lipstick on Joel Grey's emcee, the general decadence and the sense, at the end, that Nazi Germany has triumphed, make this show the most complete break with the Rodgers and Hammerstein traditions to date. Entering the cabaret, we find ourselves in a repulsive place, a place where, under the surface frivolity, lie utter degradation and total hopelessness. Just the right place to go for a good time—come to the Cabaret!

On Broadway, Jill Hayworth played Sally and Joel Grey played the epicene Master of Ceremonies, opening the show with "Wilkommen"—"Welcome!" The song, by the way, opens as a lively Kurt Weill-type European oom-pah-band 1920's pseudo-jazz number. But, at the show's finale, "Wilkommen" becomes transformed into a cacophony of instrumental dissonance, while the principals quote their lines to the ceiling. The world is falling apart and the audience has entered a nightmare.

Outside the show, "Wilkommen" and "Cabaret" lost their jagged edges and worked so well as straight songs that theatergoers, who had been attracted to the show by the songs, were often shocked by the settings that had produced the songs.

In 1957, critics were disturbed about *West Side Story*'s unwholesomeness, but 1966's *Cabaret* made *West Side Story* look like *Leave It to Beaver*. If Larry Hart's lyrics to "My Funny Valentine" are ironic, they are sweetly ironic. "Is your figure less than Greek / Is your mouth a little weak / When you open it to speak / Are you smart? / But don't change a hair for me." But, the irony in *Cabaret* is bitter and often frightening, and trapped in your theater seat, you find yourself helplessly responding to it. "Tomorrow Belongs to Me" uses a hymn-like melody by John Kander, but the lyrics lead us to the tomorrow of triumphant Nazi Germany. "The Money Song" repeats the word "money, money, money, money, money, money" so often that you find yourself irritated by the machine-gun rhythm and this blaring declaration of greed. You inwardly rebel against this ode to avarice, which is exactly what the songwriters want you to do. The song "If You Could See Her" is so subtly ironic that, if you miss the final six words of the song, you lose the whole point. The final six words are, "she wouldn't look Jewish at all!"

We have, over the decades, become increasingly thick-skinned and as a result, more unshockable. Cole Porter wrote *Anything Goes* in 1934; but, when he wrote it, a lot of things didn't go. Today, unfortunately, truly almost anything does go, and things that shocked our parents and grandparents may make us yawn. So, Broadway— even rough Broadway like *Cabaret*—has to get even rougher to keep up with the times. The original 1966 *Cabaret* ended with the Nazi takeover of Germany. You knew the decadence would be replaced by savagery and cruelty. You went home sad.

But, after I saw the Broadway revival in 1999 at the theater that was formerly Studio 54, I went home chilled to the bone, or to use a more current phrase, "creeped out." No mere suggestiveness in the newer version—instead in the final moments, as the cabaret dissolves into chaos, the emcee reappears in striped prison pajamas, with the Star of David on his chest. From the back of the stage, you see and hear the hiss of the gas chamber and the emcee walks towards it—curtain.

The fact that the 1960s begin with *Bye Bye Birdie* and end with *Hair* is a reflection of America's shift in values. The former makes light of rock 'n' roll; the latter almost deifies it.

Less dark than *Cabaret*, but just as raunchy, *Hair* racked up 1,750 performances at Broadway's Biltmore Theatre and toured until hippies eventually gave birth to yuppies. During a period when deluded youth—not excluding myself—thought that a brave new world of peace, love, and benevolent anarchy might just possibly be around the corner, *Hair* seemed liberating and hopeful.

Now, it seems like one of the most dated shows of the second half of the 20th century. It is, for those presently in their early 60s and to their children, what Sandy Wilson's *The Boy Friend* was to the 1950s—*The Boy Friend* was a quirky tongue-in-cheek-revival of the vo-do-dee-o-do Charlestoning 1920s. If *Hair* were to be presented on Broadway again in the 21st century, it would possess none of the rebellious power of Vietnam era performances. Instead, it would become whimsical nostalgia—cutesy, smirky condescension to the quaint days past, and frankly, I have no desire to relive those days. I don't think *Hair* is a revivable musical.

But *Hair*, in the '60s, was the show to see, drawing in huge audiences who had never seen another Broadway show and many of them haven't seen another Broadway show since then. Peace, love, and irresponsibility—it was the "Age of Aquarius." In my old roughhouse neighborhood in Baltimore's Highlandtown, I would hear wannabe hippies referring, un-ironically, to the song as The Age of Aquariums. "Good Morning Starshine" was full of the stupidest lyrics you every heard—"Doopy-doopy dootie-dootie"—and these kids would sing these un-hip pseudo-bop-syllables as though they weren't the least bit square. "Let the Sunshine In" was so simple and so repetitious that teenagers having parties in the parents' club-basements repeated it endlessly, like "99 Bottles of Beer on the Wall." Now, the score wasn't really stupid. It was clever, for what it was.

We had a stage full of young performers labeling themselves as "hippies," smoking grass, being "free"—which meant taking off some or all of their clothing—involving the audience, like Olsen and Johnson in *Hellzapoppin!*, by walking down the aisles and intimidating people into getting up to join the cast dancing in the aisles or, even on the stage, or even dancing and disrobing.

Galt MacDermot wrote the music and Jerome Ragni and James Rado wrote the lyrics and the book, too, what there was of it. By the way, one of the Broadway hippies on stage was destined to become one of our finest film stars, Diane Keaton. There were genuine protest songs, staged with humor, here and there.

You know at the close of the song, "Air," in talking about the air, everybody on stage is coughing. They can't catch their breath; it's a delightful touch. The song, "Initials," brings together LBJ and LSD. "Colored Spade" criticizes racist epithets by using them, as comedian Lenny Bruce had done a few years earlier.

The beat is a rock beat, but is this a rock musical? I think it is, though the lyrics are actually cleverer than most rock lyrics and the music is a little less ear-shattering. The writers want you to actually listen to what they have to say, so they write in a relatively literate manner and mute their primal screams.

 ©2006 The Teaching Company.

Hair grew out of the emotional turmoil of the Vietnam War years with its strong anti-establishment, drug-influenced, sex-obsessed ethos. With a barely-discernable storyline, the show celebrates the lifestyles of flower children who welcome the Age of Aquarius by opposing the work ethos, by opposing conventional standards of behavior and dress, and—not least of all—by opposing the draft.

The audience at *Hair*—most of it—responded as a unit, writhing along like an uncovered nest of worms. In its small way, *Hair* may have helped end the war, but, unfortunately, I think it also helped created a divisiveness, a laxness, and a self-destructiveness that plague our society to this day. Let the Sunshine In!

Lecture Sixteen
Big Bucks and Long Runs (1970s–Present)

Scope:

The final years of the 20th century saw the development of the *concept musical*, a genre created by, among others, Stephen Sondheim and exemplified by such shows as *Company*, *Cats*, and *A Chorus Line*. Sondheim has also revitalized American musical theater in other ways, exploring themes, such as mass murder and presidential assassination, that no other creator of musicals has dared to touch. Other trends in the late 20th century include a European influence on the American stage, a continuing interest in "dark" musicals, and the revival of old film musicals in Broadway shows. The late 1990s and early years of the 21st century seem to be bringing a much-needed light touch back to Broadway, with such shows as *The Producers* and the final musical we'll discuss in these lectures, *Wicked*.

Outline

I. The year 1970 gave Broadway the first of five collaborations between composer/lyricist Stephen Sondheim and producer/director Hal Prince. These five shows are: *Company* (1970), *Follies* (1971), *A Little Night Music* (1973), *Pacific Overtures* (1976), and *Sweeney Todd* (1979).

   A. Sondheim and Prince helped create a genre that only fairly recently has acquired a label: the *concept musical*. We'll define this term and describe a little about *Company* to help make it more concrete.

   B. The concept musical is a little like a revue with a serious theme. It need not have a plot, though it might have the thread of one. *Company* concerns Robert, a protagonist with whom the audience has little sympathy.

   C. Sondheim's concept musicals are not the traditional situation-conflict-resolution stories, with their build toward a climax and a satisfying denouement. That's artifice. Sondheim's presentations are more like life—or, at least, life as it exists for Sondheim: disjointed, dissatisfying, and often boring.

D. Though Sondheim's musicals don't make money (with the exception of *A Funny Thing* and his early collaborations), they are clever (often brilliant) and always artfully done. Some, like *Sweeney Todd*, are tuneful enough to compensate for the gory subject matter.

E. *Company* was pieced together from parts of 11 one-act plays George Furth had written previously, unified by the character Robert.

    1. The couples in this show live in stylized cubes that make use of stairways, an elevator, and film projections onto the set. We assume the scene is an apartment building. The couples are less than idyllically happy; the general philosophy, expressed by Robert in the show's closing song, "Being Alive," is that marriage stinks, but being alone is worse.

    2. Robert's problem is the same one that plagued most of the characters in the HBO series *Sex and the City*—an inability to make a commitment. The subject of *Company* is marriage, and one would think the subject of marriage might be romance, but this is not a romantic show. The separate lives of the characters intersect but never seem to connect.

    3. The not-particularly-witty but often zippy repartee of *Company* keeps the show's momentum rolling along but going nowhere in particular. At one point, three women join forces at a microphone as if they were the Andrews Sisters and sing, at a pace too fast for anything but a frenetic delivery, "You Could Drive a Person Crazy." It's one of the most delightful spots in the show, a moment that forces you to smile.

F. What has Sondheim done to revitalize American musical theater? He has used themes no previous creator of musicals has dared to use: mass murder in *Sweeney Todd*, presidential assassination in *Assassins*, the limits and definition of sanity in *Anyone Can Whistle*. Sondheim remains controversial, but he is unquestionably important.

II. In 1971, the year after Sondheim's *Company*, a young Andrew Lloyd Webber mounted *Jesus Christ Superstar* at the Mark Hellinger Theatre, where it ran for 720 performances. In this brief history, we've tried, in general, to focus on Broadway musicals that originated in America, but we'll spend a little time on the British Webber because his shows have set Broadway attendance records.

A. The history of *Jesus Christ Superstar* begins after composer Webber's and lyricist Tim Rice's moderate success in England with *Joseph and the Amazing Technicolor Dreamcoat*. With the success of *Joseph*, they looked around for another biblical story. Rice decided on the last six days of Jesus' life, but with Judas as the central character.

B. The theme of betrayal intrigued Tim Rice. Was there something more to the story of Judas's betrayal of Jesus than a handful of silver coins?

C. Murray Head, who had played in the London production of *Hair*, had decided to record the show's title song, which was then simply called *Jesus Christ*. Then, shortly before the recording session, Rice had the Andy Warholian inspiration to call it *Jesus Christ Superstar*—a title immediately memorable and unquestionably attention-getting. It is sung from Judas's point of view.

D. There is a suggestion, in both the song and the show, that Judas was inwardly aware that he was making himself eternally despised but that his action was, in a perverse sense, a sacrifice that would, in the end, bring Jesus a fame beyond the Romans' comprehension.

E. The single was followed by an LP that contained new songs covering other events related to those final days in Christ's life.
   1. "Everything's All Right," in 5/4 time, obviously inspired by the Brubeck Quartet's "Take Five," gave us a tender moment and a lovely tune.
   2. "Hosanna" was a lyrical shout that resembled the chants sung by the flower children in San Francisco in the mid-1960s. But the shifts from "Ho-sanna" to "Hey-sanna" and such lines as "Hey J.C., won't you smile at me?" turn the sacred into the profane.
   3. Jesus' solo, "Gethsemane," takes the limelight off Judas and makes the Christ character fully human.

F. With the success of the LP, Webber and Rice took the songs to the United States to be performed as a complete musical theater piece, directed by Tom O'Horgan, the man who had directed *Hair*. It starred Jeff Fenholt as Christ, Yvonne Elliman as Mary Magdalene, and Ben Vereen as Judas. Mary's "I Don't Know How to Love Him" became a hit even before the show reached Broadway.

G. If Sondheim appeals to a discerning minority, Webber creates shows that appeal to the masses as has no other writer of musicals since Rodgers and Hammerstein.

III. Now, let's turn to *A Chorus Line*, a unique concept with memorable music by Marvin Hamlisch.

A. "What I Did for Love" became a cabaret standard and "One" became the "Tea for Two" of 1975, the ultimate hoofers' anthem.

B. Like *Company*, *A Chorus Line* is a series of essentially disjointed stories, this time held together by the fact that nearly all the characters are fledgling dancers. The uniqueness of the stories that each of them tells grows out of the fact that they are distillations of taped interviews with real dancers talking about their lives.

IV. The year *A Chorus Line* appeared, *Chicago* also premiered, with a score by Kander and Ebb and directed by Bob Fosse. Originally running 898 performances at the 46th Street Theatre, *Chicago* has been revived on and off Broadway and made into one of the most talked-about film musicals of the past 20 years.

A. Before I talk about *Chicago*, let's listen to a song from its antecedent, the 1926 Maureen Dallas Watkins play of the same name. This song is "Chicago," with music and lyrics by Fred Fischer.

B. In the 1975 Broadway musical version of *Chicago*, Gwen Verdon played Roxy Hart, and Jerry Orbach played the razzle-dazzle lawyer Billy Flynn.

C. If this Kander and Ebb show wasn't filled with 1920s-style vaudeville music, we might be tempted to call it an opera. The songs tell the story, and long sections of the show proceed with little or no dialogue.

D. Interestingly, the show's songs exist on two levels, one accessible to younger theatergoers and the other accessible only to the over-55 crowd. Many of the songs are deliberate takeoffs on classic pieces performed by performers of the 1920s; some were revived by those same performers in films of the 1940s and 1950s. Those old enough to be familiar with these vaudevillians have the pleasure of seeing things in the show that are visible only to them.

1. Gwen Verdon sits on the piano for "Funny Honey," mimicking Helen Morgan who sat on the piano to sing "Bill" from *Show Boat*.

2. "Mr. Cellophane," sung by Roxy Hart's cuckolded husband, is awfully reminiscent of Bert William's "Nobody."

3. "When You're Good to Mama" is sung in the style of Sophie Tucker. Even the song title is a takeoff on a Sophie Tucker hit called "You've Got To See Mamma Ev'ry Night (or you can't see Mamma at all.)"

4. We hear the original 1923 "You've Got to See Mamma Ev'ry Night," with music by Con Conrad and lyrics by Billy Rose.

5. The musical *Chicago* unmasks hypocrisy with crude and obvious irony. Billy Flynn sings "All I Care about Is Love" in the style of Ted Lewis singing his Greenwich Village Follies hit "When My Baby Smiles at Me," and of course, what Billy Flynn really cares about is money and his own notoriety.

V. A current that charges Broadway during the final decades of the 20th century is the reworking of old film musicals into Broadway musicals.

A. Earlier, the procedure was to turn a stage musical into a film musical, thereby extending the show's life and earnings. Then, beginning in the 1970s, that trend was reversed, for two reasons:

1. First, it cost so much more to make a musical that producers could reduce their costs by using a property that had already gone through initial editing and revision.

2. Further, with the tremendous demand for classic revivals, the old film musicals seemed surer of success because of their popular scores and because of their previous association with Hollywood's stars.

B. Sometimes, as in the case of *42ⁿᵈ Street*, this worked beautifully; other times, as in the case of *Seven Brides for Seven Brothers*, it didn't. Among the reverse-the-trend musicals were *High Society, Singin' in the Rain, Meet Me in St. Louis, State Fair,* and *The Lion King*.

VI. Let's turn to one of the big successes, artistically and financially, of the 1980s. *42ⁿᵈ Street* premiered at the Winter Garden Theatre on August 25, 1980 [sic], where it continued for 3,486 performances.

A. Jerry Orbach played the director, Tammy Grimes played the star who breaks her leg, and the unknown chorus girl who gets to replace the star was played by Wanda Richert. It was another David Merrick-produced and Gower Champion-directed super-musical.

  1. The score for *42ⁿᵈ Street* was written by the unsung genius of film musicals, Harry Warren. Among his perfectly crafted melodies, supported by modern and lush harmonies, are "Serenade in Blue," "There'll Never Be Another You," "September in the Rain," and "I Only Have Eyes for You."

  2. The lyrics of *42ⁿᵈ Street* were written by Al Dubin, whose relationship with Warren is reminiscent of that of Richard Rodgers and Larry Hart. Warren was steady and dependable; Dubin was a glutton and an alcoholic. Their original score for the 1933 film *42ⁿᵈ Street* was supplemented on Broadway by songs from several of their other 1930s Warner Brothers films, including *Lullaby of Broadway*.

  3. In the show *42ⁿᵈ Street*, Peggy Sawyer is in Grand Central Terminal, sitting on her suitcase, about to give up on New York and Broadway. The director, Jerry Orbach, appears, to beg her to return and save the show.

  4. Orbach sings, "Come on along and listen to…the lullaby of Broadway," and the stage fills with electricity. The rest of the cast appears from all directions. The number builds until it fills the auditorium with smiles.

B. We should mention a little about the great and powerful—and totally untrustworthy—David Merrick, Broadway's greatest producer of the 1960s to late 1970s.

1. A critic once said, "David Merrick would destroy you for a Cracker Jack prize if the mood struck him," but he also takes fabulous risks. The capital for *42nd Street* came entirely out of his pocket—all $2.5 million of it.

2. However, what David Merrick did on the night *42nd Street* opened was unforgivable. We hear the star of the show, Tammy Grimes, describe his tasteless grab for publicity in announcing the death of director Gower Champion onstage after the final curtain call.

VII. Having talked about shows that were film musicals, let's go back one year, to 1979, and look at Sondheim again.

   A. *Sweeney Todd* is Sondheim simultaneously at his darkest and at his most melodious. His lyrics in this show are clever, and the music is dramatic and compelling. The opening ballad of *Sweeney Todd* sets the tone for the entire show—both terrifying and funny.

   B. *Sweeney Todd* is easily the most grisly musical ever to do a successful run on Broadway and, unquestionably, one of Sondheim's best. Premiering at the Uris Theatre on March 1, 1979, it ran for 557 performances.

   C. The operatic Sweeney Todd was sung by a mad barber (played by Len Cariou) who returns home from an unjust imprisonment, determined to get back at the world. Mrs. Lovett (played by Angela Lansbury) becomes his accomplice in murder, helping him to turn corpses into meat pies. All of this is accomplished through broad comedy.

VIII. Before we close, let's look at a blockbuster: The critical response paralleled the audience response for *The Producers*, which premiered at the St. James Theatre in 2001.

   A. *The Producers* won an incredible 12 Tony Awards and Mel Brooks's new songs simply added luster to a story that had already become a classic film comedy. This is a show about doing a show called *Springtime for Hitler*; it sounds like a sure-fire failure for a musical which, in *The Producers*, it's supposed to be. The idea is that Max (Nathan Lane) and Leo (Matthew Broderick) plan for the show to fail so that they can make off with the "angels'" investment. The problem is that, to their chagrin, the show becomes a hit.

B. This show has everything that only Mel Brooks could imagine, including Adolf Hitler, reincarnated as a vaudevillian, and a chorus of "little old ladies" tapping in unison with the feet of their aluminum walkers.

IX. Knowing that we have to stop somewhere, let's end with a recent blockbuster that has played to sold-out houses at the Gershwin Theatre. The show, with music and lyrics by Stephen Schwartz and book by Winnie Holzman, is *Wicked*.

A. Gregory Maguire's 1995 novel *Wicked* explored the tortured history of the green-skinned, so-called "wicked" Witch of the West, called Elphaba by Maguire. She and the good witch, Glinda, used to be friends. We see the friendship from Elphaba's point of view and are forced to reevaluate our picture of her.

B. Winnie Holzman ably adapted the story. Eugene Lee's set for the show is filled with "futuristic" machinery, overseen by a ferocious metal dragon that rests on top of the proscenium. Susan Hilferty created costumes for the ensemble that make them look, in one critic's description, "like the creeping, mutating figures in a Hieronymus Bosch painting." Wayne Cilento's munchkin choreography consists of a series of rather spasmodic movements, each ending in a bizarre pose.

C. The show has been described as having "more glitter than heart," but no show can be successful for this long without a heart. Stephen Schwartz's music, like Marvin Hamlisch's, has seldom been singled out for critical praise, but it does exactly what it needs to do in order to make this musical work.

D. With the end of the course in sight, we have a special treat. Composer/lyricist Stephen Schwartz shares some backstage information on the evolution of the song "The Wizard and I" from *Wicked*. This tale has never before been told in public. The interview was done by Dave Wilkes in New York.

X. Over the past 16 lectures, my challenge was to capture the evolution of musical theater. If many of your favorite shows weren't discussed, don't feel disappointed. Many of mine weren't either.

A. For instance, I far prefer Jerry Herman's *Mame* to his *Hello, Dolly!*, but I had to represent him with a single show, and I chose the blockbuster. *Carousel* is my favorite Rodgers and Hammerstein show, as it was theirs, but I focused more on *Oklahoma!*.

B. The huge corporations who currently produce musicals bank on choreographers with such names as Michael Bennett, Susan Stroman, Tommy Tune, and Bob Fosse, despite the fact that Fosse has been dead for 25 years. The choreographer now dominates Broadway and sees his or her name on the marquee above the show's title.

C. To some extent, this trend is unhealthy. When the theater is a writer's theater, the songs, stories, and characters are more likely to be worth reviving in new productions by new choreographers and directors. That the writer's art is less valued may be partially responsible for the limited number of interesting new songs on Broadway today.

D. Let me hasten to add that musical theater on Broadway is in no danger of disappearing. As to how the form will change over the next few decades, we're all in the dark, which is exactly where we need to be in order to enjoy the show, whatever it might be.

Suggested Reading:

Gerald M. Berkowitz, *New Broadways*.

Steven Suskin, *More Opening Nights on Broadway*.

Questions to Consider:

1. In terms of European influence, how is the end of the 20th century like and unlike the end of the 19th century?

2. Define the *concept musical* and give reasons why *A Chorus Line* is considered, perhaps, the most successful example to date.

 ©2006 The Teaching Company.

Lecture Sixteen—Transcript
Big Bucks and Long Runs (1970s–Present)

The year 1970 gives Broadway the first of five collaborations between composer-lyricist Stephen Sondheim and producer-director Hal Prince. These five shows are *Company*, 1970; *Follies*, 1971; *A Little Night Music*, 1973; *Pacific Overtures*, 1976; and *Sweeney Todd*, 1979.

For the 1970s, these shows are roughly equivalent to Rodgers and Hammerstein's four classics of the 1940s—*Oklahoma!, Carousel, Allegro,* and *South Pacific.* Rodgers and Hammerstein, during the '40s, created the template for the book musical. Sondheim and director Hal Prince helped create a genre that only fairly recently has acquired a label—the concept musical. It's a term that doesn't say much and doesn't mean much, but since it's presently in wide use, we'll have to define it and describe a little about *Company* to help make the term more concrete.

The concept musical, as created by Sondheim, is a little like a revue with a serious theme. It need not have a plot, though it might have the thread of one. *Company* concerned Robert, played by Dean Jones and later by Larry Kert—the original Tony in *West Side Story.* Robert is a protagonist with whom the audience has little sympathy and that seems to suit Sondheim, Prince, and librettist, George Furth, just fine. We're never really concerned about Robert's fate any more than we're concerned about the fates of those damned felines in *Cats*, another concept musical. Interestingly, in *A Chorus Line*, perhaps the greatest concept musical of them all, we care a great deal about the kids who are desperately trying to audition for a show.

Sondheim's concept musicals are not the traditional situation-conflict-resolution stories, with their build toward a climax and a satisfying denouement. That's artifice. Sondheim's presentations are more like life—or at least life as it exists for Sondheim—disjointed, dissatisfying, or often boring. Its greater satisfactions seem to be cynicism and derision.

Though Sondheim's musicals don't make money—with the exception of *A Funny Thing...* and his early collaborations—they do appeal to an audience who shares his view of life and, consequently, are quite willing to bankroll the shows. The shows are clever—often brilliant—and always artfully done. Some, like *Sweeney Todd*, are tuneful enough to compensate for the gory subject matter.

The year 1970's *Company* was pieced together from parts of 11 one-act plays George Furth had written previously. The character of "Robert" unifies the disconnected vignettes. The couples in this show live in stylized cubes that make the use of stairways, an elevator, and film projections onto the set. We assume the scene is an apartment building. The couples who live in these cubes are less than idyllically happy—they argue, smoke pot, plan to divorce each other from time to time, and drink too often and too much. The general philosophy, expressed by Robert in the show's closing song, "Being Alive," is that marriage stinks, but being alone is worse.

This show ran at the Alvin Theatre for 760 performances, so it probably made money for its backers. *Company* is a unique show and a good one. And, urban marriage among the affluent may be as dissatisfying in life as it is in *Company*. Good—that should make those of us who aren't affluent feel grateful for what we don't have.

Robert's problem is the problem that plagued most of the characters in the HBO series, "Sex and the City"—an inability to make a commitment. The subject of *Company* is marriage and one might think that that subject might be romance, too, but this is not a romantic show. We're not sure if Robert likes these friends in the other cubes. One of the couples talks about their kids, but we don't see them. These separate lives intersect, but never seem to connect.

The not-particularly-witty, but often zippy repartee of *Company* keeps the show's momentum rolling along, but going nowhere in particular.

At one point, three women join forces at a microphone as if they were The Andrews Sisters and sing, at a pace too fast for anything but a frenetic delivery, "You Could Drive a Person Crazy." It's one of the most delightful spots in the show, a moment that forces you to smile—at last!

What has Sondheim done to revitalize American Musical Theater? He's used themes no previous creator of musicals has dared to use. He used mass murder in *Sweeney Todd*; Presidential assassination in *Assassins;* the limits and definition of sanity in *Anyone Can Whistle*. In that sense, he's remarkably like Oscar Hammerstein, who—in every other way—is the antithesis of Stephen Sondheim.

Hammerstein created a musical decrying racism at a time when to do so was dangerous; the musical was *Showboat*. The difference here is that Hammerstein's experiments with untried themes became big box office and are cherished today as milestones in the theater.

But, Sondheim remains controversial, attracts a rather clique-ish and supercilious coterie of loyal fans, and gets mixed reviews from the critics. Is he important? Unquestionably.

In 1971—the year after Sondheim's *Company*—a young Andrew Lloyd Webber mounted *Jesus Christ Superstar* at the Mark Hellinger Theatre, where it ran for 720 performances. Between Webber's *Cats* and Schoenberg's *Miss Saigon*, the 20th century's final decades are a little like the final decade of the 19th century, when the operettas of Irishman Victor Herbert and Englishmen Gilbert and Sullivan dominated Broadway. In this brief history, I try, in general, to focus on Broadway musicals that originated in America. But, I'll spend a little time on Webber since his shows have set Broadway attendance records.

Of all Andrew Lloyd Webber shows, *Jesus Christ Superstar* most belongs in this retrospective because, though the songs originated in England, the show itself originated here in the United States.

The history of the show begins after composer Andrew Lloyd Webber's and lyricist Tim Rice's moderate success in England with their show, *Joseph and the Amazing Technicolor Dreamcoat*. With the past success of *Joseph*, they looked around for another biblical story.

Rice decided on the last six days of Jesus' life. But, Jesus would not be the central character; Judas would. After all, we're living in the age of the anti-hero.

The theme of betrayal intrigued Tim Rice. Would a handful of silver coins have been enough to cause Judas to betray his teacher and his friend? Or was there more to it than that? Interestingly, in both Webber and Rice shows, we find the theme of betrayal. Joseph's brothers sold him into slavery and Christ's apostle set him up for crucifixion. Judas—as created by Tim Rice—was more complex than all 11 of Joseph's brothers put together.

Murray Head, who had played in the London Production of *Hair*, had decided to record the song, which was then simply called *Jesus*

Christ. A song they wrote, not even sure if they were going to turn it into a show. Then, shortly before the recording session, Rice had the Andy Warholian inspiration to call it, instead, *Jesus Christ Superstar*—a title immediately memorable and unquestionably attention-getting. It is sung from Judas's point of view:

> Every time I look at you I don't understand
>
> Why you let the things you did get so out of hand.

There is a suggestion, within the song and within the entire show, that Judas was inwardly aware that he was making himself eternally despised, but that his action was—in a perverse sense—a sacrifice, which would, in the end, bring Jesus a fame beyond the Romans' comprehension.

The record, *Jesus Christ Superstar*, was banned by the BBC, condemned by the establishment as heretical, and called "blasphemous" by the Church of England. In other words, it was an instant hit!

The single was followed up by an LP that contained new songs that covered other events related to those final days in Christ's life. "Everything's All Right," in 5/4 time, obviously inspired by the Brubeck Quartets's "Take Five," gave us a tender moment and a lovely tune. "Hosanna" was a lyrical shout that resembled the chants sung by the flower children in San Francisco in the mid-'60s. But, the shifts from Ho-sanna to Hey-sanna and lines like "Hey J.C., won't you smile at me?" turn the sacred into the profane. Jesus' big solo, "Gethsemane," takes the limelight off Judas and makes the Christ character fully human. He sings:

> Now I'm sad and tired.
>
> Bleed me,
>
> Beat me,
>
> Kill me,
>
> Take me now,
>
> Before I change my mind.

With the success of the LP, Webber and Rice took the songs to the United States to be performed not as a concert, but as a complete musical-theater piece, directed by Tom O'Horgan, the man who had directed *Hair*. It starred Jeff Fenholt as Christ, Yvonne Elliman as Mary Magdalene, and Ben Vereen as Judas. Mary's "I Don't Know How to Love Him" became a hit even before the show reached Broadway.

If Sondheim appeals to a discerning minority, Webber creates shows that appeal to the masses as has no other writer of musicals since Rodgers and Hammerstein. Sondheim is kept writing by contributions from his wealthy sponsors; Webber has become fabulously wealthy, himself, by consistently selling out his box offices. Yet, the work has its detractors who feel the music is full of grand effects easily achieved.

Now, let's looks at *A Chorus Line*, a unique concept and a unique concept musical, with memorable music by Marvin Hamlisch. "What I Did for Love" became a cabaret standard and "One" became the "Tea for Two" of 1975, the ultimate hoofers anthem. I only wish that Hamlisch—whose talents move him from conducting symphony orchestras to creating film classics like "The Way We Were" and "Nobody Does It Better"—I only wish that Hamlisch had written more than a few scores for musical theater. Broadway would have been richer for his contribution.

Like *Company, A Chorus Line* is a series of essentially disjointed stories, this time held together by the fact that nearly all the characters are fledgling dancers. The uniqueness of the stories that each of them tells grows out of the fact that they're not really made-up stories, but they're actually distillations of real taped interviews with real live dancers, who had done all this long before the show existed. *A Chorus Line, Company,* and *Cats* are, as we said, concept musicals, inhabiting the no-mans-land between the book show and the revue. One way to test them is move the songs around. You couldn't do that in a book show, but you could in any of these concept musicals just mentioned.

The year *A Chorus Line* appeared, 1975, *Chicago* also premiered with a score by Kander and Ebb and directed by Bob Fosse. Originally running 898 performances at the 46th Street Theatre, *Chicago* has been revived on and off-Broadway and made into one of the most talked about film musicals of the past 20 years.

Before I talk about *Chicago* the musical, I'd like to talk about its antecedent, the 1926 Maureen Dallas Watkins play of the same name. Some music was used in the play, most notably a 1922 song with music and lyrics by Fred Fischer—by far the best song Fischer ever wrote and, by far, the best song, in my opinion, ever written about Chicago. *(Plays piano—"Chicago.")* Kander and Ebb briefly considered using that song in their score, but decided not to.

In the 1975 Broadway musical version of *Chicago*, Gwen Verdon played Roxy Hart and Jerry Orbach—of "Law and Order" fame—played the razzle-dazzle lawyer, Billy Flynn.

If this Kander and Ebb show weren't 1920s-style vaudeville music, you might be tempted to call it an opera. The songs do tell the story, and long, long sections of the show proceed with little or no non-musical dialogue. What's interesting is that this show's songs exist on two levels, one accessible to younger theatergoers—those under 50, maybe under 55—and the other accessible possibly only to the over-55 crowd, unless their really movie buffs, because many of the songs are deliberate takeoffs on pieces performed by classic performers of the 1920s. Now, many of these were revived by the same performers in the '30s and the '40s on film. Those old enough to be familiar with these old vaudevillians will have the pleasure of seeing things in the show that are visible only to them.

For example, Gwen Verdon sits on the piano for "Funny Honey," mimicking Helen Morgan who sat on the piano in the '30s to sing "Bill" from *Showboat*. "Mr. Cellophane," sung by Roxy Hart's cuckolded husband, is awfully reminiscent of an old Bert William's song called "Nobody." "I ain't never done nothing to nobody / No time and ain't never got nothing from nobody / No time." "When You're Good To Mama" is sung in the style of Sophie Tucker, the big-voiced "last of the red-hot-mamas," and even the song title is a takeoff on a Sophie Tucker hit called "You've Got To See Mama Every Night Or You Can't See Mama At All." Now of course, the only purpose for Sophie's song is to please the audience, but when *Chicago*'s prison matron sings "When You're Good to Mama," the purpose is to expose the corruption of the system by lampooning it.

But here's the original 1923 "You've Got to See Mama," with music by Con Conrad—whose song "The Continental," by the way, was destined to win the very first Academy Award for "Best Song" in 1933. The lyrics were written by Billy Rose who later married Fanny Brice and went on to become one of the most important producers on Broadway. Rose produced, during the 1930s, the last musical to play

 ©2006 The Teaching Company.

New York's Hippodrome Theatre before it was torn down—the show was Rodgers and Hart's *Jumbo*.

Now here's Conrad and Rose's 1923 hit "You've Got to See Mama." It's a really great blues number and in order to illustrate that, I'm gonna sing it the first time around and then play it in a bluesy manner, and improvise on it a little bit. *(Plays piano—"You've Got to See Mama.")*

The musical *Chicago* unmasks hypocrisy with crude and obvious irony. Billy Flynn sings "All I Care about Is Love" in the style of Ted Lewis singing his Greenwich Village Follies hit, "When My Baby Smiles At Me." And of course, what Billy Flynn really cares about is money and his own notoriety.

A current that charges Broadway during the final decades of the 20th century—let's move past *Chicago* and look at this now—the reworking of old film musicals into Broadway musicals. Now, the procedure was, beginning with 1928's *Whoopee*, to turn a stage musical into a film musical, thereby extending the show's life and earnings. But then, beginning in the '70s, we reversed that trend. Why? Well, there were really two reasons. It costs so much more to make a musical that producers could greatly reduce their costs by using a property that had already gone through initial editing and revision; and two, with the tremendous demand on Broadway for revivals of classic shows, the old film musicals seem surer of success because of their popular scores and because of their previous association with Hollywood's best stars.

Sometimes, as in the case of *42nd Street*, this worked beautifully. Other times, as in the case of *Seven Brides for Seven Brothers*, Broadway built it, but they did not come. Among the reverse-the-trend musicals were *High Society, Singin' in the Rain, Meet Me in St. Louis, State Fair,* and *The Lion King*. Some of these shows were SRO—standing room only—others were SR-No!

Now, let's talk about one of the big successes, both artistically and financially, of the 1980s—*42nd Street*. Premiering at the Winter Garden Theatre on August 25, 1981 [sic 1980], it continued for 3,486 performances. Jerry Orbach played the director, Tammy Grimes played the star who breaks her leg, and the unknown chorus girl who gets to replace the star was played by Wanda Richert. It was another David Merrick-produced and Gower Champion-directed super-musical. You remember *Hello, Dolly!*? It ran for years in London's Drury Lane Theatre and 13 years after it closed on Broadway, its revival appeared, filling every seat again.

The score for *42nd Street* was written by the unsung genius of film musicals, Harry Warren. The fact that we don't recognize his name is due partly to his shyness and partially to the fact that he wrote for films, a medium in which songwriters tend to be anonymous. Warren, when he wanted to, could muster up the lyricism of a jazz-Puccini. He was one of the many first-rate Gershwin-inspired composers of the 1930s. Among his perfectly crafted songs, supported by modern and lush harmonies, are "Serenade in Blue," "There'll Never Be Another You," "September in the Rain," and "I Only Have Eyes for You."

The lyrics of *42nd Street* were written by Al Dubin, whose relationship with Warren is reminiscent of that of Richard Rodgers and Larry Hart. Warren was steady and dependable, like Richard Rodgers; Dubin was a glutton and an alcoholic and undependable, like Larry Hart. But, like Larry Hart, he also wrote great lyrics. The original score for the 1933 film, *42nd Street*, was supplemented on Broadway by songs from several of their other 1930s Warner Brothers' films, including the perennial favorite from Warner Brothers's *Golddiggers of 1935*, "Lullaby of Broadway."

In *42nd Street*, the Broadway show, Peggy Sawyer is in Grand Central Terminal, sitting on her suitcase about to give up on New York and about to give up on Broadway. The director, Jerry Orbach, appears and begs her to return and save the show.

No cues are needed here. Orbach just opens up and sings, "come along and listen to…the Lullaby of Broadway" and the stage fills with electricity. The rest of the cast suddenly appears from all directions. The number builds until it fills the entire auditorium with smiles. The show never failed to receive a standing ovation.

Now, a little about the great and powerful—and totally untrustworthy—David Merrick, Broadway's greatest producer of the 1960s through the late '70s. Once a critic said of David Merrick, "David Merrick would destroy you for a Cracker Jack prize if the mood struck him." But, he also took fabulous risks. The capital for this show, *42nd Street*, came entirely out of his own pocket—all 2.5 million of it. But what David Merrick did on the night *42nd Street*

©2006 The Teaching Company.

opened was unforgivable. Let's let the star of the show, Tammy Grimes, tell you about it in her own words. *(Plays recording— Tammy Grimes interview on "42nd Street"):*

> **Bob Allen**: On opening night, the cast received 14 curtain calls. And as the cheers were still echoing through the Winter Garden Theatre, producer David Merrick took to the stage and told the shocked audience and cast that the show's director, Gower Champion, had died that afternoon at Sloan-Kettering National Cancer Institute. Tammy Grimes was standing next to her costar when she heard that shocking news.

> **Tammy Grimes**: I looked at Wanda Richert, who was the lead dancer, and I thought, "Oh, David. Oh, David. Don't do this." Don't do this to these young kids who were dancing because their faces would just awash with tears and shock and it was, for me, it was, yes, it was a shock. But I didn't really think about anything except David. Do you realize, can you see those faces? Don't do this. It's not meant to be shown, these reactions. Have the curtain stay down and come on and tell us. Because there they were, bravo-ing, everyone was standing, and bravo-ing to this piece of work. And everybody was so happy and then to do this should not have been seen by the audience. This is not part of theater. This is, this is publicity; in a crass sense, it is publicity. But it has nothing to do with the production, per se. They didn't pay their money to hear this piece of news. They would certainly pick up any paper in the world the next day and read it on the front page, but I went out with David for dinner two weeks after we had opened and I said, "David, why did you do that?" David said, "I couldn't resist."

Now, having talked about shows that were film musicals first, let's go back one year and look at Sondheim again. Nineteen seventy-nine's *Sweeney Todd* is Sondheim simultaneously at his darkest and at his most melodious. His lyrics in this show are clever, and the music is dramatic and compelling. The opening ballad of *Sweeney Todd*—in a minor key—has the lilt of a sea chantey like "The Drunken Sailor" with a little hint of something like *Gilligan's Island* in it. This is not a slur; Sondheim, by making the song both terrifying and light, sets the tone for the entire show. There is a nice variety of songs in this show, from the blithely romantic to the foreboding. We see hilarious dark humor here juxtaposed with actual horror.

This is easily the most grisly musical ever to do a successful run on Broadway and, unquestionably, one of Sondheim's best. Premiering at the Uris Theatre on March 1, 1979, it ran for 557 performances.

The operatic Sweeney Todd was sung by mad barber, played by Len Cariou, who returns home from an unjust imprisonment, determined to get back at the world. Mrs. Lovett, played by Angela Lansbury, becomes his accomplice in murder, helping him to turn the corpses into meat pies. The cutting and the meat grinding take place before your eyes, splattering the stage with blood. All of this is accomplished through the medium of broad comedy and I confess that the songs and the situations made me laugh, despite my revulsion.

Now, let's look at a real blockbuster! The critical response paralleled the audience response for *The Producers*, another show still running years after its premiere at the St. James Theatre in 2001.

The Producers won an incredible 12 Tony Awards and Mel Brooks's new songs simply added luster to a story that had already become a classic film comedy.

Though none of the newer leads have had the charisma of Nathan Lane and Matthew Broderick, the show continues to do its dark magic. Here's a show about doing a show called "Springtime for Hitler," in which the dancers goose-step in the chorus line. It sounds like a sure-fire failure for a musical, which, in *The Producers*, it's supposed to be. The idea is that Max, Nathan Lane, and Leo, Matthew Broderick, plan on having the show fail so they can make off with the "angels" investment. The problem is that, to their chagrin, the show becomes a hit.

This show has everything that only Mel Brooks could imagine— Adolph Hitler reincarnated as a vaudevillian who dances and sings in a style reminiscent of Al Jolson or Judy Garland or a little of both. It has a chorus of "little old ladies"—why are they never "big" old ladies?—little old ladies tapping in unison with the feet of their aluminum walkers. That's taste! No, it's not; it's Mel Brooks. And, it's hilarious. It's also, if you think about it—think about the rest of this course—it's 21st-century Weber and Fields travesty. Think about that. Leo is the *schlemiel* and Max is the *schlimazel*! *The Producers* is a first-rate film that was made into a first-rate musical that was then made into a first-rate film musical. It makes you wonder if the '50s, the Arthur Freed era at MGM, could be coming back?

Knowing we have to stop somewhere, let's focus on a recent blockbuster that continues to play to sold-out houses at the Gershwin Theatre. The show, with music and lyrics by Stephen Schwartz and book by Winnie Holzman, is *Wicked*.

It all started with Gregory Maguire's 1995 novel of the same title. His *Wicked* explored the tortured history of the green-skinned, so-called "wicked" witch of the West. She didn't have a name in Baum's book or in the film, so Maguire called her Elphaba. You see, she and the good witch—Glinda—used to be friends. We see the friendship from Elphaba's point of view and are forced to re-evaluate our picture of her.

Winnie Holzman ably adapted the story. Eugene Lee's set for the show is futuristic in the old-fashioned sense, you know like something out of Fritz Lang's classic German sci-fi film, *Metropolis*. Wheels, cogs, and futuristic doo-dads are overseen by a ferocious metal dragon that rests on top of the proscenium. And Susan Hilferty created costumes for the ensemble that made them look, in one critic's description, "like the creepy, mutating figures in a Hieronymus Bosch painting." Wayne Cilento's munchkin choreography consists of a series of rather one-of-a-kind spasmodic movements—it reminds me of Elaine dancing on "Seinfeld"—each ending in a bizarre pose. It all works together.

The original Glinda the Good Witch was played and sung brilliantly by past Tony winner Kristin Chenoweth. But, it was Idina Menzel's Elphaba—Glinda's green-skinned roommate at sorcery school—who won the Tony award for this show.

The show has been described as having "more glitter than heart," but no show can be this successful for this long without a heart. Stephen Schwartz's music, like Marvin Hamlisch's music in *Chorus Line*, has seldom been singled out for critical praise, but it does exactly what it needs to do in order to make this musical work.

By 2004, *Wicked* had more than recouped its 14 million-dollar original capitalization; and in December 2004, it had advanced ticket sales of 30 million dollars and consistently sold out at the Gershwin

Theatre; it is still selling out today and the Gershwin Theatre is one of the largest theaters on Broadway.

Now, with the course's end in sight, we have a really special treat. Composer-lyricist Stephen Schwartz is going to share some backstage information on the making, or I shouldn't say "the making," it's the evolution of a song. It's interesting how a song can go through so many stages and become in the end something that seemed to have little or nothing in common with whatever it started as. This is the evolution of the song "The Wizard and I" from *Wicked*. This bizarre tale has never before been told in public. The interview was done by our man in New York City, Dave Wilkes. (Plays recording—Stephen Schwartz interview):

> **Steven Schwartz**: The advent of the book musical pioneered back by Rodgers and Hammerstein in the '40s. One of the songs that has come to be more or less thought of as obligatory is termed the "I Want" song where the leading character, within the first two or three songs of the show, comes out and basically tells you what he or she wants and is gonna fight for the rest of the show; and *Wicked* is no different in that regard. Our leading character, Elphaba, who becomes the Wicked Witch of the West starts out as a young girl who, because she is green and has a rather spiky personality, has been scorned by her father and rejected by the people in Munchkinland, where she has grown up and she wants love and acceptance from all of Oz.
>
> When I first began to approach that as a song, I had the notion of doing a song entitled, "Making Good." I liked the title because it had a double meaning, of course, that it meant making good in the sense of becoming a success, but also making good in the terms of doing good deeds. And, her notion when she starts out is that she's gonna do something so good and so wonderful that she's going to become beloved by all of Oz, which is, I think, an ironic idea to be sung by someone who becomes the Wicked Witch of the West.
>
> Anyway, I wrote a song called, "Making Good." This is a bit of that song. *(Plays piano—"Making Good.")* So, the song went on for a while and in the course of preparing the show, we did a series of readings. And, as the song was performed

©2006 The Teaching Company.

in the various readings, I sensed from the audience response and from the feeling I got hearing it within the context of the show that it really wasn't delivering as much as I wanted it to. It wasn't really landing the character. And my first thought was that it needed to be a more energetic song. And so, I kept the title, "Making Good," but I did an entirely different melody about Elphaba, the character Elphaba, getting on a train for the first time to leave Munchkinland and go off to school and this is how that version of "Making Good" went. *(Plays piano.)* Hear how it sounds like a train, get it? *(Plays piano.)*

And, so on. And again, we did this song in a couple of readings and again, I felt that, while the response was perhaps a little bit stronger, it still wasn't completely going over the top the way I felt the first song for our leading character needed to do. So, I began to think that maybe the whole idea of a song called "Making Good" wasn't the right idea. And I thought about, "Well, if somebody wants something in the Land of Oz, what do they do about it?" Well, we all know from the movie, *The Wizard of Oz*, what they do is, they go to see the Wizard and the Wizard answers their prayers or gives them what they wish for. And I thought, "Well, Elphaba really should be no different. She should want to hook up with the Wizard." So, I came up with the idea of doing a song called "The Wizard and I" and that's the song that wound up being in the show and it works very successfully within the contexts of the show. It starts out with a brief intro in which Elphaba is surprised and delighted that these magical powers she's had that have embarrassed her all her life actually have begun to be recognized as something that could be used positively to get her into favor with the Wizard. And, you'll notice that this intro, with a different feel, is the exact same tune as the second version of "Making Good" and the title "Making Good" appears at the very, very end of this intro, going into a new song called "The Wizard and I." Here's an abbreviated version of that song which is the song being sung on Broadway every night. *(Plays piano—"The Wizard and I.")*

Nearing the end of this entire course, I have regrets, but not too few to mention. Over the past 16 lessons, my challenge was to capture the evolution of musical theater in 16 lessons. If many of your favorite shows weren't discussed, don't feel bad. Many of mine weren't either.

I far prefer Jerry Herman's *Mame* to his *Hello, Dolly!*, but I had to represent him with a single show, and I chose the blockbuster. *Carousel* is my favorite Rodgers and Hammerstein show—as it was theirs—but, again, I focused more on the perennial blockbusters. As I speak, there are at least six shows on Broadway I wish I had time to talk about, and maybe I will, but not here and not now.

The huge corporations who currently produce musicals will bank on choreographers with names like Michael Bennett, Susan Stroman, Tommy Tune, and Bob Fosse—despite the fact that Fosse's been dead for 20some years. The choreographer—who first showed her importance in *Oklahoma!*—the choreographer now dominates Broadway and sees his or her name on the marquee above the show's title. No one could have imagined that 50 years ago.

To some extent, this trend may be unhealthy. When the theater is a writer's theater, the songs, the stories, the characters are more likely to be worth reviving in new productions by new choreographers/directors. That the writer's art is less valued may be partially responsible for the limited number of interesting new songs that appear on Broadway today. "Not hummable," some people say about these new songs, but I don't ask for that. I really don't. I think what I'd like is "interesting," "compelling," "memorable"! Sondheim probably isn't awfully memorable except for one or two songs; Bernstein certainly memorable even if he's not "hummable." Those adjectives are what Broadway needs, and it gets them, but with less frequency than in the distant past.

Where do we go from here? I only hope I can come up with an answer that's less of a cliché than that question. The only certain answer is that musical theater on Broadway is in no danger of disappearing. As to how the form will change over the next few decades, we're all in the dark, which is exactly where we need to be in order to enjoy the show, whatever it might be. Thank you.

©2006 The Teaching Company.

Timeline

1828 .... Thomas Dartmouth Rice dons blackface, learns plantation dances, and sings his pre-ragtime song "Jump Jim Crow."

1842 .... Daniel Decatur Emmett expands Rice's Jim Crow act and creates America's first minstrel show.

1866 .... *The Black Crook*, America's first hit musical, appears at Niblo's Garden in New York City.

1881 .... Tony Pastor gives birth to vaudeville by opening his music hall in New York City's Union Square.

1889 .... Charles K. Harris writes the first song to sell a million copies of sheet music, thus firmly establishing an interdependence between the music publishing industry and the Broadway musical stage.

1904 .... George M. Cohan creates his first hit Broadway musical, *Little Johnny Jones*.

1914 .... Irving Berlin writes his first Broadway show, *Watch Your Step*, a dance-focused musical starring Vernon and Irene Castle.

1914 .... Kern's first classic song, "They Didn't Believe Me," appears as an interpolation in the Broadway show *The Girl from Utah*.

1915 .... Cole Porter mounts his first Broadway show, a flop called *See America First*.

1918 ....George Gershwin writes "Swanee," a song that Jolson made into an international hit.

1924 ....Richard Rodgers and Larry Hart's "Manhattan" becomes the hit of the Garrick Gaieties.

1927 ....*Show Boat*, the first serious integrated book musical, appears on Broadway.

1928 ....With the production of Warner Brothers' *The Jazz Singer*, the birth of sound movies precipitates the death of vaudeville.

1931 ....George and Ira Gershwin's Broadway show *Of Thee I Sing* wins the first Pulitzer Prize ever given to a musical.

1935 ....Gershwin's *Porgy and Bess* is an artistic success and a critical and financial failure.

1940 ....The age of the anti-hero begins with Rodgers and Hart's *Pal Joey*, the story of a sleazy, self-absorbed, second-rate performer in a seedy nightclub.

1943 ....Larry Hart dies, and Richard Rodgers begins his long and illustrious career with Oscar Hammerstein, starting with *Oklahoma!*.

1946 ....Irvin Berlin writes his greatest musical, *Annie Get Your Gun*.

1948 ....Cole Porter mounts his masterwork, *Kiss Me, Kate*.

©2006 The Teaching Company.

1949 .... Rodgers and Hammerstein end the decade with their fourth collaboration, *South Pacific*.

1950 .... Frank Loesser writes music and lyrics to his most successful show, *Guys and Dolls*.

1950 .... Broadway is treated to Gertrude Lawrence's and Yul Brynner's performances in *The King and I*.

1956 .... The Lerner and Loewe show that Brooks Atkinson called "the greatest musical of the century" appears— *My Fair Lady*.

1957 .... The Bernstein/ Robbins/ Laurents/ Sondheim collaboration confuses the critics because of its dark, pessimistic tone, but the show proves to be tremendously influential in the remainder of the Broadway century— *West Side Story*.

1959 .... Stephen Sondheim writes lyrics to Jule Styne's music for *Gypsy*.

1959 .... The decade ends with Hammerstein's death; unfortunately, he does not live to see *The Sound of Music*, his final collaboration with Richard Rodgers.

1960 .... *The Fantasticks* opens its 40-year run at the tiny (150-seat) Sullivan Street Playhouse in Greenwich Village.

1962 .... For his first solo effort as composer and lyricist, Stephen Sondheim writes a brilliant score for the hilarious musical *A Funny Thing Happened on the Way to the Forum*.

1964	Jerry Herman writes music and lyrics for the biggest show of the decade to date—*Hello, Dolly!*.
1964	Broadway is treated to one of the 20th century's most enduring and beloved musicals—*Fiddler on the Roof*.
1966	*Cabaret*, the biggest success of Kander and Ebb's early career, sustains the pessimistic tone established by *West Side Story* in 1957.
1968	The rebellious spirit of the Vietnam era is encapsulated in the rock musical *Hair*.
1971	The team of Andrew Lloyd Webber and Tim Rice (music and lyrics) takes its first trip together across the Atlantic to mount *Jesus Christ Superstar* at the Mark Hellinger Theatre.
1975	*A Chorus Line* begins its 15-year run on Broadway, breaking attendance records and winning the Pulitzer Prize.
1982	*Cats*, another Webber and Rice production, becomes the "must-see" show on Broadway.
1987	The team of Claude-Michel Schönberg and Herbert Kretzmer mounts *Les Miserables* at the Broadway Theatre.
1988	With *The Phantom of the Opera*, it becomes clear that American musical theater, for the next decade, will be dominated by Andrew Lloyd Webber.

©2006 The Teaching Company.

1989 ....Jerome Robbins firmly asserts the importance of the choreographer, whose name, by the 1990s, often appears above the title of the show.

1989 ....*Miss Saigon*, another Claude-Michel Schönberg musical, dark, tragic, and compelling, runs on Broadway for 11 years.

1993 ....Kander and Ebb's *Kiss of the Spider Woman* continues the gay subject matter and the dark tone of their first success, *Cabaret*; this show focuses on the daydreams of a transvestite locked in a South American prison cell.

1998 ....Disney turns its blockbuster film *The Lion King* into an ingeniously staged Broadway musical.

1999 ....*Fosse*, another musical tribute to a choreographer, appears during a period when Susan Stroman dominates the marquees as the most prominent Broadway choreographer of the 1990s.

2001 ....Mel Brooks's *The Producers* may have dark and perverse underpinnings, but this musical about making a musical about Adolf Hitler is a laugh-a-minute show with well-crafted, memorable songs; the darkness is pierced with light.

2002 ....Twyla Tharp choreographs the old top-40 hits of Billy Joel to create the revue-ish musical *Movin' Out*.

2002 ....*Thoroughly Modern Millie*, based on the 1967 Julie Andrews film, brings lightness and gaiety back to

Broadway; after a decade of well-crafted but dark musicals, the first decade of the 21st century has audiences exiting the theater whistling and grinning.

2003 .... *Wicked*, a sympathetic view of the Wicked Witch of the West, manages, by 2004, to make back its incredible $14 million investment and, since then, turns pure profit; this dark comedy was Broadway's number-one musical as of 2005.

Glossary

accent: To emphasize a note.

altered chord: A chord in which one or more tones has been raised or lowered For example, C–E–G is a C-major triad, while C–E–G-flat is a C-major triad with a flatted fifth (an altered chord).

appoggiatura: A non-harmonic grace note that resolves stepwise to a chord tone (a harmonic note).

blue note: The lowered third, seventh, and (sometimes) fifth degrees of a major scale that help create the characteristic sound of the blues.

chord: Three or more different tones sounded simultaneously.

concept musical: A presentation in which normal sequential storytelling is abandoned in favor of events connected by a common theme. Examples are Stephen Sondheim's *Company*, which revolves around the vicissitudes of people who all happen to dwell in the same apartment building, and *A Chorus Line*, whose vignettes are created by young dancers revealing themselves as they audition for parts in a musical.

counterpoint: See **polyphonic**. A musical composition with two or more melodies played simultaneously.

extended chord: A chord more complex than the triad, containing four, five, six, or more different tones.

form: The organization and structure of a musical composition.

harmonic rhythm: The frequency with which harmonies change within a piece of music.

harmony: The results produced when different tones are sounded simultaneously.

homophonic: Music with one melodic part that is supported by a chordal accompaniment.

integrated musical: A musical in which dialogue, song, and dance all directly contribute to telling the story.

key: The tonal center of a composition. (The first note of a scale is the *keynote*.) Most often, a song will end on the keynote.

major triad: A triad in which the root and the third consist of the first and third steps of the major scale (for example, C–E–G).

measure: The notes and rests between two bar lines. (A measure here is also referred to as a *bar*.)

meter: The pattern of beats by which the movement of a musical composition is measured. Most of the songs heard and discussed in this course move in a pattern that equals two beats per measure, three beats per measure, or four beats per measure. The two-beat songs are usually called *marches*; the three-beat songs are usually called *waltzes*.

minor triad: A triad in which the third has been lowered (for example,
C–E-flat–G).

modulation: To change key within a musical composition.

overture: In the case of a Broadway show, the overture is an orchestral composition created out of musical themes taken from songs in the show.

pentatonic scale: A scale having five different tones to the octave; the five black keys (in groups of two and three) are identical to the pentatonic scale.

polyphonic: Two or more melodic lines overlapping or sounding simultaneously.

step: A narrow melodic movement from one scale tone to the next (C–D equals a *whole* step; E–F equals a *half* step).

syncopation: An off-the-beat accent or an accent on a normally weak beat.

triad: A three-note chord consisting of a root, a third, and a fifth (for example, the first, third, and fifth notes of a major scale, C–E–G or F–A–C).

©2006 The Teaching Company.

Biographical Notes

Andrews, Julie (1935–). Julie Andrews's phenomenal voice was first heard in America when the British musical *The Boy Friend* played Broadway. After Mary Martin had turned down the lead in *My Fair Lady* (1956), Alan J. Lerner approached 19-year-old Andrews about doing the show. The rest is one of the most pleasant chapters in Broadway history.

Bayes, Nora (1880–1928). Vaudeville star, Ziegfeld Follies star, musical theater star, and one of America's most successful pre-World War I recording stars. Bayes's original song (co-written with her husband) "Shine on Harvest Moon" was one of the top-ten moneymakers of the first decade of the 20th century. George M. Cohan chose Nora Bayes to make a bestselling recording of his song "Over There" during World War I. Though accounting methods during this period may be questionable, Bayes's recording of "Over There" appears to have been the number-one bestselling recording of the World War I era.

Berlin, Irving (1888–1989). Berlin was America's most successful songwriter (music and lyrics) of the first half of the 20th century. Years after his death, a generation that knows none of the standards written by the other members of the big five (Gershwin, Rodgers, Kern, Porter, and Berlin) instantly recognizes such Berlin songs as "White Christmas," "Easter Parade," "There's No Business Like Show Business," and "God Bless America." Berlin's pre-World War I songs caught the spirit of ragtime as did those of no other songwriter. His musical theater masterwork, *Annie Get Your Gun*, is arguably the most "hit-packed" musical ever written.

Bernstein, Leonard (1918–1990). One of the few composers since Gershwin who could successfully work with equal facility in both classical and popular music. Bernstein's most renowned theater score was his collaboration with Stephen Sondheim for *West Side Story*. As a music educator to the masses, he has no peers in the 20th century, leaving behind a treasure of televised lessons for both children and adults that run the gamut from Baroque composers and humor in music to jazz styles and musical theater.

Bland, James (1854–1911). Appearing near the end of the minstrel era, minstrel James Bland has often been called the "black Stephen

Foster." Like Foster, he wrote timeless minstrel songs, including "Carry Me Back to Old Virginny" and "Oh, Them Golden Slippers."

Bock, Jerry (1928–). (See **Harnick, Sheldon**.) Bock wrote for television and films before his songs were heard on Broadway.

Brice, Fannie (1891–1951). One of the best-loved figures of vaudeville and the Ziegfeld Follies, because of the remarkable versatility with which she stepped back and forth from wisecracking Jewish comedy to the tear-stained ballads of the Bowery. Brice's life was dramatized in one Broadway musical—*Funny Girl* (1964), starring Barbra Streisand, and three films—*Rose of Washington Square* (1939), *Funny Girl* (1968), and *Funny Lady* (1975), which chronicled her later years.

Cantor, Eddie (1892–1964). One of America's best-loved entertainers on Broadway, on the screen, on radio, and on recordings. Cantor introduced many first-rate standards, including the timeless song "Makin' Whoopee." In 1953, he was the subject of a Hollywood musical biography called *The Eddie Cantor Story*, starring Keefe Brasselle. In 1956, Cantor was awarded a special Oscar for his distinguished service to the film industry.

Champion, Gower (1919–1980). During the 1950s, Gower was half of the MGM dance team of Marge and Gower Champion. The Champions became known for their work in such films as *The Clouds Roll By* (1946) and *Show Boat* (1951). Gower left MGM after the golden age of film musicals to choreograph Broadway musicals. *Hello, Dolly!* (1964) owes much of its success to Champion's choreography. Champion's final show on Broadway was *42nd Street*.

Cohan, George M. (1878–1942). Cohan was responsible for an important shift in the development of the American musical. At a time when musicals were, essentially, a potpourri of songs tied together by creaky plots, Cohan wrote songs that grew directly out of his stories. The value of the stories and the value of many of the songs may be questionable, but the value of the man is not. Cohan represents stage two in the evolution of the musical, a necessary precursor to stage three, the truly integrated musical.

De Mille, Agnes (1905–1993). A member of the famous theatrical family that included her grandfather, 19th-century playwright Henry de Mille, and her uncle, director Cecil B. DeMille. With her background in classical ballet, Agnes revolutionized musical theater dance. She increased the importance of dance in the musical, as well as the prestige of the choreographer, thus paving the way for Jerome Robbins, Bob Fosse, Gower Champion, Michael Bennett, and Susan Stroman, who is currently considered Broadway's most important choreographer.

Edwards, Gus (1879–1945). Famous vaudevillian and songwriter who is remembered for his kiddie shows, which starred Edwards and assorted child performers and always ended with his song "School Daze." Edwards also composed "By the Light of the Silvery Moon" and "In My Merry Oldsmobile."

Emmett, Daniel Decatur (1815–1904). Creator of the minstrel show and composer of what became the anthem of the South during the Civil War. An abolitionist from Mount Vernon, Ohio, Emmett later regretted writing what appeared to him to be the "battle cry of the enemy." Lincoln appeased Emmett by having the White House orchestra play "Dixie" immediately after the South's surrender and announcing, "*Now* 'Dixie' belongs to the entire country."

Fosse, Bob (1927–1987). Fosse first showed his gift for choreography in the number "Steam Heat" from *Pajama Game* (1954). He allowed his performers to dance with snapping fingers and clicking tongues, as well as their feet. Every part of the body, particularly the hips and shoulders, became important in his dances. The Fosse moves revolutionized theater dance for the final four decades of the 20th century.

Foster, Stephen (1826–1864). Foster was both America's first great popular songwriter and America's first full-time professional songwriter. If he owes his success not only to his talent but also to the rise of the minstrel show, we can say that the minstrel show owes *its* success, at least partially, to the drawing power of Foster's imaginative and well-crafted songs. When Thomas Edison perfected cylinder recordings, Foster's were among the first songs to be recorded. His tragic descent from affluence to drunkenness and poverty has been the basis for novels, plays, and films, and his melodies seem to have been the inevitable choices of barroom piano players in the B-westerns that Hollywood churned out during the 1940s and 1950s.

Frohman, Charles (1860–1915). The most important producer of musical theater productions during the first 15 years of the 20th century. Frohman discovered Jerome Kern and became his mentor. Their partnership might be compared to that of David Merrick and Jerry Herman or of Hal Prince and Stephen Sondheim.

Gershwin, George (1898–1937). George Gershwin was the only songwriter of the golden age to transcend successfully the limits of popular song form. In addition to writing such standards as "The Man I Love," "A Foggy Day," and "They Can't Take That Away from Me," he wrote some of the most popular concert works of the century, including *Rhapsody in Blue* and the ballet *An American in Paris*. Blending the sounds of the early-20th-century symphonic masters with the elements of blues and jazz, Gershwin wrote a unique opera, *Porgy and Bess*, which may be the finest and most permanent creation of its kind in the history of American music.

Gershwin, Ira (1896–1983). Brother of George, who survived him by more than 40 years and continued to write songs with Jerome Kern, Vernon Duke, Kurt Weill, and Harry Warren.

Hamlisch, Marvin (1944–). A composer, pianist, arranger, and conductor, Hamlisch composed the Scott Joplin score for the movie *The Sting* in 1973, which attracted the attention of choreographer/director Michael Bennett. Bennett encouraged Hamlisch to work with lyricist Ed Klaban to create music for a work that eventually came to be called *A Chorus Line*, which ran on Broadway for 15 years and was awarded the Pulitzer Prize. Currently, Hamlisch is focusing on his career as a conductor.

Hammerstein, Oscar (1895–1960). Aside from his immeasurable contributions of libretto and lyrics for shows with Richard Rodgers in the 1940s and 1950s, Hammerstein has the distinction of being the guiding force behind the first modern musical, 1927's *Show Boat*, written with composer Jerome Kern. (See **Rodgers and Hammerstein** and **Kern, Jerome**.)

Handy, William Christopher (1873–1958). With more than 1,500 recordings, Handy's "St. Louis Blues" vies with "Stardust" as the most-recorded song of the 20th century. Musicologist Isaac Goldberg wrote (about the blues): "Handy is its Moses, not its Jehovah. It was he, first of musicians, [who] first codified the new spirit of African music and set it forth upon its conquest of the North." If we see echoes of Gershwin in the great songwriters of the 1920s and 1930s, we see echoes of Handy in Gershwin himself. Singer Nat King Cole portrayed Handy in the 1958 film biography *St. Louis Blues.*

Harnick, Sheldon (1924–). Although he has made a name for himself as a lyricist, Harnick received a thorough musical education. Like his partner, Jerry Bock, he started by writing college musicals at Northwestern University. His 1964 musical *Fiddler on the Roof* is the work for which he will be remembered. His lyrics are perfect character pieces and, like the great lyrics of Oscar Hammerstein, they help create brilliantly staged scenes without calling attention to themselves.

Harrigan, Ned (1844–1911). Creator and performer in the yearly Mulligan Guard forces that were the hit of Broadway in the 1870s and early 1880s. George M. Cohan's famous song "H-A-Double R-I-G-A-N Spells Harrigan" was a tribute to his idol, Ned Harrigan.

Harris, Marion (1896–1944). Broadway, vaudeville, and cabaret headliner; one of Gershwin's favorite singers; and perhaps, the first person to record Gershwin's song "The Man I Love." For its era, the Marion Harris singing style is quite understated and modern.

Hart, Lorenz (1895–1943). This distinguished first partner of Richard Rodgers was, along with Cole Porter, the wittiest and most sophisticated of Broadway lyricists. Hart's lyrics created wit and worldliness through his blending of learned references and complex interval rhymes. His ability to rhyme words that shouldn't rhyme has been equaled only by competitor Yip Harburg. In 1924's "Manhattan," Hart writes, "The great big city will never spoil…The dreams of a boy and goil." In a 1924 song, "Any Old Place with You," he writes, "I'd go ta hell fa ya…or Philadelphia."

Hart, Tony (1855–1891). Though Hart's humor had an Irish sensibility and even some of his biographers referred to him as Irish, Hart was Jewish; however, his thousands of Irish fans accepted him as an honorary Hibernian. Harrigan's success was largely the result of Hart's amazing comic abilities as a mimic and female impersonator.

Herbert, Victor (1859–1924). Herbert was the first classically trained musician to involve himself in popular music in America. Though he had little influence on those who followed him, he was the first important composer of the American musical stage. Working primarily in the operetta genre, he is, perhaps, best remembered for *Naughty Marietta*, which MGM made into a film starring Jeanette MacDonald and Nelson Eddy, and for *Babes in Toyland*, which continues to be revived in community theaters throughout the country during the Christmas season.

Herman, Jerry (1933–). Before writing his attendance-breaking show *Hello, Dolly!* (1964), Herman wrote special material (music and lyrics) for such stars as Tallulah Bankhead, Jane Froman, and Hermione Gingold. *Dolly* was followed by *Mame*, another highly successful show with a theme song that reached the top of the pop charts. Herman's songs are among the last Broadway songs to become popular hits before rock 'n' roll nudged Broadway songs off the edge of a cliff.

Hogan, Ernest (1865–1909). Born Reuben Crowders in Bowling Green, Kentucky, as Ernest Hogan, Crowders moved to New York City, where he became a major writer, actor, singer, dancer, and director of all-black Broadway musicals during the first decade of the 20th century.

Jolson, Al (1886–1950). America's most popular entertainer during the decade before World War I, Jolson was also the first person during this period to do a one-man show on Broadway. He has the further distinction of having had two film biographies—*The Jolson Story* and *Jolson Sings Again*.

Jones, Ada (1873–1922). The leading female recording artist from 1905 to 1912. Her duets with Billy Murray are considered among the finest recordings of that era.

Kander and Ebb (John Kander, 1927– ; Fred Ebb, 1932–2004). Beginning with the hit musical *Cabaret*, the team of Kander and Ebb continued, throughout the 20th century, to produce blockbuster hit shows with dark themes and lively, memorable scores. Among these are *Chicago* and *Kiss of the Spider Woman*.

Kern, Jerome (1885–1945). Once described as a giant with one foot in Europe and the other in America, Kern's songs from *Show Boat* can be linked to European operetta ("We Could Make Believe," "Why Do I Love You?") and the new jazz-influenced American style ("Can't Help Lovin' That Man," "Pick Yourself Up"). Kern and Hammerstein's *Show Boat* represents the beginning of modern American musical theater.

Lauder, Sir Harry (1879–1950). In American vaudeville, Harry Lauder was the lovable and amusing personification of Scottish kitsch. When he sang his original songs, such as "Roamin' in the Gloamin'," he winked as he steamrolled his *r*'s and played the Scotchman (which he was) to the hilt (and to the kilt).

Lerner, Alan Jay (1918–1986). Many called the Lerner and Loewe musical *My Fair Lady* (1956) the greatest musical of the 20th century. The show achieved Rodgers and Hammerstein's ideal of a perfectly integrated score, but it also provided the country with the number-one bestselling LP and a half-dozen standards that everyone in America was soon singing. Lerner, son of the founder of the Lerner dress shops, followed Oscar Hammerstein's lead in writing both lyrics and librettos. His ability to channel George Bernard Shaw's wit and style in his lyrics is singular, to say the least.

Lewis, Ted (1890–1971). Broadway and vaudeville performer who was known for his battered top hat and half-spoken, half-sung style of song performance. Also a band leader, Lewis and his band backed up Sophie Tucker on the classic recording of her theme song, "Some of These Days."

Loewe, Frederick (1904–1988). Loewe grew up in Vienna and was at his best in the Viennese musical style (*Gigi*), but with the Lerner-Loewe collaboration, he showed amazing versatility by writing music that ran the gamut from cowboy ballads (*Paint Your Wagon*) to English beer-hall ditties (*My Fair Lady*). (See **Alan J. Lerner**.)

Murray, Billy (1877–1954). The most popular recording artist of the pre-electric era, though less well known today than such singers as Jolson and Cantor because his stage appearances were infrequent. Murray has the distinction of recording both the original Cohan song "You're a Grand Old Rag" and the more popular expurgated version, "You're a Grand Old Flag."

Porter, Cole (1891–1964). Of the five most important theater composers of the 20th century (Gershwin, Kern, Berlin, Rodgers, and Porter), only Porter wasn't Jewish, but he was fond of pointing out that he was the only one of the group who *wrote* Jewish. He was referring to his use of Semitic scales in such songs as "My Heart Belongs to Daddy" and to his love of minor-key melodies that almost sounded cantorial, such as "I Love Paris," "It's All Right with Me,"

"I Love You," and others. Porter's *Kiss Me, Kate* remains one of the masterworks of the American musical theater.

Rice, Thomas Dartmouth ("Daddy," 1808–1860). The "grandfather" of the minstrel show, Rice created a blackface stage persona called Jim Crow in 1828, touring the country with his act. Rice was the inspiration for Dan Emmett's creation of the first minstrel troupe, the Virginia Minstrels, in 1842.

Robbins, Jerome (1918–1998). Robbins's association with Leonard Bernstein resulted in the creation of *West Side Story* (1957), which like de Mille's work in *Oklahoma!* (1943), revolutionized theater dance. He created incredibly athletic dances that made greater demands on his dancers and helped make dance, in his shows, as important as music and dialogue in telling stories and revealing character.

Rodgers and Hammerstein (Richard Rodgers, 1902–1979; Oscar Hammerstein, 1895–1960). During the 1940s and 1950s, Rodgers and Hammerstein brought about profound changes in the Broadway musical. From *Oklahoma!* (1943) onward, song, dance, and story were "craftfully" interwoven to create what was soon to be called the *integrated musical*. Their approach helped determine the course of musical theater from that time until the present. Although the Rodgers and Hammerstein shows produced a body of work that has merited almost continuous revival, the earlier (1930s) Rodgers and Hart work produced a huge body of songs that continues to be the heart of the jazz musician's and the cabaret singer's repertoire; among these songs are "Lover," "Bewitched," "My Funny Valentine," "The Lady Is a Tramp," "I Could Write a Book," "Manhattan," "My Heart Stood Still," and "Blue Moon."

Schwartz, Stephen (1948–). Schwartz's first work on Broadway was the theme song for the 1969 play *Butterflies Are Free*. The immense success of the music and lyrics for 1971's *Godspell* propelled him to write a series of musicals during the final three decades of the 20th century, culminating in *Wicked*, among the most successful musicals ever to appear on the Broadway stage.

Sondheim, Stephen (1930–). The composer/lyricist of the often-recorded "Send in the Clowns," Sondheim was the most influential Broadway composer of the 1970s and 1980s. His most successful Broadway show, *Sweeney Todd*, appeared in 1979. Sondheim is

©2006 The Teaching Company.

known for his lyrical wit, his dark tone, and his uncompromising dedication to his own artistic ideals.

Stroman, Susan (1954–). Susan Stroman is a Broadway director, choreographer, and performer who grew up in Wilmington, Delaware. In 1992, she won her first Tony Award, for Best Choreography, for *Crazy for You*. In the next few years, she won three more Tonys for Best Choreography, for *Show Boat* (1995), *Contact* (2000), and *The Producers* (2001), and one Tony for Best Director, for *The Producers*.

Tucker, Sophie (1884–1966). Early on, Sophie Tucker became the first white blues shouter, with a voice that Janice Joplin (who probably never heard of Tucker) seemed to channel out of the past. Tucker was the first person to record W. C. Handy's classic "St. Louis Blues," and she was one of the biggest stars of the vaudeville era.

Webber, Andrew Lloyd (1948–). Possibly the most popular composer of musicals at present, Webber's shows are marked by oversized theatricality and memorable special effects. His Broadway triumphs include *Evita*, *Cats*, and *Phantom of the Opera*.

Williams, Bert (1874–1922). Bert Williams was one of the first and one of the greatest names in African-American show business. A star of the Ziegfeld Follies (he received top billing in the show), Williams, during the second decade of the 20th century, was America's highest paid African-American Broadway star. His ability to focus his comedy on foibles common to *all* people makes his the only comedy of that early era that still retains its wit. His original songs, particularly "Nobody," were international hits for several decades.

Ziegfeld, Florenz (1869–1932). The most important producer of musical extravaganzas in the theater's history. His Follies featured America's greatest songwriters (Berlin and Kern), performers (Will Rogers, Eddie Cantor, Fannie Brice, and Bert Williams), and sets and costumes so lavish that even the great beauties who performed in his shows were diminished by such opulence.

Bibliography

Essential Reading:

Bergreen, Lawrence. *As Thousands Cheer*. New York: Viking, 1990. No other Berlin biography has done the difficult job of re-creating this complex and somewhat peculiar man in all his light and shadow. When you finish the final page of this book, you'll feel, at least momentarily, that you've actually lived with Berlin.

Berkowitz, Gerald M. *New Broadways*. New York: Applause Books, 1997. The final few decades of the 20th century, rife with revivals, bizarre experiments (that often succeeded), and neo-traditional productions, are covered, in detail, in this text.

Bordman, Gerald. *American Musical Theatre: A Chronicle*. London: Oxford University Press, 1992. This is the bible of musical theater reference books, with data on nearly every show of the past 150 years.

Church, Maryann, et al. *The Schuberts Present (100 Years of Musical Theater)*. New York: The Schubert Organization, Inc., 2001. A century after it was founded, the Schubert empire continues to be a vital part of the New York musical theater scene. This highly readable book sheds a bright light on the family and its impact on theater.

Fantle, David, and Patrick Byrne. *The Vaudeville Songbook*. Milwaukee, WI: Hal Leonard Corp., 1995. Strictly for those who sing or play piano a little, this is a primary source for understanding the world of vaudeville. Includes mini-bios of great vaudevillians.

Forte, Allen. *Listening to Classic American Popular Songs*. New Haven: Yale University Press, 2001. A scholarly approach to the Great American Songbook, this text is accompanied by a CD and suggestions for listening activities.

Frommer, Myrna, and Harvey Frommer. *It Happened on Broadway: An Oral History of the Great White Way*. New York: Harcourt Brace, 1998. Primary sources are usually superior to secondary sources, and you can't get much more primary than this. Frommer's book is the history of Broadway told by the people who created the musicals and performed in them.

Furia, Philip. *Ira Gershwin: The Art of the Lyricist*. New York: Oxford University Press, 1996. During his lifetime, Ira was the unknown Gershwin, living quietly in the background of his flamboyant brother's dramatic life. (People were known to look at the sheet music to a Gershwin song and say, "Oh, look, George wrote this with his sister, Ira!") This book establishes Ira as an artist in his own right and as an important behind-the-scenes decision maker in the creation of not only the songs but also the Gershwin concert pieces.

Gänzl, Kurt. *The Musical: A Concise History*. Boston: Northeastern University Press, 1997. Gänzl, being German, includes more about European musicals than one usually finds in an American text, but he covers the 200-year sweep of the American musical in a manner that is readable without sacrificing depth.

————. *Song/Dance*. New York: Smithmark Publishers, 1995. Knowing that dance has become increasingly important to the American musical—these days, the choreographer's name often appears above the title—I feel that this profusely illustrated book is essential to a full understanding of the evolution of American musical theater.

Hamm, Charles. *Irving Berlin: Songs from the Melting Pot: The Formative Years, 1907–1914*. New York: Oxford University Press, 1997. Hamm makes an excellent case for the idea that our popular songs reflect our social history. His analysis of the early Berlin songs clearly proves his point.

Hardy, Phil, and Dave Laing. *The DaCapo Companion to 20th-Century Popular Music*. New York: DaCapo Press, 2000. An inexpensive paperback reference book with a broad scope and concise articles on most of the personalities and topics covered in this course.

Hylands, William G. *Richard Rodgers*. New Haven: Yale University Press, 1998. In past biographies, to make maximum use of the real contrast between dependable Rodgers and wild-man Hart, Rodgers has tended to come off a little saint-like. This biography, however, tosses away Rodgers's halo and creates a less puritanical and more human picture.

Jasen, David A., and Gene Jones. *Spreadin' Rhythm All Around: Black Popular Songwriters, 1880–1930*. New York: Schirmer Books, 2002. This is a long-overdue book that, at last, gives neglected black writers of theater music their due.

Mordden, Ethan. *Rodgers and Hammerstein*. New York: Harry Abrams, Inc., 1992. This book probably contains everything you ever wanted to know about the collaboration of these two important writers of classic American musical theater.

Nolan, Frederick. *Lorenz Hart: A Poet on Broadway*. London: Oxford University Press, 1994. Larry Hart was the greatest lyricist of the 20th century. That statement may be arguable, but it's an argument that inevitably stimulates stirring discussion. The man had no control over alcohol and drugs, but *wow*, did he have control over and delight in words!

Raph, Theodore. *The American Song Treasury: 100 Favorites*. New York: Dover Publications, 2000. Raph provides us with a vast sampling of American songs that run the gamut from colonial times to the mid-20th century. Included are the biographies of the songwriters and brief stories behind each song.

Riss, Thomas. *Just Before Jazz: Black Musical Theater in New York, 1890–1915*. Washington, DC: Smithsonian Institution Press, 1989. This excellent book on early black musical theater fills a gap that, unfortunately, most histories of Broadway have created.

Rosenberg, Deena. *Fascinatin' Rhythm*. London: Lime Tree Press, 1991. Though this is a book about the collaboration of George and Ira Gershwin, it's also a book about the business, in general, of wedding music to lyric; wonderful insights into the working and personal relationship of two talented brothers.

Rubin, Marin. *Showstoppers: Busby Berkeley and the Tradition of Spectacle*. New York: Columbia University Press, 1993. The eye-popping extravaganza dominated the 19th century and continued to influence shows throughout the 20th century. Berkeley's massed numbers, first on the stage and later in Hollywood, come from a long theatrical tradition of spectacle, explored here in detail.

Smith, Cecil, and Litton, Glenn. *Musical Comedy in America: From The Black Crook through Sweeney Todd*. New York: Routledge Publishers, 1978. For more than fifty years, a classic reference on American musical theater; covers everything from the minstrel shows of the 1800s to the blockbusters of the late 1970s.

Steyn, Mark. *Broadway Babies Say Goodnight: Musicals Then and Now*. New York: Routledge Publishers, 1999. Steyn's writing is witty, informative, and loaded with interesting musical anecdotes.

Suskin, Steven. *More Opening Nights on Broadway*. New York: Schirmer Books, 1997. Here you'll find opening-night reviews and long-term evaluations of classic Broadway musicals.

 ©2006 The Teaching Company.

Wilder, Alec. *American Popular Song: The Great Innovators, 1900–1950*. London: Oxford University Press, 1972. This is the Holy Grail of America's greatest songs, the majority of which originated in Broadway musicals. Wilder focuses on 800 songs, evaluating each as an effective (or ineffective) work of art. He points out musical and lyrical strengths and weaknesses, unrelenting in his quest to identify and quantify *quality*.

Supplementary Reading:

Berlin, Edward. *Ragtime: A Musical and Cultural History*. Los Angeles: University of California Press, 1984. This book contains something for everyone—detailed analysis of ragtime for the musicologist and the sociology of the music for the armchair historian. Berlin's concrete examples and his quotes from periodicals of the times help bring the ragtime era to life.

Brantley, Ben. *The New York Times Book of Broadway*. New York: St. Martin's Press, 2001. This text covers everything you might want to know about Broadway shows that you won't find in other references.

Brooks, McNamara. *The Schuberts of Broadway*. New York: Oxford University Press, 1990. Lee and Jake Schubert, in addition to other family members, created and ran a theater empire that spanned the country for the entire 20th century. This is a complex story of the family, the theaters, and the Schuberts' important role in creating shows and stars.

Brooks, Mel, and Tom Meehan. *The Producers: How We Did It*. New York: Hyperion, 2004. It's rare to find a step-by-step description of the creation of a musical by its creators. This book makes a delightful and insightful read.

Cockrell, Dale. *Demons of Disorder: Early Blackface Minstrels and Their World*. Cambridge: Cambridge University Press, 2000. While this Teaching Company course has chosen to emphasize the positive aspect of the bizarre business of minstrelry, Cockrell often focuses on the negative, with erudition and dark wit. A good follow-up to our introduction to the minstrel show.

Freedland, Michael. *Jerome Kern: A Biography*. New York: Stein and Day, 1989. Because Kern spent many of his early years in England, married an Englishwoman, and wrote most of his early shows with P.G. Wodehouse (noted British wit), Freedland (a British biographer) captures Kern more completely than any other author to date.

Gracyk, Tim. *Popular American Recording Pioneers, 1895–1925*. London: The Haworth Press, 2000. When you come across an old LP reprint or an ancient 78-RPM recording, one of the frustrating things for the curious is the lack of information available on the performers. This book compensates for that lack.

Green, Stanley. *The World of Musical Comedy*. New York: DaCapo Press, 1980. This was once *the* text to read to acquire an understanding of the evolution of musical theater; nothing new has done a better job, and though the book is out of print, because of its past popularity, hundreds of used copies are available at Amazon.com.

Groce, Nancy. *New York: Songs of the City*. New York: Watson-Guptil Publications, 1999. This is a beautifully designed coffee-table book; readers will probably be surprised to discover that "East Side, West Side" and "New York, New York" are just a few of the hundreds of songs written about Manhattan. Interesting stories behind each song.

Hischak, Thomas. *The American Musical Theatre Song Encyclopedia*. Westport, CT: Greenwood Press, 1995. If you've been wondering which show that song came from, regardless of how obscure the song or the show, this is the reference you've been looking for.

Iger, Arthur. *Music of the Golden Age, 1900–1950*. Westport, CT: Greenwood Press, 1998. This is a useful, compact reference to hundreds of composers, lyricists, and songs, with very short bios on each songwriter.

Jasen, David A. *Tin Pan Alley: An Encyclopedia of the Golden Age of American Song*. New York: Routledge Publishers, 2003. This work contains more than you'll ever need to know about Tin Pan Alley. Can be browsed through for a pleasant read or used as a reference to answer nearly every question you might have about Tin Pan Alley.

Lehman, Engel. *The Making of a Musical: Creating Songs for the Stage*. New York: MacMillan, 1973. Engel has conducted and/or composed music for more than 170 shows and operas and is a three-time Tony Award winner. While the views in this book are strongly opinionated, its author writes with unquestionable authority.

Lissauer, Robert. *Encyclopedia of Popular Music in America*. New York: Facts on File, 2004. What Bordman is to the shows, Lissauer is to the songs. He relates essential details (creators, performers, recordings, etc.) on literally thousands of songs.

Maeder, Jay, ed. *Big Town, Big Time: A New York Epic, 1898–1998*. New York: New York Daily News, 1999. A unique view of New York musicals and other events, told through 100 years of articles from the *New York Daily News*.

Maltby, Richard, ed. *Passing Parade: A History of Popular Culture in the 20th Century*. New York: Oxford University Press, 1989. This huge, photo-filled book covers a century of fads, follies, and entertainment; makes delightful skimming.

Paymer, Marvin. *Facts Behind the Songs*. London: Garland Publishing, 2002. This book is more than a song reference; it is (for those who would make the effort) a complete source for self-instruction in the basics of musical form, melody, harmony, lyric writing, and almost anything else that pertains to popular song from the 19th century to the near-present.

Peyser, Joan. *The Memory of All That: The Life of George Gershwin*. New York: Simon and Schuster, 1993. Peyser won the Pulitzer Prize for her biography of Leonard Bernstein, thus, we know her to be erudite, incisive, and capable of making sound judgments. Though she does the same here, she dwells on Gershwin's private life, particularly on his sexual excesses, more than any other writer to date. Though at times her tone seems a little shrill, the book is a fascinating read.

Sanjek, Russell, and David Sanjek. *Pennies from Heaven: The American Popular Music Business in the 20th Century*. New York: DaCapo Press, 1996. Broadway as an art couldn't exist without Broadway as a relatively solvent business. This book covers the music business over the century in great detail. A good reference that makes enjoyable skimming.

Sutherland, Susan. *About Musicals*. London: Teach Yourself Books, 1998. All the essentials in 234 pages; very simple, generally accurate, and a quick overall view of musical theater.

Ziegfeld, Richard, and Paulette Ziegfeld. *The Ziegfeld Touch: The Life and Times of Florenz Ziegfeld, Jr.* New York: Harry Abrams, Inc., 1993. A huge book (it weighs several pounds) crammed with art nouveau and art deco scenes and costume designs and rare photographs. The words of Ziegfeld's own children make him (and the Follies) come to life.

Music Credits

Ed Goldstein and Company

"A Wonderful Guy" by Richard Rodgers and Oscar Hammerstein II
Williamson Music (ASCAP)

"Edelweiss" by Richard Rodgers and Oscar Hammerstein II
Williamson Music (ASCAP)
℗ Under License From The SONY BMG Custom Marketing Group,
SONY BMG MUSIC ENTERTAINMENT

"Oh, What A Beautiful Mornin'" by Richard Rodgers and Oscar
Hammerstein II, Williamson Music (ASCAP)
℗ Under License From The SONY BMG Custom Marketing Group,
SONY BMG MUSIC ENTERTAINMENT

"My Funny Valentine" by Richard Rodgers and Lorenz Hart
Williamson Music (ASCAP) and © Chappell & Co.

"The Man I Love"
(George Gershwin / Ira Gershwin)
© WB Music Corp.

"Someone To Watch Over Me"
(George Gershwin / Ira Gershwin)
© WB Music Corp.

"Prelude # 1" from "Preludes for Piano"
(George Gershwin)
© WB Music Corp.

"Somebody Loves Me"
(George Gershwin / Ballard McDonald / B.G. Desylva)
© WB Music Corp.

"'S Wonderful"
(George Gershwin / Ira Gershwin)
© WB Music Corp.

©2006 The Teaching Company.

"The Wizard and I"
From the Broadway musical *Wicked*
Music and Lyrics by Stephen Schwartz
Copyright © 2003 by Stephen Schwartz
All Rights Reserved. Used by Permission.

Notes